# MACMILLAN MODERN NOVELISTS

**General Editor:** Norman Page

D0988082

# MACMILLAN MODERN NOVELISTS

*Published titles*

MARGARET ATWOOD  Coral Ann Howells
SAUL BELLOW  Peter Hyland
ALBERT CAMUS  Philip Thody
ANGELA CARTER  Linden Peach
FYODOR DOSTOEVSKY  Peter Conradi
GEORGE ELIOT  Alan W. Bellringer
WILLIAM FAULKNER  David Dowling
GUSTAVE FLAUBERT  David Roe
E. M. FORSTER  Norman Page
ANDRÉ GIDE  David Walker
WILLIAM GOLDING  James Gindin
GRAHAM GREENE  Neil McEwan
ERNEST HEMINGWAY  Peter Messent
CHRISTOPHER ISHERWOOD  Stephen Wade
HENRY JAMES  Alan W. Bellringer
JAMES JOYCE  Richard Brown
FRANZ KAFKA  Ronald Spiers and Beatrice Sandberg
D. H. LAWRENCE  G. M. Hyde
ROSAMOND LEHMANN  Judy Simons
DORIS LESSING  Ruth Whittaker
MALCOLM LOWRY  Tony Bareham
NORMAN MAILER  Michael K. Glenday
THOMAS MANN  Martin Travers
GABRIEL GARCÍA MÁRQUEZ  Michael Bell
TONI MORRISON  Linden Peach
IRIS MURDOCH  Hilda D. Spear
VLADIMIR NABOKOV  David Rampton
V. S. NAIPAUL  Bruce King
GEORGE ORWELL  Valerie Myers
ANTHONY POWELL  Neil McEwan
MARCEL PROUST  Philip Thody
BARBARA PYM  Michael Cotsell
JEAN-PAUL SARTRE  Philip Thody
MURIEL SPARK  Norman Page
MARK TWAIN  Peter Messent
JOHN UPDIKE  Judie Newman
EVELYN WAUGH  Jacqueline McDonnell
H. G. WELLS  Michael Draper
PATRICK WHITE  Mark Williams
VIRGINIA WOOLF  Edward Bishop
SIX WOMEN NOVELISTS  Merryn Williams

*Forthcoming titles*

SIMONE DE BEAUVOIR  Terry Keefe
IVY COMPTON-BURNETT  Janet Godden
JOSEPH CONRAD  Owen Knowles
JOHN FOWLES  James Acheson
SALMAN RUSHDIE  D. C. R. A. Goonetilleke
ALICE WALKER  Maria Lauret

MACMILLAN MODERN NOVELISTS

# ANGELA CARTER

Linden Peach

First published 1998 by
MACMILLAN PRESS LTD
Houndmills, Basingstoke, Hampshire RG21 6XS
and London
companies and representatives
throughout the world

ISBN 0–333–67615–7 hardcover
ISBN 0–333–67616–5 paperback

A catalogue record for this book is available
from the British Library.

This book is printed on paper suitable for recycling and
made from fully managed and sustained forest sources.

10   9   8   7   6   5   4   3   2   1
07  06  05  04  03  02  01  00  99  98

Typeset by Forewords, Oxford/Longworth Editorial Services
Longworth, Oxfordshire.

Printed in Malaysia

**Series Standing Order**
If you would like to receive future titles in this series as they are published,
you can make use of our standing order facility. To place a standing order
please contact your bookseller or, in case of difficulty, write to us at the
address below with your name and address and the name of the series. Please
state with which title you wish to begin your standing order. (If you live
outside the United Kingdom we may not have the rights for your area, in
which case we will forward your order to the publisher concerned.)

Customer Services Department, Macmillan Distribution Ltd
Houndmills, Basingstoke, Hampshire, RG21 6XS, England.

*For Angela*

# Contents

# Acknowledgements

The author and publishers wish to thank the Estate of Angela Carter, c/o Rogers, Coleridge and White Ltd, 20 Powis Mews, London W11 1JN, for permission to use copyright material from *Shadow Dance*, © Angela Carter 1966; *The Magic Toyshop*, © Angela Carter 1967; *Several Perceptions*, © Angela Carter 1968; *Heroes and Villains*, © Angela Carter 1969; *Love*, © Angela Carter 1971; *The Infernal Desire Machines of Doctor Hoffman*, © Angela Carter 1972; *The Passion of New Eve*, © Angela Carter 1977; *Nights at the Circus*, © Angela Carter 1984; and *Wise Children*, © Angela Carter 1991.

# General Editor's Preface

The death of the novel has often been announced, and part of the secret of its obstinate vitality must be its capacity for growth, adaptation, self-renewal and self-transformation: like some vigorous organism in a speeded up Darwinian ecosystem, it adapts itself quickly to a changing world. War and revolution, economic crisis and social change, radically new ideologies such as Marxism and Freudianism, have made this century unprecedented in human history in the speed and extent of change, but the novel has shown an extraordinary capacity to find new forms and techniques and to accommodate new ideas and conceptions of human nature and human experience, and even to take up new positions on the nature of fiction itself.

In the generations immediately preceding and following 1914, the novel underwent a radical redefinition of its nature and possibilities. The present series of monographs is devoted to the novelists who created the modern novel and to those who, in their turn, either continued and extended, or reacted against and rejected, the traditions established during that period of intense exploration and experiment. It includes a number of those who lived and wrote in the nineteenth century but whose innovative contribution to the art of fiction makes it impossible to ignore them in any account of the modern novel; it also includes the so-called 'modernists' and those who in the mid- and late twentieth century have emerged as outstanding practitioners of this genre. The scope is, inevitably, international; not only, in the migratory and exile-haunted world of our century, do writers refuse to heed national boundaries – 'English' literature lays claim to Conrad the Pole, Henry James the American, and Joyce the Irishman – but geniuses such as Flaubert,

Dostoevsky and Kafka have had an influence on the fiction of many nations.

Each volume in the series is intended to provide an introduction to the fiction of the writer concerned, both for those approaching him or her for the first time and for those who are already familiar with some parts of the achievement in question and now wish to place it in the context of the total *oeuvre*. Although essential information relating to the writer's life and times is given, usually in an opening chapter, the approach is primarily critical and the emphasis is not upon 'background' or generalisations but upon close examination of important texts. Where an author is notably prolific, major texts have been made to convey, more summarily, a sense of the nature and quality of the author's work as a whole. Those who want to read further will find suggestions in the select bibliography included in each volume. Many novelists are, of course, not only novelists but also poets, essayists, biographers, dramatists, travel writers and so forth; many have practised shorter forms of fiction; and many have written letters or kept diaries that constitute a significant part of their literary output. A brief study cannot hope to deal with all of these in detail, but where the shorter fiction and non-fictional writings, private and public, have an important relationship to the novels, some space has been devoted to them.

NORMAN PAGE

# 1

# Introduction

*Be advised . . . this writer is no meat-and-potatoes hack; she is
a rocket, a Catherine Wheel.*

(Salman Rushdie, introduction to *Burning Your Boats*)

I

When Angela Carter died of cancer in 1992, aged only 51, she
became, as Nicci Gerrard (1996) observed four years later, 'one of
our most missed, lost contemporaries' (p. 20). Her early death has
coloured the way in which her writing is now received. Paul Barker
(1995) has wryly recalled:

> She dies untimely, and everyone suddenly bursts out weeping.
> The obituaries give her better notices than anything she ever
> received in her lifetime. Her books sell out within three days of
> her death. She becomes the most read contemporary author on
> English university campuses. Her last story, finished during her
> final illness, sells 80,000 copies in paperback. She has arrived. But
> she is dead. (p. 14)

It does not matter how much of this is exact. We do not need
evidence that within months of her death she became the most read
author on English university campuses. Neither is it necessary to
point out that not all her reviewers had given her worse notices

1

than her obituaries. For Barker's point is that Angela Carter, having died young, has been canonised. Rather like Angela Carter herself, Barker's primary concern here is with perception rather than fact.

As the author of a collection of essays entitled *Nothing Sacred*, Carter would probably have found her own canonisation amusing. She would have found less amusing, however, that as a result she is frequently misunderstood. She may be one of the most read contemporary writers on English university campuses but she is not always the best read. As Gerrard (1996) points out, her 'mocking iconoclasm' has sometimes been reduced to something more comfortable and less radical. It is sometimes forgotten as, Gerrard says, that she has 'more in common with Salvador Dali than Virginia Woolf' (p. 22).

Carter completed nine novels. Although most of them are relatively short, they are crammed with an extraordinary range of ideas, themes and images: *Shadow Dance* (1966; reprinted in America as *Honeybuzzard*, 1966), *The Magic Toyshop* (1967), *Several Perceptions* (1968), *Heroes and Villains* (1969), *Love* (1971), *The Infernal Desire Machines of Doctor Hoffman* (1972; reprinted in America as *The War of Dreams*, 1977), *The Passion of New Eve* (1977), *Nights at the Circus* (1984) and *Wise Children* (1991). She was, however, more than a novelist; she was a prolific writer of short stories and non-fiction and a teacher of writing.

In addition to the novels, she published several collections of short stories, *Fireworks: Nine Profane Pieces* (1974), *The Bloody Chamber and Other Stories* (1979), *Black Venus's Tale* (1980), *Black Venus* (1985; reprinted in America as *Saints and Strangers*, 1987) and, posthumously, *American Ghosts & Old-World Wonders* (1993). Of her non-fiction the most relevant to an appreciation of her novels are *The Sadeian Woman: An Exercise in Cultural History* (1979; reprinted in America as *The Sadeian Woman and the Ideology of Pornography*, 1979), *Nothing Sacred: Selected Writings* (1982) and *Expletives Deleted: Selected Writings* (1992). There are also four collections of children's stories, a work in verse entitled *Unicorn* (1966) and four radio plays. The fact that she edited fairy stories is particularly important to an appreciation of her fiction. She edited and translated *The Fairy Tales of Charles Perrault* (1977) and *Sleeping Beauty and Other Favourite Fairy Tales* (1982) and also edited two collections for Virago: *The Virago Book of Fairy Tales* (1990) and *The Second Virago Book of Fairy Tales* (1992).

Despite Paul Barker's contention that Carter received better notices after her death, her work won favourable reviews as well as prizes during her lifetime. Carter's second novel, *The Magic Toyshop*, won the John Llewellyn Rhys Prize, and *Several Perceptions*, her third novel, the Somerset Maugham Award. *Nights at the Circus* was the joint winner of the James Tait Black Memorial Prize in 1985. In the same year, the film, *Company of Wolves* based on *The Bloody Chamber* and a rewriting of 'Red Riding Hood' was released. During the period 1976–8, Angela Carter was Arts Council of Great Britain Fellow in Sheffield. Further recognition of her work and her skill as a teacher of writing came with prestigious appointments which included Visiting Professor at Brown University, Rhode Island, USA; tutor on the MA in Writing at East Anglia University, UK; and writer-in-residence at the University of Adelaide, South Australia. Soon she achieved international recognition as a teacher as well as a writer, holding writing residencies at Austin, Texas; Iowa City, Iowa; and Albany, New York State in America.

There are many aspects, then, to Carter's life as a writer. It is always difficult to separate out the various strands in an author's biography and this is especially difficult in Carter's case. While her non-fiction, short-fiction, children's fiction and novels all interconnect, Carter was always interested, too, in blurring the boundaries between them, challenging our perceptions of what we mean, for example, by a short story or a novel. Not surprisingly, much of the criticism of Carter's work has ranged over the whole of her *oeuvre* and while it has tried to do justice to the totality of her intellectual life, Carter's engagement with, and contribution to the development of particular genres, has tended to get lost.

The subject of this book is Carter's contribution to the development of the novel. In this introduction, I have tried to highlight some of the contexts and frameworks which are particularly appropriate to a discussion of her work. Inevitably, there are features of Carter's novels which it is impossible to overlook such as their contentious and subversive nature. However, as I will argue shortly, we must be wary of applying convenient critical labels, such as 'magic realism', to Carter's non-realistic, philosophical writing which explores the 'actualities' in which many of us live. Indeed, in the following pages, I have tried to draw attention to some of the implications for literary criticism of the cultural critique in Carter's work. These include the need to recognise how her novels deconstruct the processes that produce social structures and shared meanings, evident, for example, in her recurrent demythologising of the mother figure and in the way in which the manifestation of the female body in her work disrupts the social construction of women as Woman.

I have also thought it important to highlight early in this book the significance of Carter's perception of post-war Britain – a trope in several of her works including her last novel, *Wise Children* (1991) – even suggesting that it may repay reading in psycho-analytical terms. The recalcitrant 1960s, in which Carter's early work is set, clearly provided an important initial context for her fiction. However, the differences between the 1960s and the 1950s may have proved a more significant influence on her creative imagination than either one of those decades as such.

Although the starting point of my discussion is the recalcitrant, mocking iconoclasm of Carter's fiction, I recommend throughout the book that this aspect of her work be approached as an intellectual strategy in tandem with the unusually dense, allusive nature of her texts. Subsequent chapters examine the hybrid nature of individual novels and how this is a literary device that Carter deliberately mines and exploits, often as part of a wider intertextuality in which traditions, mythologies and conventions are subjected to scrutiny. Through a consideration of Carter's use of different and competing frameworks within her fiction, I argue that intertextuality becomes a boldly thematised part of her work, in which her own culture is rendered as 'foreign'. As I suggest toward the end of this intro-duction, we need to reassess the commonly held view of the period which Carter spent in Japan as a watershed in her literary career. It should be seen in terms of continuities as well as discontinuities. Primarily, Japan provided valuable confirmation of the ways in which she was developing intellectually and as a writer and cultural critic. Its impact upon her writing was pronounced because it encouraged those aspects of her work, such as the sense of the foreignness of her own culture and her interest in the blurred boundaries between realism and illusion, which were already making her novels distinctive in the late 1960s. Without an appreciation of the period which Carter spent in Japan, it would be impossible to understand fully the nature of the short fiction which followed or of the novels which are set outside Britain.

II

Even with hindsight, Carter's novels are unusually provocative. Indeed, one critic, Elaine Jordan (1992), has admitted: 'I'll please no one least of all her, by trying to say she's not offensive' (p. 120). Generally regarded as one of the most important post-1945 English novelists, responses to her work have sometimes been extreme – at both ends of the critical continuum – and contradictory. Whilst John Bayley (1987), writing mainly with reference to *Love*, can criticise Carter's novels as vehicles for hard-line feminist ideologies and the fashionable perceptions of the moment, Suzanne Kappeller (1986) can take issue with Carter's depiction of Juliette in *The Sadeian Woman* for ignoring her complicity in a system that oppresses women.

The representation of women in Carter's work certainly seems to have been a bone of contention among critics. Paulina Palmer (1989) is critical of the female characters in *The Passion of New Eve* who seek to liberate themselves from qualities associated with feminity in the early 1970s – such as dependency, passivity and masochism – but are 'composed of attributes which are predominantly "masculine"' (p. 16). Robert Clark (1987) has criticised Carter for unwittingly repeating the 'self-alienation' to which patriarchal power relationships give rise. Even Jordan (1992), a self-confessed devotee of Carter who takes Clark to task, admits: 'Reading back through Angela Carter's work from the Sixties on, I had my moment of horror and cold feet at what I was letting myself in for . . . she started out writing as a male impersonator, with a strong streak of misogyny' (p. 16). In reading *The Infernal Desire Machines of Doctor Hoffman* (1972), Sally Robinson (1991) too had her moment of cold feet, but it seemed to have passed with further consideration. Although she found that 'there is, quite simply, *no place* for a woman reader in this text', she is prepared to argue that the novel challenges 'the reader to occupy a position on the outside of that narrative' (p. 105). Perhaps the extent to which Carter set out to be provocative is indicated in a note she sent to Elaine Jordan, referring to two leading feminist writers: 'If I can get up Suzanne Kappeller's nose, to say nothing of the Dworkin proboscis, then my living has not been in vain' (Sage, 1994, p. 332).

The purpose of the Macmillan Modern Novelists Series is to examine how modern novelists 'continued and extended, or reacted against and rejected' the traditions created by their predecessors. Although this would appear to be an apposite approach to a writer as innovative as Carter, it is also one of the most difficult. Carter's literary career defies summary and her novels deny, resist and subvert definitions and frames of all kinds – literary, cultural, social, sexual, religious, ontological. She does not write from a particular worldview and throughout her work sociohistorical assumptions and conventions which have prescribed and organised our thinking are disrupted. As she argues in *The Sadeian Woman* (1979):

> Fine art, that exists for itself alone, is art in a final state of impotence. If nobody, including the artist, acknowledges art as a means of *knowing* the world, then art is relegated to a kind of rumpus room of the mind and the irresponsibility of the artist and the irrelevance of art to actual living becomes part and parcel of the practice of art. (p. 13)

It would be a mistake, however, to confuse Carter's concept of *knowing* the world with social realism, an elision that is often made in discussing the novel as a literary form. Even though realism is based on a particular, historically located mode of awareness as partial as any other, over the last few hundred years it has been the preferred mode for writers with a commitment to social change who, in depicting society, have been concerned to bring out the social forces within it. Carter's novels, however, are essentially ludic, characterised by linguistic play. Even the more 'realistic' early texts are parodic, allusive and, sometimes, elusive. Such artistic innovation has been regarded by social realist Marxist critics and writers, such as George Lukacs, as too decadent, introverted and 'bourgeois'. However, as myself and Angela Burton have argued elsewhere (Peach and Burton, 1995), writers like Dennis Potter have recognised that as society changes, so different strategies and techniques are needed to write effective social critiques (p. 31). Social realist fiction 'naturalises' what it portrays so that we trust what we are reading. Non-realistic fiction distances, or even alienates, us so that we are disturbed, puzzled, confused and possibly very critical of what we are reading. As a student of English at Bristol University, Carter would have been familiar with 'alienating techniques' through the work of Bertolt Brecht and through his writings on Chinese theatre where he found that 'everything put forward' has 'a touch of the amazing' (Willett, 1964, p. 92). Certainly in Carter's fiction, as in Brecht's work, everyday things are 'raised above the level of the obvious and automatic' (ibid.).

Non-realistic fiction usually presents the reader with new insights into how society is structured, into the forces behind it and into how it is organised according to the interests of particular powerful groups. In *Heroes and Villains* to some extent but especially in the post 1970 novels, as I shall discuss later, Carter acknowledges that the mode of awareness which in the last three hundred years or so has been associated with realism is breaking down. Although these novels do not offer any clear, coherent alternatives, they are written from the realisation that many of the traditional principles which have governed our perception and organisation of 'reality' have been brought into question by modern and post-modern European and Euro-American thinking.

As Jordan (1992) points out, 'there are no naturalistically credible imitations of experience in Carter's work and no role models either, not in any simple sense' (p. 121). Helen Carr (1989), believing this has posed a particular problem for Carter's readers, has even suggested that 'Carter's novels became much more acceptable in Britain after the discovery of South American magic realism: her readers discovered that she was writing in a genre that could be named' (p. 7). Associating Carter with 'magic realism', however, creates more problems of definition than it solves. Carter herself has explained that the kinds of social forces that produced Gabriel García Márquez, who is most often associated with this mode of writing, were very different from those that produced her (Haffenden, 1985, p. 81). Even if we were to accept the term 'magic realism' as unproblematic, it would be misleading to apply the same label to all of Carter's work. For example, 'magic realism' seems a more appropriate description of the later fiction written in the 1970s than the earlier work. The early novels of the 1960s employ a fusion of realist, Gothic and fantasy conventions, but, as Marc O'Day (1994) points out, they nevertheless 'invite readings in terms of quite traditional literary criticism' (p. 24).

This distinction between the fiction written in the 1960s and Carter's subsequent work is one that readers will encounter frequently in criticism on Carter's work. Often the later work is referred to as 'speculative fiction' as if all writing were not speculative to some degree. In Carter's case, such distinctions are problematic because all her novels, including the early works, blur the boundaries between fiction and philosophy. Nevertheless, if 'speculative fiction' is taken to mean 'non-realistic philosophical fiction' then it may be an appropriate way of describing her post-1960s writing. For the later work is more intensely theoretical than the earlier writing and Carter's interest in cultural myths did develop into a more pronounced exploration in her fiction of the part they have played, are playing and are likely to play in the transformation and break-up of conventional social structures.

The label 'magic realism', however, even when applied to the novels of the 1970s and 1980s because they are less 'realist' and more intensely philosophical than the earlier work, creates difficulties. Admittedly, Isabel Allende's definition of magic realism suggests some of the characteristics of Carter's later work: 'Magic realism really means allowing a place in literature to the invisible forces that have such a powerful place in life . . . dreams, myth, legend, passion, obsession, superstition, religion, the overwhelming power of nature and the supernatural' (Lewis, 1993, p. 26). But the term, first coined by Franz Roh in 1925 in relation to post-expressionist art, has been applied slackly since the 1940s to Latin American writers and more recently to those from the Caribbean, Nigeria and India to emphasise their difference from mainstream Euro-American culture. It has not been rigorously defined or adequately distinguished from related literary concepts such as fabulation, the fantastic and the uncanny.

David Punter (1991) has suggested that if Carter is to be described as a 'magic realist' then it must be recognised that 'magic realism', often associated with magical or boundary-breaking events in everyday reality, has to do 'with seeing the recognisable world . . . through transformed eyes' (p. 143). Whilst this is a valid proposition, what is at the heart of 'magic realism', and Carter's work, as Allende's elaboration of her definition suggests, is the representational code of realism locked in a continuous dialectic with that of fantasy. As Selmon (1989) argues, the term 'magic realism' signifies 'resistance to central assimilation by more stable generic systems' (p. 10). Although both these explanations of 'magic realism' suggest that the term might prove appropriate to Carter's writing after all, they are also suggestive of Brecht's work – a much more likely influence on Carter – and especially his essay, 'The Popular and the Realistic', in which he argues that 'reality can be represented in a factual or a fantastic form' (Willett, 1964, p. 110). However, even though Brecht was probably an important influence on Angela Carter's fiction, Carter is more prepared to stress the dialectic between the two codes of representation which for Allende is central to 'magic realism'. Thus while we might acknowledge the influence of Brecht on Carter's work, pushing Carter toward what has been called 'magic realist', her fiction cannot even be labelled Brechtian. Moreover, while in Carter's work generally the conflation of the fantastic and the factual inscribes a tension between the 'the representational code of realism' and fantasy, in the later novels there is also tension between the celebration of that dialectic – through the figure of Fevvers, for example, in *Nights at the Circus* – and a subversive, analytic framework that cannot accept even that celebration at face value.

It is difficult to quarrel with Margaret Atwood (1992), who observed in her obituary, with only a hint of exaggeration, that Carter 'was born subversive'. Even readers who come to Carter with only a limited knowledge of the English novel, will recognise, as Gerrard (1995) has said, that she was 'the one-off'. And what makes her 'the one-off' is the subversive nature of her 'strange, ribald novels': 'undecorous, overripe and mocking tales in which nothing is sacred and nothing natural' (p. 20). The latter is again a feature which Carter's work shares with Brecht's. As he explained, 'the new alienations are only designed to free socially conditioned phenomenon from the stamp of familiarity which protects them against our grasp today' (Willett, 1964, p. 192). Carter's fiction encourages us to perceive for ourselves the processes that produce social structures, sociohistorical concepts and cultural artefacts. For example, Carter persistently demythologises the idealisation of the mother figure. In *The Sadeian Woman*, she not only argues that 'maternal superiority is one of the most damaging of all consolatory fictions' (p. 106) but maintains:

> All the mythic versions of women, from the myth of the redeeming purity of the virgin to that of the healing, reconciling mother, are consolatory nonsenses; and consolatory nonsense seems to me a fair definition of myth, anyway. Mother goddesses are just as silly a notion as father gods. (p. 5)

Desiderio, the narrator of *The Infernal Desire Machines of Doctor*

*Hoffman* (1972), relates how an African chief described his army of women:

> examine the bases of the traditional notions of the figure of the female, you will find you have founded them all on the remote figure you thought you glimpsed, once, in your earliest childhood, bending over you with an offering of warm, sugared milk, crooning a soft lullaby while, by her haloed presence, she kept away the snakes that writhed beneath the bed. Tear this notion of the mother from your hearts. Vengeful as nature herself, she loves her children only in order to devour them.  (p. 160)

Although the African chief's account of his army is mediated through Desiderio's masculinised worldview, Carter's work regularly includes descriptions of women, albeit ironically or parodically, that cut across conventional mythic representations. It is frequently critical of essentialising notions such as the eternal feminine, the benevolent or destructive mother, the virgin and the whore, because, as Robinson (1991) says, they obscure 'a socially conditioned female subjectivity and sexuality under a blanket of myth' (p. 118).

The emphasis throughout Carter's work, as in her depictions of women, on manifestations of the body is a product of the dialectic between the representational code of realism and fantasy which Allende identifies as characteristic of 'magic realism' but which is also a feature of Brecht's work. Such an emphasis emerges, however, as Fredric Jameson (1986) argues, when larger historical perspectives lose their validity and older more complex narratives are neutralised. Carter's work, in which conventional narratives are deconstructed and their lack of relevance exposed, would seem to confirm Jameson's thesis. According to Jameson, in such situations when everything else appears to have been stripped away, only 'body manifestations are retained' (p. 321).

The appearance of the body, Jameson argues, is potentially one of the most important disruptive elements in narratives. Although it disturbs the logical progression of realist narrative, the disruption is checked by the fetishisation of the body as image. In narratives which question the validity of grand narratives such as civilisation and progress, however, the appearance of the body, according to Jameson, usually produces 'an awakening of fresh sight' which 'diverts a conventional narrative logic of the unfolding story in some new vertical direction' (p. 307). This is evident, for example, in *The Magic Toyshop* (1967) – a novel especially sceptical of grand narratives – which begins with Melanie's discovery that 'she was made of flesh and blood'. From the outset, this realisation disrupts the fetishisation of the female body as image:

> For hours she stared at herself, naked, in the mirror of her wardrobe; she would follow with her finger the elegant structure of her rib-cage, where the heart fluttered under the flesh like a bird under a blanket, and she would draw down the long line from breast-bone to navel (which was a mysterious cavern or grotto), and she would rasp her palms against her bud-wing shoulderblades. (p. 1)

The excitement and sense of self-satisfaction Melanie experiences in this narcissistic enjoyment of her own physical being fragments, and is threatened by, the social construction of Woman. As Melanie tries on various preconceived images of Woman and female sexuality, the reader becomes more aware than Melanie of the cultural history at her shoulder. Instead of seeing only herself in the mirror, Melanie measures herself against different images of the female body as Woman.

In *Love* (1971), Lee's body is eroticised and deconstructed at the same time:

> [Annabel] took a technical pleasure in observing the musculature of his shoulders and the play of snowlight on the golden down which covered them for he was of a furry texture. He was colourful to look at and also reminded her of Canova's nude, heroic statue of Napoleon in Wellington House. . . . She was especially pleased when she caught a glimpse of his leonine left profile. She found him continuously interesting to look at but it hardly occurred to her the young man was more than a collection of coloured surfaces. (p. 30)

As in the opening of *The Magic Toyshop*, this particular manifestation of the body is disruptive. Whilst it is unusual for a text to eroticise the male nude, this attempt to do so is especially contentious. Lee is mediated through the eyes of Annabel and the eroticisation says more about her than Lee's body. The description of Melanie's body at the beginning of *The Magic Toyshop* employs words which associate it with the larger world of nature: 'fluttered', 'like a bird', 'bud-wing', 'cavern'. There is an element of mystery and, through the references to birds, of spirituality. But the description of Lee's body is undercut by some of the words which are used; 'musculature', 'play', 'texture', 'profile', 'surfaces' are words which belong to the language of art criticism. The focus shifts from the body – which is placed and yet not placed within a particular heroic tradition of the male nude – to the observer. The representation of the body here is the product of a worrying detachment. In her later fiction, which I shall discuss in subsequent chapters, Carter became increasingly interested in the grotesque body as a site where the body as fetishised in realist narrative is challenged.

### III

One of the difficulties in trying to relate the subversive elements of Carter's work, including those which have been associated with 'magic realism', to a particular context is knowing which particular aspect of that context has the most significant bearing on the work. Born in 1940, Carter began writing in the 1960s, by the end of which she had completed five novels, and the subversive terms in which Gerrard describes her novels are similar to those in which Carter herself recalled the 1960s in 'Notes From the Front Line':

> towards the end of that decade there was a brief period of public philosophical awareness that occurs only very occasionally in human history; when truly, it felt like Year One, that all that was holy was in the process of being profaned . . . I can date to that time and to some of the debates and to that sense of heightened awareness of the society around me in the summer of 1968, my own questioning of the nature of my reality as a *woman*.
>
> (Wandor, 1983, p. 70)

However, the radical nature of her work is rooted not just in the 1960s but in the contrast between the 1960s and the 1950s in which Carter grew up. Admittedly, the 1940s/1950s saw the introduction of the National Health Service, increased educational opportunities and social mobility. And the 1950s was a radical decade for the arts which saw the 'Angry Young Men' in Britain, the Beat Generation in America and the existentialists in France. But Carter also experienced rationing, advertising campaigns which encouraged women to believe their place was in the home, and the austerity of the 1950s. As Lorna Sage (1994) has pointed out 'the prevailing style of British writing and of film-making (and of grey-and-white television) was neo-realistic – of a piece with the general atmosphere of austerity' (p. 2). The protest voices of the 1950s were male and men benefited more than women from the increased educational and social opportunities. So in locating Carter's origins in the dialectic between the 1950s and the 1960s, we can begin to appreciate Atwood's point that Carter seemed to be born subversive, having experienced the increasing frustration with the conformist neo-realism of the 1950s, but, as a woman especially, also experiencing the limited nature of the radical movements.

If the subversive nature of Carter's novels is the first aspect likely to strike a new reader, then probably the second is that they are, as Gerrard has said, 'savage' and 'ribald'. To some extent, this feature of her work can also be said to have its origins in Carter's post-war upbringing. Or rather, it can be said to have its origins in how Carter perceived the post-war Britain in which she grew up: 'I am the pure product', she wrote in 'Notes From the Front Line', 'of an advanced, industrialised, post-imperialist country in decline' (Wandor, 1983, p. 73).

As Connor (1996) reminds us, in the post-war period, 'Britain came progressively to lose its confident belief that it was the subject of its own history' (p. 3). Instead Britain appeared increasingly subject to outside pressures and influences including the more rampant and unpredictable forces of international capitalism which lay beyond the control of any one state. For Carter, there were positive aspects to Britain's changing position: 'The sense of limitless freedom that I, as a woman, sometimes feel *is* that of a new kind of being. Because I simply could not have existed, as I am, in any other preceding time or place' (Wandor, 1983, p. 73). But whatever one's perspective on the matter, there could be no denying that the psychology of Britain was changing. Indeed, in her early novels, she depicts a Britain which is in what one school of psychoanalysis might call 'a depressive condition'.

In psychoanalysis, the depressive condition is the one in which infants begin to separate themselves from their mothers and experience a sense of loss. Carter herself did not regret the passing of imperialist Britain as such. In fact, she believed it was possible that because 'Western European civilisation as we know it has just about run its course' that 'for the first time for a thousand years or so, its inhabitants may at last be free of their terrible history' (Wandor, 1983, pp. 72–3). Not everyone saw things this way, of course, and the experience of decline for the country after the war was also for many the cultural experience of loss.

In *Several Perceptions* (1968) and in *Wise Children* (1991), Britain's waning power is linked with the decline in the prestige and influence of the English theatre. Whatever the subsequent benefits for women, Carter acknowledges that Britain as 'post' – post-imperialist, post-industrial – is cast, albeit temporarily, into a condition of loss; as a nation, Britain after 1945 began to separate from its mythical 'mother' – industrialised, imperialist Britain. This view of Britain is incorporated in her first novel, *Shadow Dance* (1966). An auction sale is held in the gutted corpse of what had once been an Edwardian department store, 'where tall, thin pillars topped with fading garlands of gilded leaves insinuated hints of departed elegancies' (p. 23). The two junk shop owners know that there is a market for objects which evoke a period of lost elegance and glory. They are interested in a cake tin because it was produced as a souvenir of the coronation of Edward VII and a bidet because it depicts a pastoral scene of nymphs and shepherds. In *Several Perceptions*, the decline of imperialist Britain is reflected in the bohemian district of Bristol in which the novel is set:

> Many of the shops were boarded up, to let, or sold second-hand clothes, or had become betting shops but, nevertheless, this street had once been the shopping promenade of a famous spa and still swooped in a sinuous neo-classic arc from the Down. Plaster mouldings of urns and garlands decorated upper storeys of rusticated stone and rosy brick where . . . broken windows were roughly patched with cardboard, if at all. The pavements were spattered green and white with droppings of fat pigeons who strutted among the maimed and old as smugly as if the district had not seen the last of its good times long ago. (pp. 9–10)

Joseph Harker also alludes to this sense of cultural loss later in the novel when he regrets the passing of 'Victorian shooting jackets, Eskimo anoraks lined with wolf fur and military greatcoats of the elegant past' (p. 123). Indeed, as I shall discuss in the next chapter, the elision of a historical sense of loss and a psychoanalytic sense of lack is an important trope in this novel. In Carter's final novel, which is discussed in chapter 5, a sense of cultural loss is pursued through the disappearance of some of the icons associated with London such as the Lyons teashops and through the figure of a stand-up comedian who has the Empire tattooed on his body. Performing on stage, flexing his muscles to patriotic tunes, his ageing body positions parts of the Empire in less than complimentary places.

In Carter's 1960s novels, the loss of an industrialised, imperialist Britain in the post-war years, like the infant's loss of the mother, is experienced not only as the loss of something. It is experienced, too, as the presence of something else – the presence of something tangible and frightening. Although Carter may have enjoyed the recycling economy of the 1960s, the stark unpleasantness-cum-horror of the emergent milieu is anticipated in the description of the bar which opens her first novel, *Shadow Dance*, set in the early years of the decade:

> The bar was a mock-up, a forgery, a fake; an ad-man's crazy dream of a Spanish patio, with crusty white walls (as if the publican had economically done them up in leftover sandwiches) on which hung unplayable musical instruments and many bull-fight posters, all blood and bulging bulls' testicles and the arrogant yellow satin buttocks of lithe young men. Nights in a garden of never-never Spain.

At one level, this is the postmodern world of simulacra, in which there is no reality behind the images other than further images. At another level, however, we are presented with a disturbing combination of maleness, of the absence of anything female, of blood and violence, of death and of unplayable musical instruments – the significance of which for the novel as a whole I shall discuss in the chapter on *Shadow Dance*.

Given the nature of Carter's work, it is appropriate to discuss her perception of post-war Britain in terms borrowed from psychoanalysis. All her novels demonstrate an interest, albeit a characteristically sceptical one, in psychoanalysis and the ways in which it has influenced our thinking about our selves, our identities, our sexuality and our relationships with others. As Elaine Jordan (1990) points out: 'playing the psychoanalytically questionable distinction between the real world of sense and the fantasy world of dreams, she collapses the one into the other' (p. 91). However, there are further reasons why Carter's realisation of a sense of loss in post-war Britain can be discussed in terms of the child's experience of the loss of its mother.

Whilst there is an absence of mothers in Carter's fiction, there are often characters who experience the loss of their mothers. For example, Morris' mother in *Shadow Dance* is killed in an air raid during the war; Melanie in *The Magic Toyshop* loses both her parents in a plane crash; Lee's mother in *Love* is lost to him when she suffers a nervous breakdown; and Marianne's mother in *Heroes and Villlains* dies broken hearted two years after her son's death. During the war years, of course, a generation of children suffered enforced separation from their mothers. Carter herself experienced this, having been taken from London in the year in which she was born to live with her grandmother in the coal-mining village of Wath-upon-Deane in South Yorkshire. Her experiences of evacuation coloured her view of industrial Britain. She came to see it as 'matriarchal' – 'a community where women ruled the roost' – and, through a lens which, as she admits, was 'romantic' (p. 8). Carter's account of her upbringing during these years in 'The Mother Lode' in *Nothing Sacred*, originally published in the *New Review* (1976), reinforces the appropriateness of discussing her perception of Britain's post-war decline within psychoanalytic paradigms. The essay provides us with a clear indication of how for Carter loss is replaced by something tangible and apprehensive. Although Carter grew fond of her grandmother, the initial account of her suggests that Carter's mother has been replaced by a disturbing presence:

> My maternal grandmother seemed to my infant self a woman of such physical and spiritual heaviness she might have been born with a greater degree of gravity than most people . . . she effort-lessly imparted a sense of my sex's ascendancy in the scheme of things, every word and gesture of hers displayed a natural dominance, a native savagery, and I am very grateful for all that,

now, although the core of steel was a bit inconvenient when I was looking for boyfriends in the South in the late fifties, when girls were supposed to be as soft and as pink as a nursuree. (pp. 8–9)

In *The Magic Toyshop*; the mother is replaced by an aunt who has been rendered dumb and by a frightening patriarchal figure, Uncle Philip, whose entry into the novel is delayed so that his presence, described in terms which evoke primal fears and anxieties, precedes him.

As I shall argue in the next chapter, Carter seems interested in melancholic figures for whom, in the words of the French psychoanalyst, Julia Kristeva (1987), 'sadness is in reality the only object' (p. 22). Kristeva quarrels with Freud's interpretation of the melancholic/depressive as simply displacing hatred of an 'other' into his or her own ego. For Kristeva, the melancholic is unable to displace the loss of the mother into language. Whereas others are able to deal with the loss of the mother by, for example, eroticising the lost object, the melancholic in Kristeva's view dies in her place:

> Signs are arbitrary because language begins with a *denegation* (*Verneinung*) of loss, at the same time as a depression occasioned by mourning. 'I have lost an indispensable object which happens to be, in the last instance, my mother', the speaking being seems to say. But no, I have found her again in signs, or rather because I accept to lose her, I have not lost her (here is the *denegation*), I can get her back in language. (p. 55)

Whilst I do not suggest that the melancholic figure in Carter's work can only be understood in terms of the failure of the *denegation* to which Kristeva refers, there is a connection to be drawn between the absence of mother figures in Carter's novels, the preponderance of characters who have lost their mothers and an abiding interest in the early novels in melancholy.

IV

Carter's novels are, as Gerrard says, 'undecorous' and 'mocking'. However, their subversion, irony and ribaldry are not just literary techniques – they are intellectual strategies. All texts inevitably contain traces of other texts which signal different ways of reading them. Julia Kristeva (1969) has pointed out: 'Tout texte se construit comme mosaique de citations, tout texte est absorption et trans-formation d'un autre texte' [Every text builds itself as a mosaic of quotations, every text is absorption and transformation of another text] (p. 146). This is something which Carter exploits in her work, but its hybridity is actually part of a wider intertextuality in which traditions, mythologies and conventions are subjected to scrutiny and inverted. As Pam Morris (1993) points out, *Nights at the Circus*, for example, is:

> One of the most triumphant examples of a woman writer's dialogic engagement with male literary language . . . a brilliant tapestry of parodied snatches from every conceivable form of novel: Dickensian eccentricity and comedy, Zolaesque realism, hard-boiled American detective fiction, travel narrative, popular sentiment and romance.  (p. 156)

Carter's novels frequently, explicitly and implicitly, refer to mythology, the Bible, European and English literary works, Renaissance drama, fairy stories, European art, film, especially Godard and Buñuel, opera, ballet, music, and psychoanalytic and linguistic theory. It is an indication of the subversive nature of Carter's work that often she refers to two or three different frameworks for the same referent in the same paragraph! For example, in *Shadow Dance* when Morris enters the cellar of the house where his friend is to kill their woman friend, he is compared to a character in a nursery tale and to a protagonist in a Greek tragedy (p. 135). Indeed, Carter's voice as a novelist is located, even though it is difficult to uncover, in the intertextuality of her work.

At Bristol University, Carter became familiar with European art – the French Symbolists and Dadaists are an obvious influence on her writings; and with Shakespeare and medieval literature in particular. Later, she became more conversant with European critical theorists especially the poststructuralists and the feminist psycho-analysts. The literary influences on her work include Chaucer, Boccaccio, Shakespeare, Jonathan Swift, William Blake, Mary Shelley, the Marquis de Sade, Edgar Allan Poe, Herman Melville, Dostoevsky, Lewis Carroll and Bram Stoker. Her close friends included postmodernist fiction writers such as Robert Coover and Salman Rushdie. Indeed, perhaps one of the reasons why Carter's work has aroused such controversy is that it is not typically English. Her novels are closer to the speculative fiction of writers such as Swift, the fiction of European Romantic writers, folk tales, fairy stories and the American Gothic than the traditional English novel.

In the succeeding chapters, I have attempted to show that the intertexts are exploited in Carter's writing as part of a general scepticism about frameworks. Her novels often exploit the creative possibilities in shifting between different frames of reference and in subverting the cultural forms and traditions which structure our thoughts, perceptions and actions. Whereas the early works are, to employ Kristeva's viewpoint, a 'mosaique de citations', the intertext in subsequent novels is often more clearly the totality of a particular cultural or literary tradition. Eventually, intertextuality becomes not so much a characteristic of her writing but a boldly thematised part of it. These novels – *The Magic Toyshop* is an obvious early example – are less likely than the Bristol trilogy to be read satisfactorily from a realist perspective. For their chief area of interest is the way in which meanings, boundaries and identities are rendered 'real' through cultural and linguistic metaphors. In these novels, Carter renders Western culture as 'foreign'. The texts are driven by the twin processes of 'defamiliarisation' – making the literary and the familiar strange – and 'deconstruction'. The latter provides a means of looking critically at what we take for granted – the original meaning of the word 'deconstruction' is 'to take things apart'. However, Carter's novels, which frequently employ, challenge and invert pairings of many kinds, are 'deconstructionist' in the more precise way in which the term is defined in critical practice. Our thinking often takes place within binary opposites – male:female; work:leisure; light:dark and so forth – in which one part is more highly valued in society than the other. Deconstructionists, like Carter, are concerned with questioning this relative assignment of value as a means of unravelling larger cultural and ideological implications.

Since the seeds of the defamiliarisation and deconstruction which are so pronounced in the post-1970s work are evident in the early fiction, I am reluctant to see the period, 1969–72, which she spent in Japan after she and her first husband, Paul Carter, separated, solely in terms of a watershed. Sage (1994b) has suggested that it was 'the impetus she had built up through her own early work that had sent her on her travels' (p. 29). Clearly, the period in Japan, according to Salman Rushdie (1993) 'a country whose tea-ceremony formality and dark eroticism bruised and challenged Carter's imagination' (p. x), was important. As Gerrard (1996) points out, Carter herself said of the period: 'In Japan, I learned what it was to be a woman, and became radicalised' (p. 23). But all these state-ments need further consideration in the light of ideas, interests and preoccupations around the concept of Woman and 'radicalism' in the pre-Japan fiction. Much of what she wrote about Japan and produced after her stay there provides a gloss on the early fiction. The account of the puppet master in 'The Loves of Lady Purple' from *Fireworks: Nine Profane Pieces* (1974) is clearly a product not only of Japan but of her experience of having written *The Magic Toyshop*. It recalls, for example, the sinister nature of Uncle Philip, the novel's toy maker and puppet master, the way in which he tries to transform his niece into a puppet and the way in which he serves as a parody of patriarchy:

> The puppet master is always dusted with a little darkness. In direct relation to his skill he propagates the most bewildering enigmas for, the more lifelike his marionettes, the more godlike his manipulations and the more radical the symbiosis between inarticulate doll and articulating fingers.
>
> (*Burning Your Boats*, p. 41)

The relationship between Marianne and Jewel in *Heroes and Villains* clearly informs her assessment of the Japanese attitude to romance in *Nothing Sacred*:

> But human relations either have the stark anonymity of rape or else are essentially tragic. Even at the level of the lowest art, the Japanese, it would seem, cannot bring themselves to borrow that simplistic, European formula: 'then they lived happily ever after'.
>
> (p. 43)

A gloss on this novel, as I shall explain in a later chapter, is also provided by her essay, 'People as Pictures' which is concerned with the Japanese art of tattooing. In other words, Japan did not simply provide her with new ideas, but confirmed her in the way in which she was developing.

The post-Japan period was initially difficult for Carter because she had no secure relationship with a publisher and her work was not well received by mainstream critics. Nevertheless, she seems not to have lost faith in the subjects on which Japan had confirmed her views. Indeed, the influence of Japan on the later novels is evident in their more pronounced sense of the artificiality of culture and of the self as a product of social and cultural processes. The impact of her Japanese experiences upon her view of other cultures, indeed culture in general, is evident in *The Infernal Desire Machines of Doctor Hoffman* (1972) and *The Passion of New Eve* (1977). Both these texts are set mainly abroad, the former in South America and the latter in the USA. Hoffman's purpose is the same as that which Carter, in 'A Souvenir of Japan', believed informed Japanese rituals, the transmutation of 'life itself to a series of grand gestures' (*Burning Your Boats*, p. 33). Hoffman's means of achieving this is provided by the mass media, anticipating Carter's concern with American culture, and the grand illusions spun by Hollywood, in *The Passion of New Eve* and *Wise Children* especially. Indeed, *The Passion of New Eve* brings 'A Souvenir of Japan' specifically to mind for the illusions are, as Carter said of those she found in Japan, 'as moving as they are absurd' (p. 33). As Sage (1994b) says, Japan 'confirmed her in her sense of strangeness' (p. 29). In *The Infernal Desire Machines of Doctor Hoffman* (1972), Mendoza is said to have claimed 'that if a thing were sufficiently artificial; it became absolutely equivalent to the genuine' (p. 102). This is a concept which Carter explores from various perspectives and in different levels of detail throughout the post-Japan fiction. The impact of Japan in this respect is evident in the first collection of 'stories' published after she had left there. In 'Flesh and the Mirror' from *Fireworks: Nine Profane Pieces* (1974), two strangers make love, and one of them sees their reflections in the mirror above them:

> But the selves we were not, the selves of our own habitual perceptions of ourselves, had a far more insubstantial substance than the reflections we were. The magic mirror presented me with a hitherto unconsidered notion of myself as I . . . I beset me. I was the subject of the sentence written on the mirror.
>
> (*Burning Your Boats*, p. 70)

The notion of the subject as located in an endless series of reflected images is central to the cultural critique which Carter developed after her period in Japan. In 'A Souvenir of Japan', Carter associates what she perceives as the insubstantiality of Japan with the Japanese obsession with mirrors:

> But, as if in celebration of the thing they feared, they seemed to have made the entire city into a cold hall of mirrors which continually proliferated whole galleries of constantly changing appearances, all marvellous but none tangible. If they did not lock up the real looking-glasses, it would be hard to tell what was real and what was not. (*Burning Your Boats*, p. 32)

After her period in Japan, Carter's writing displays a heightened concern with ways in which the boundaries between reality and illusion are blurred. While retaining a critique of identity and culture in late capitalist society, Carter's post-Japan novels are set in postcultural locations which are geographically and temporally farther and farther from 1960s Bristol and the London of *The Magic Toyshop*.

Carter's works are best read not as independent texts, but as part of an ongoing process of writing. Whilst to some degree this may be true of any author, it is especially true of Carter. In the chapters that follow, although I have tried to respect the independence of each text, the emphasis is upon how each of the novels is related to the other works. Although many valuable insights are to be gained from a chronological consideration of her work, there is also a strong cyclical dimension to her *oeuvre*. Carter herself seems at pains to draw attention to it. Apart from the recurring preoccupation with key themes and ideas, details such as the names of characters are repeated across a range of the texts. Honeybuzzard in *Shadow Dance* (1966), for example, recurs as two characters in *Love* (1971); Toussaint in *Several Perceptions* (1968) is resurrected in *Nights at the Circus* (1984); and the names of two of the characters in *The Passion of New Eve* (1977) are borrowed from a passage in *Heroes and Villains* (1969). There are pointed similarities between characters in different novels, as, for example, between Mrs Boulder in *Several Perceptions* and Fevvers in *Nights at the Circus* or between Desiderio in *The Infernal Desire Machines of Doctor Hoffman* (1972) and Walser in *Nights at the Circus*. Carter employs similar scenarios in different contexts such as the psychiatrist–client interview between Joseph and Ransome in *Several Perceptions* which occurs again between Lee and Annabel's doctor in *Love*. Moreover, where Carter engages with the characteristics of a literary tradition, for example the fairy story or the apocalyptic novel, rather than with particular texts, the engagement is frequently carried over a number of her novels.

In the chapters that follow, discussions of individual works are structured to help readers who may not be familiar with all of Carter's novels and are designed to illuminate important interpretative issues in her work as a whole whilst providing extended treatment of topics and features particular to each book. Each of the chapters are based on more than one novel, so that at the outset of each a brief *raison d'être* is provided for reading those particular texts together. The discussion of *Shadow Dance, Several Perceptions* and *Love* acknowledges that these novels do constitute a trilogy concerned with a bohemian district of Bristol with which Carter was familiar in the 1960s and that unlike the later fiction they invite being read as realist narratives. However, the emphasis of the chapter is on the combination of Gothic and psychological fantasy in each of these texts, particularly the way in which the Gothic genre becomes a means of engaging with other perspectives including realism, Jungian philosophy and twentieth-century psychoanalytic theory. The chapter explores the extent of Carter's indebtedness to American and European literature which in turn places her outside the tradition of the English novel. *Shadow Dance* (1966) is discussed at length because it has received relatively little critical attention over the years. It is seen as a novel particularly indebted to the work of Melville and Dostoevsky and to Carter's own critique of the Marquis de Sade in its pursuit of key Euro-American literary tropes such as the 'man of sorrows', body horror associated with 'necrophagy' and the 'double'. However, it is also suggested that the novel can be approached through a particular psychoanalytic framework provided by what has become known as object relations theory.

*Several Perceptions* (1968) is seen as pursuing the interest in the previous novel with the particular type of melancholy to be found in German Romantic and early nineteenth-century American literature. The emphasis of the critical discussion, however, falls on the significance for the novel of David Hume's concept of the mind as a kind of theatre and upon the importance of the influence of Shakespeare's last plays in which the distinction between reality and illusion is blurred in potentially stunning pieces of experimental theatre. While *Love* (1971) shares many of the preoccupations of the other two parts of the trilogy, the novel is seen as primarily, but not exclusively, concerned with a preoccupation that Carter no doubt discovered in the work of the nineteenth-century American writer, Edgar Allan Poe: the price paid by those who take too subjective a view of the world. The third chapter is concerned with two novels written during the same period as the trilogy, which do have certain features in common with those three texts, but which in other respects are closer to the later non-realistic fiction.

Unlike the novels of the trilogy, *The Magic Toyshop* (1967) and *Heroes and Villains* (1969) are each narrated from the perspective of a female consciousness, specifically an adolescent girl. They also confirm that Carter's work is different from the conventional English novel in the extent to which she is indebted to European literature and to pre-novelistic modes of writing such as fairy stories, 'warning tales', the European picaresque narrative and German Romantic tales. Although they are different novels in many respects, *The Magic Toyshop* and *Heroes and Villains* have much in common. Literary allusions are more sharply focused and coherent than in the trilogy and as such are used to call into question some of the grand narratives of Western culture – particularly those pertaining to the way in which female subjectivity and sexuality are normally constructed.

The salient narratives and assumptions of Western culture are also subjected to scrutiny in the two novels discussed in chapter 4. *The Infernal Desire Machines of Doctor Hoffman* (1972) and *The Passion of New Eve* (1977) were written during or after Carter's period in Japan. They develop ideas to be found in the earlier work, especially the unusual sense of 'foreignness' with which Carter, although born and brought up in England, tended to see English and Western culture. However, they stand apart from the other novels in the boldness of their treatment of this theme, their less realist and more philosophical mode of writing, and the way in which they each pursue their themes and tropes through a number of differently imagined societies. The chapter focuses on Carter's engagement with key debates of the 1970s such as biological essentialism, the masculinist bias in Freudian psychoanalysis, separatist feminist movements, and American survivalist movements as well as wider philosophical and social issues.

Carter's final novels, *Nights at the Circus* (1984) and *Wise Children* (1991), are discussed in relation to Carter's interest in the circus and the theatre in chapter 5. As Salman Rushdie (1993) has observed, although Carter made the fable-world her own, her 'other country is the fairground, the world of the gimcrack showman, the hypnotist, the trickster, the puppeteer' (p. xi). In particular, the chapter explores the ways in which Carter exploits the traditional connection between the theatre, the circus and what has come to be called the carnivalesque. These three areas are seen as cohering around Carter's interest in illegitimacy with which the theatre in the seventeenth century was associated.

# 2

# Euro-American Gothic and the 1960s

## *Shadow Dance* (1966), *Several Perceptions* (1968) and *Love* (1970)

I

*Shadow Dance, Several Perceptions* and *Love* are Angela Carter's first, third and fifth novels respectively. In between writing them, she published two novels, *The Magic Toyshop* and *Heroes and Villains*, which anticipate the less realistic style of the later fiction. Although Sue Roe (1994) has argued that formally *Love* stands alone in Carter's *oeuvre*, these three novels, despite the differences between them, have much in common. Indeed, acknowledging that they all share a recognisable contemporary setting, O'Day (1994) has called them Carter's Bristol trilogy, a view supported by Lorna Sage (1994b, p. 22). Sage, however, is troubled by O'Day's description of them as realist texts. Whilst, as O'Day argues, they do not possess the 'magic realist' qualities of Carter's later fiction, she believes that they have 'the extra density of fiction squared' (p. 22).

O'Day's main argument for seeing these three novels as a trilogy is that each is a fictional mediation of aspects of the area of Bristol in which Carter lived: the auction room, junk shop and derelict houses in *Shadow Dance*; a bedsit, a large mansion and the Downs in *Several Perceptions*; and a two-room flat, the park and (Mecca) ballroom in *Love*. More significantly, the trilogy presents us with an imaginative response to provincial bohemian life as it happened at the time in bedsits, flats, cafes and coffee bars where somehow the boundaries between art and life became blurred. However, O'Day also suggests that the novels all deploy a similar array of characters, variants of a similar plot structure, comparable forms of narration, and themes and motifs concerning 1960s counterculture.

There are further reasons why these novels may be regarded as a trilogy which I want to explore in this chapter. Each novel, at various levels, including parody, is indebted to Euro-American Gothic. In particular, through a combination of Gothic and psychological fantasy, Carter pursues themes and motifs from nineteenth-century American writers, especially Herman Melville and Edgar Allan Poe. Carter's view of American Gothic writing was undoubtedly mediated through Leslie Fiedler's *Love and Death in the American Novel* (1960) which quickly became required reading for students of literature. One of the epigraphs to *Heroes and Villains* (1969) is from Fiedler's book and suggests that Carter was particularly interested in his perception of Gothic American literature: 'The Gothic mode is essentially a form of parody, a way of assailing clichés by exaggerating them to the limit of grotesqueness.' Certainly many of the characteristics of Carter's early writing recall Fiedler's summary of the principal features of Gothic writing: the substitution of terror for love as a central theme; the vicarious flirtation with death; an aesthetic that replaces the classic concept of 'nothing-in-excess' with the 'the revolutionary doctrine that nothing succeeds like excess'; and a dedication 'to producing nausea, to transcending the limits of taste and endurance' (p. 126).

Each of the novels constituting the Bristol trilogy explores the negative aspects of the psyche – a project which leads inevitably to the Gothic tale, traditionally a vehicle for ideas about 'psychological' evil rather than evil as a force exterior to the mind. In the afterword to the first edition of *Fireworks* (1974) Carter makes clear that even in the mid-1970s this was how she thought of European Gothic tales although, as Warner (1994) points out, she removed it from subsequent editions having become by then more interested in the connection between folktales and the imaginations of 'ordinary' people:

cruel tales, tales of wonder, tales of terror, fabulous narratives that deal directly with the imagery of the unconscious – mirrors; the externalised self, forsaken castles, haunted forests; forbidden sexual objects. . . . Characters and events are exaggerated beyond reality, to become symbols, ideas, passions. Its style will tend to be ornate, unnatural – and thus operate against the perennial human desire to believe the word as fact. Its only humour is black humour. It retains a singular moral function – that of provoking unease. (pp. 244–5)

Carter's early novels, however, are not simply Gothic in the traditional sense of the term. The Gothic genre is itself subversive, giving expression to what is culturally occluded such as sexual fantasy and female desire. However, Carter's novels are frequently subversions of the genre; themes and ideas first explored – albeit however crudely – in Gothic writing are re-examined, challenged and expanded. The Gothic becomes a mode of awareness within the novels which challenges, contradicts or confirms other perspectives, as diverse as social realism, Jungian psychoanalysis and 'projection' theory, and is in turn subverted and/or expanded by them. This hybridity creates different possible ways of reading the texts, giving them the 'extra density of fiction' to which Sage refers. However, the dominance of the Gothic mode of writing within these early novels subverts the close relationship between word and referent which characterises realism. As Elizabeth MacAndrew (1979) points out, the all pervading symbolism of the Gothic tale is 'almost, though not quite allegorical' – the 'referents are deliberately hazy' (p. 8). In the early novels – as in the later non-realistic, philosophical fiction – Carter exploits the hybridity of Gothic writing and its capacity for ambivalence and ambiguity.

In this trilogy, Carter appears to be re-visioning the sequence novel which according to Connor (1996) underwent a remarkable revival after the Second World War. As he points out:

The world of the sequence has the self-sufficient density it supposes of the 'real' world. It is closed and complete in itself, a parallel universe or working simulacrum of the real not only in the encyclopaedic abundance of its narrative detail but also in its plethora of different possible perspectives; typically the novel-sequence will combine and juxtapose not only different experiences of different characters but also the same experiences revisited from different points of view. (p. 136)

Unlike the conventional novel-sequence which Connor describes, and more like Beckett in his *Trilogy*, Carter's sequence resists offering the reader a complete, coherent and self-sufficient world. Each of the novels in the Bristol trilogy enacts a complex, repetitious and paradoxical narrative.


II


*Shadow Dance* (published in the USA as *Honeybuzzard*) was completed in 1964 whilst Carter was a student of English literature at Bristol University. It is the novel which has received least attention, partly because it was out of print from 1966 until 1994 and may be because it has a number of obvious weaknesses which Claire Harman (1994) has identified; for example, the surreal characters, the constant threat of melodrama and its loose ends.

Although the novel is narrated in the third person, the story is told from the point of view of one of the male characters, Morris Grey, and, as Lorna Sage (1994b) says, 'the female characters are scattered at large in a man's world' (p. 10). The specifically male focus is evident, for example, in Morris's attempt to justify what his friend, Honeybuzzard, has done to Ghislaine, the attractive woman with whom Morris has a disastrous one-night stand: 'She was asking for trouble . . . Running around like she used to do, daft bitch, late at night, and nothing on under her mackintosh' (p. 33). It is also apparent in the way he describes his junk shop as a worthwhile place to work because it attracts lots of Americans in the summer – 'Especially females. In Bermuda shorts' (p. 35). Nevertheless, *Shadow Dance* is a complex, feminist and psychoanalytical exploration of post-1950s England. Morris's perspective, as one of many in the novel, is challenged and undermined by the wider interaction of voices within the text which also encourages the reader to regard it sceptically.

At one level, the narrative takes the reader, as Harman (1994) says, 'through a brilliantly evoked provincial urban landscape of the early 1960s (full of diverting 'period' detail), complete with a moribund newsagent's shop, a filthy laundry, a cafeteria of 'inescapable, undistinguishable brownness', vomiting girls and peeing dogs'. However, as I suggested in the introduction, drawing on Allende's definition of 'magic realism', the representational codes of realism in Carter's work, even in the more realistic writing of the 1960s, are locked in a continuous dialectic with fantasy. In *Shadow Dance*, the distinction between the two is blurred in the focalisation of Morris himself as well as in much of its imagery, as in the exchange between an owl and a child who mimics the bird's call so that the two sounds, the real and the fictitious, become indistinguishable. But the dialectic between the two modes is present in the novel as ironic comedy and, with more *gravitas*, in the spirit of Melville and the German Romantic writers.

Honeybuzzard, at one level, appears as a comic version of the Gothic villain – he likes to wear false noses, false ears and plastic vampire teeth, retaining only his habitual dark glasses. Morris is a less parodic adaptation of the German Romantic protagonist pursued by the guilty secret of some terrible past deed. In pursuing these two approaches to Gothic material, Carter appears to be reflecting on the difficulty of transposing nineteenth-century Romantic tropes to the late twentieth century, especially for readers whose taste for the Gothic has been influenced by Hammer horror films and their subsequent parodies. Nevertheless, it is at the level of horror-fantasy that *Shadow Dance* is a shocking book.

After the disastrous one-night stand with Ghislaine, Morris tells his flamboyantly violent friend, Honeybuzzard, with whom he runs the junk shop, to 'teach her a lesson'. He is unprepared for what Honeybuzzard does. In a graveyard, she is raped and slashed with a knife after which her face is left monstrously scarred. However, she returns from hospital to haunt Morris in ways which are reminiscent of 'the bride of Frankenstein' and of Dracula and eventually to take Honeybuzzard away from his new woman-friend, Emily. But once Emily has seen Ghislaine's scars, she is more than prepared to let him go! Bizarrely, Ghislaine, however, is willing to accept Honeybuzzard as her master. Taking her to an old house, though, he murders her near a plaster crucifix of Christ.

The fact that Ghislaine is mutilated in a graveyard and murdered close to a crucifix, on which Honeybuzzard had envisaged taking turns with Morris to lay her, are significant. These details compound the horror arising from the way in which women are seen as 'flesh' and 'meat' – especially as Honeybuzzard also thinks of selling pornographic photographs of Ghislaine on the crucifix. The interrelated but contrasting tropes of flesh signifying pleasure and of meat as signifying economic objectification occur throughout

Carter's fiction which seeks to explore the boundaries between them. In *The Sadeian Woman*, Carter explains:

> The word 'fleisch', in German, provokes me to an involuntary shudder. In the English language, we make a fine distinction between flesh, which is usually alive, and, typically, human; and meat, which is dead, inert, animal and intended for consumption . . . the pleasures of the flesh are vulgar and unrefined, even with an element of beastliness about them, although flesh tints have the sumptuous succulence of peaches because flesh plus skin equals sensuality.  (pp. 137–8)

Investigating and challenging the distinction between 'flesh' and 'meat' was not peculiar to Carter's work in the 1960s and not confined to fiction. For example, Carolee Schneeman's performance art piece, *Meat Joy*, first performed in 1964, was based on what was then a scandalous amount of nudity and 'forbidden' contact with the raw flesh of fish and chickens. Carter's critique of the work of the Marquis de Sade, however, provides a retrospective commentary on how the flesh/meat trope is developed by what happens to Ghislaine in *Shadow Dance* in distinctive ways and upon the particular dimension of 'body horror' which the novel explores. As Carter says in *The Sadeian Woman:* 'Sexuality, stripped of the idea of free exchange, is not in any way humane; it is nothing but pure cruelty. Carnal knowledge is the infernal knowledge of the flesh as meat' (p. 141). This is reinforced by the proximity of Ghislaine's murder to an image of the crucifixion, one of the assumptions of which it also makes real. As Carter explains in her reading of de Sade: 'The strong, abuse, exploit and meatify the weak' (p. 140).

The image of 'meatifying' the weak also occurs in Carter's parody of de Sade in the later novel, *The Infernal Desire Machines of Doctor Hoffman* (1972). There the women who are kept in the Count's cages have 'hides . . . streaked, blotched and marbled' (p. 132). The 'meaty' connotations of the word 'hides' are developed in the description of the girl who appears to have been recently whipped: 'torn and bleeding she was the most dramatic revelation of the nature of meat that I have ever seen' (p. 133). Moreover, in that novel, the Reality Testing Laboratory, in which the Determination Police – a latter day equivalent of the German SS of the 1930s and 1940s – torture their suspects, smells of roast pork (p. 22).

In *The Sadeian Woman,* Carter observes that it is 'the shocking tragedy of mortality itself, that all flesh may be transformed, at any moment, to meat' (p. 140). This sense of horror at the transformation of 'flesh' into 'meat' in death is very strong in *Shadow Dance.* Morris, for example, is reminded of it every time he opens the door of his junk shop and is 'punched in the stomach' by the smell of rotting meat from the butcher's shop next door. Indeed, this may be what encourages him to think of his sick wife, Edna as 'a poor flat fillet on the marble slab of her bed' (p. 13). This image is disturbing for what is absent – there is nothing alive or sensual about it. It anticipates Edna's condition as a corpse, bereft of any compensatory symbolism. As Jean Baudrillard (1993) has pointed out every society has

> always staved off the abjection of natural death, the *social* abjection of decomposition which voids the corpse of its signs and its social force of signification, leaving it as nothing more than a substance, and by the same token, precipitating the group into the terror of its own symbolic decomposition.  (p. 180)

Julia Kristeva (1982) argues, 'refuse and corpses *show me* what I permanently thrust aside in order to live' (p. 3). However, the fillet metaphor is particularly disturbing because not only does it turn Edna's body into meat but, in turning the bed into a butcher's slab, associates it with necrophagy.

Necrophagy – 'the exposition of the meatiness of human flesh' – as Carter points out in *The Sadeian Woman* 'parodies the sacramental meal' (p. 140), thereby associating Edna with Ghislaine's death close to the crucifix. In *The Sadeian Woman,* Carter explains: 'Substitute the word "flesh" in the Anglican service of Holy Communion; "Take, eat, this is my meat which was given for you . . ." and the sacred comestible becomes the offering of something less than, rather more than, human' (p. 137). 'Fillet' suggests not only the pleasure of carving meat, associating Morris's fantasy of his wife with Honeybuzzard's mutilation of Ghislaine's face, but the anticipatory pleasure of eating meat. It is the suggestion of necrophagy in Honeybuzzard's face that exacerbates the horror of what he has done to Ghislaine: 'It was impossible to look at the full rich lines of his dark red mouth without thinking: "This man eats meat" ' (p. 56). The association with a bird of prey in his name is reinforced by the nature of his mouth which is said to suggest 'snapping, tearing, biting'.

Meat eating is a recurring trope in Carter's work, evident in *The Bloody Chamber and Other Stories* (1979) which, as Margaret Atwood (1994) has pointed out, is 'arranged according to categories of meat-eater' (p. 122). Although these stories are based on fairy tales – such as Perrault's 'Little Red Riding Hood' – they are not 'versions' or, as the American edition of the book said, 'adult' fairy stories. Carter herself explained that she sought 'to extract the latent content from the traditional stories and to use it as the beginnings of new stories' (Haffenden, 1985, p. 84). In them, Carter develops the connection, first mooted in *Shadow Dance*, between the perception of women as property and the objectification of women as 'flesh' in ways which elide the connotations of 'flesh' and 'meat'. However, the association is taken further in the emphasis placed upon an active, unruly female sexuality which women have been taught might devour them. The first three stories, 'The Bloody Chamber', 'The Courtship of Mr Lyon' and 'The Tiger's Bride', are cat family narratives where, as Merja Makinen (1992) argues, the wild felines signify 'the sensual desires that women need to acknowledge within themselves' (p. 11). The last three stories in the book are wolf family stories, concerned with a more unruly, animalistic sexuality. Critics have argued over how to read these stories. Makinen suggests that the beasts be seen as the 'projections of a feminine libido' and challenges critics, such as Patricia Duncker, who see the beasts as men. I would suggest that the stories invite a number of different and, even competing, readings, as does most of Carter's fiction. The stories are a development from *Shadow Dance* in that they are not only an exploration of women's sexuality but of the ways in which men have sought to control that sexuality, of how both men and women need to reconfigure their sexualities, and of the commodification of women as 'flesh'.

The trope of cannibalism in Carter's work is closely connected to its interest in oppression for, as she explains in *The Sadeian Woman*, she saw cannibalism 'as the most elementary act of exploitation, that of turning the other directly into a comestible; of seeing the other in the most primitive terms of use' (p. 140). In the opening story of *The Bloody Chamber and Other Stories*, Carter provides a male protagonist drawn particularly closely on the Marquis de Sade's cannibal, Minski. Although not the organising principle, cannibalism is an important trope, too, in the earlier *The Infernal Desire Machines of Doctor Hoffman* (1972). Not only is Desiderio adopted by river people who intend to eat him because they believe in that way they will acquire his knowledge, but in a parodic scene, the Count is boiled alive by an African tribe where the chief's cannibalistic methods of discipline maintain his authority. There is, however, a difference between cannibalism as it is practised by the river people and that employed by the chief or suggested by the 'buzzard' part of Honeybuzzard's name. As Baudrillard (1993) maintains, cannibals 'don't just eat anybody . . . whoever is eaten is always somebody worthy, it is always a mark of respect to devour somebody since, through this, the devoured even becomes sacred' (p. 138). This is very different from the meat eating which takes place in Western European society: 'We think of anthropophagia as despicable in view of the fact that we despise what we eat' (ibid.).

Contentiously, *Shadow Dance* associates the mutilation of Ghislaine with a latent necrophagy in society as a whole. It is surely significant that when Emily first sees the mutilated Ghislaine she is standing in the street outside the junk shop when the butcher next door receives a delivery of meat. The description of the meat underlines its transformation from flesh – 'great joints of meat, red sides of beef and amber-rinded pork and white legs of lamb and rosy shoulders of mutton' (p. 152). The nouns which remind us of animals – joints, sides, shoulders, legs – also remind us of what is human. But they are combined with words that deny the origins of meat as flesh – 'beef', 'rinded', 'mutton', 'pork'. Yet what is denied is reintroduced by the description of the butcher in his 'filthy blue apron and bloodstained straw boater, around which the flies already buzzed'.

The last verb in the above quotation reminds us of Honeybuzzard himself and significantly occurs before the account of Ghislaine standing in the street, waiting to confront Emily with what he has done to her face. It also recalls the fly that buzzed as Morris confronted Honeybuzzard over what he did to Ghislaine, while the Janus nature of Honeybuzzard's face – cherub and buzzard – is reflected in the description of the butcher. However, in developing the comparison between the butcher and Honeybuzzard, Carter focuses on the process of denial. The boater signifies a traditionally English view of what is elegant and civilised, but the bloodstains suggest what civilisation tends to deny or render as 'other'. This denial is suggested also by the fact that before Emily sees Ghislaine she is on her way to the lavatory – signifying the disposal of unpleasant matter – and when Ghislaine and the meat appear the laundry starts up and begins to 'hum'. Indeed, the presence of the laundry not only reinforces the notion of removing what is unpleasant from public view, but places the process in an institutionalised context.

In the description of the butcher receiving his order of meat, then, Carter inscribes the tension between society's recognition of its scatological elements, albeit in order to remove them, and its denial of them. Honeybuzzard's mutilation of Ghislaine is contextualised within this Janus aspect of society. Society turns flesh into meat on a daily basis, but simultaneously denies this by locating abattoirs out of public view and in reconfiguring flesh as cooked food, masking its origins. The word 'hum', of course, can suggest a musical sound – something attractive and transcendental – or the smell of rotting matter.

Emily's obsessive cleanliness enables her to cope with the contradictory nature of society and of the roles which she is required to perform. This is evident after her one-night stand with Morris in which she serves as his surrogate mother as much as, if not more than, his lover – she is able to expel him like so much dirt. Significantly, when Ghislaine arrives shortly afterwards at her door, she cries 'Let me in!' (p. 154). Ghislaine is, of course, asking to be admitted not just to the shop but to Emily's consciousness. In making Emily kiss her scar, Ghislaine forces her to acknowledge Honeybuzzard's violence: 'he would cut me up like that if I did anything he didn't like. Like going to bed with anyone else. Or getting pregnant' (p. 166).

A key to the association of flesh with meat, necrophagy and the crucifix in Carter's early work is provided by the psychoanalytical criticism of Julia Kristeva (1987), albeit in another context. In an analysis of the painting *The Corpse of Christ in the Tomb*, by Hans Holbein the Younger (1521), Kristeva responds to the minimalism of the work: that Christ is entirely alone in the tomb; that the body is not idealised in any way; and that there is no suggestion of transcendence nor of passion. In other words, Kristeva is concerned with the way in which the painting brings the viewer into close proximity with death, bereft of any compensatory symbolism. At one level of signification, the crucifix is a transcendental symbol. Normally, representations of Christ provide us with a way of enlarging our imaginary and symbolic means of coping with death. However, at another level, the crucifix reminds us that at one time the cross was a cruel and commonplace instrument of torture and execution. Bereft of any compensatory symbolism, death, as in Holbein's painting and Carter's *Shadow Dance*, disrupts the symbolic, as a depression. Both texts challenge our imaginary capacities. For the novel, like Holbein's painting, forces us to imagine what is in the gap between death and its *denegation* through symbolic language, and between flesh and meat.

Kristeva attributes the kind of detachment and coldness in Holbein's presentation of death to the Reformation and the emergence of a 'melancholic moment'. Here she makes a connection, essential to our understanding of Carter's work, between Holbein's view of death and the state of mind of the melancholic. As John Lechte (1990) argues 'Holbein's dead Christ . . . goes very close to illustrating the denial of *denegation* and the evacuation of drive affect characteristic of the melancholic's constructions' (p. 188). Similarly, in her depiction of melancholia, Carter focuses on the failure of the imaginative and the symbolic, as I shall discuss in the next section.

### III

Carter's use of the concept of the 'Shadow' may have been triggered by Fiedler's *Love and Death in the American Novel* (1960) in which he points out that the Shadow is 'the most variously developed of all the Gothic symbols' (p. 125). The word 'Shadow' in the title of the novel has a number of connotations. At one level, it invokes Jungian psychology. But, at another level, *Shadow Dance*, refers the reader to Psalm 23 where we are said to 'walk through the valley of the shadow of death'. This is certainly appropriate to both Morris and his friend, Honeybuzzard, who specialise in stealing Victoriana from derelict houses which they subsequently sell in their junk shop. This line of work only serves to feed Morris's dark, brooding personality:

Beds with the shallow depressions in them that men and women, like rivers, mould out for themselves over the years. And piles of photographs of other people's darlings, smiling from outmoded clothes in forgotten summers at Torquay and elsewhere. And books signed inside, with love; up for sale, now, dead love for sale. (p. 25)

An important influence here is a story, 'Bartleby', by Melville, whom Carter regarded, according to 'Notes From The Front Line', as one of her 'male literary heroes' (p. 75). The story concerns a man who, it is suggested, was affected by his work as a clerk in the Dead Letter Office. The Dead Letter Office, as the name suggests, was concerned with documents and personal effects, such as rings, enclosed with them, relating to people who had died. Like Morris, Bartleby spends much of his life meditating upon mortality, the brevity of life, and upon objects that were once part of someone's life, but are now 'junk' or of value only as antiques.

In creating Bartleby, Melville drew upon a figure well established in European romance, which he had read in Carlyle's translations – the 'man of sorrows' (Peach, 1982, pp. 155–6). The stranger in Tieck's 'The Runnenberg', for example, typically admits to Christian: 'tonight I grew so sad as I never was in my life before: I seemed so lost, so utterly unhappy; and even yet I cannot shake aside that melancholy humour'. Melville and his European predecessors approached this type of melancholy within a particular metaphysical framework of the time. The optimistic disposition of a confident protagonist, such as the narrator of 'Bartleby', is undermined by the presence of the 'man of sorrows', a figure whom we might describe today as suffering from melancholia, just as Bartleby is affected by his work in the Dead Letter Office. The presence of the 'man of sorrows' disturbs the binarism between a positive subject position, or optimistic mode of thought and being, which Carlyle summarised in *Sartor Resartus* as the 'Everlasting Yea', and a negative subject position, arising from a sceptical turn of mind, which Carlyle summarised as 'the Everlasting No'. Melville , like Dostoevsky – another of Carter's male literary heroes – found the latter subject position so horrific as to be almost beyond contemplation. As the narrator of 'Bartleby' concludes: 'What miserable friendlessness and loneliness are here revealed! His poverty is great; but his solitude, how horrible!' Nevertheless, Melville suspected that the 'Everlasting No' may have offered a more accurate reflection of life and the human condition than the 'Everlasting Yea'. Throughout Melville's work, *pace* Carlyle, 'the articulate lovely' appears to the enquiring mind but a veil for 'the inarticulate chaotic' (Peach, 1982, p. 144). This aspect of Melville's and also of Dostoevsky's work certainly interested Carter. In 'Notes From The Front Line', she observes: 'both of them lived so close to the edge of the existential abyss that they must often, and with good reason, have envied those who did not have enquiring minds' (p. 75).

In *Shadow Dance*, Carter approaches Morris from different yet overlapping perspectives. Whilst one can be appropriately discussed in terms of the nineteenth-century metaphysical framework which she undoubtedly found in Melville's work, the other is influenced by twentieth-century psychoanalysis and anticipates the work of French psychoanalysts such as Julia Kristeva. According to Kristeva, the melancholic is someone for whom despair and pain, as in Bartleby's case, provide the only meaning. The melancholic's identification with suffering and death, evidenced by Morris and Bartleby, is thus part of their failure to transform suffering in imaginative language. Kristeva (1987) argues that the melancholic's sadness is:

the most archaic expression of a non-symbolisable, unnameable narcissistic wound that is so premature that no external agent (subject or object) can be referred to it. For this type of narcissistic depressive sadness is in reality the only object. More exactly, it is an ersatz of an object to which he attaches himself, and which he tames and cherishes, for want of something else.  (p. 22)

From this perspective, the fact that Morris is a failed painter is an index of his melancholia, providing evidence of his failure to develop his imaginary and symbolic capacities. In fact, Morris tends to translate life into death. He imagines the old woman who works as a skivvy at the cafe, for example, creeping nearer and nearer the grave and envisages the loneliness of her death. He thinks of her as the Struldbrug, the name given to the immortals in Swift's *Gulliver's Travels* who only get older and uglier. Confessing to his friend, Oscar, that the cafe makes him sad, he sees his meringue as 'whited sepulchres with dead men's bones inside them' (p. 32).

Although Morris is a failed painter, the fact that he struggles to paint distinguishes him in a crucial respect from Emily and Honeybuzzard. For instance, he is at least able to appreciate the loss of life in the destruction of a bluebottle's eggs, unlike Emily who manifests her failure to develop the imaginary. Her only response to one of Morris's paintings, which she tries to 'read' as a visually impaired person feels Braille, is that it is 'quite big reely' (p. 104). Indeed, Melville's argument that an important aspect of the enquiring, symbolic imagination was the capacity to appreciate 'the inarticulate chaotic' makes Emily's initial reaction to Morris's junk shop significant. When Morris pointedly tells her that 'the unseemly chaos around her was the norm', a sentence which has metaphysical ramifications beyond the shop to which it refers, she seems unperturbed, even spitting out a raisin pip as if in defiance.

Suffering comes with love and a capacity to believe in, that is the struggle to symbolise, some ideal. In his regret over what happens to Ghislaine and over the mistaken killing of the Stuldbrug, Morris demonstrates a capacity, albeit undeveloped, for love. His troubled conscience is symbolised by his constant aching teeth which when he tells Edna that Honey mutilated Ghislaine begin 'to ache, all together, in concert; all the canines and molars sang in chorus' (p. 50).

Morris's troubled state of mind stands in contradistinction to Honeybuzzard's indifference, a concept for which Carter is again indebted to Melville who, unlike Carlyle, saw the state of indifference as more than a transitory condition. The influence of Melville's preoccupation with what he called 'bitter blanks' is evident in the way Carter, too, associates 'indifference' with an inner void. When Morris tells Honeybuzzard that Ghislaine has been discharged from hospital, he notes how Honeybuzzard's face is 'a mask of nothing' (p. 59). However, Dostoevsky is an additional influence on Honeybuzzard, who is also described as having 'Raskolnikov eyes, like dead coals' (p. 42). Like Dostoevsky's Raskolnikov prior to his redemption, who cannot believe that his murder of an old woman was a crime, Honeybuzzard does not feel any remorse over what he has done to Ghislaine or over his apparent killing of the old woman from the cafe. Indeed, the emphasis shifts from his cruelty, evidenced in the extent of Ghislaine's injuries, to his indifference: ' "I don't care. Let her go, let her go!" He flung Ghislaine to the winds, with the gesture of the sower in the parable' (p. 61).

As I indicated earlier, in Western European culture the figure of the crucified Christ became one of the most potent symbols for the transformation of suffering and death, providing a way of enlarging the symbolic means of coping with death. As Kristeva (1987) explains,

> In the light of this identification, admittedly too anthropological and psychological in the eyes of a strict theology, man is nevertheless bequeathed a powerful symbolic device enabling him to live his death and resurrection even in his physical body, thanks to the power of imaginary unification – and its real effects – with the absolute Subject (Christ).  (p. 145)

Hence, Honeybuzzard's indifference to the crucifix which he and Morris find in a derelict house is an important indicator of his psychic disposition: '[Christ's] plaster nose was chipped, there were cobwebs in his beard and Honey's booted foot crunched a hand to dust in the darkness' (p. 131) However, indifference in Carter's work becomes 'in differance', the portmanteau term coined by the French philosopher, Jacques Derrida, to conflate the senses of 'difference' and 'deferment'. Derrida's thesis that meaning is never finite but always 'deferred' because of its dependency upon an endless interplay of shifting signifiers within language is appropriate to Carter's representation of Honeybuzzard.

In the previous chapter, I suggested that all texts contain traces of other texts which signal different ways of reading them. In *Shadow Dance*, there are allusions to a famous film of the 1960s, Hitchcock's *Psycho*. For example, in the dream in which Morris mutilates his wife, Edna, he screams that there is too much blood. In *Psycho*, the film's chief protagonist, Norman Bates, reacts in a similar way to the amount of blood after the infamous 'shower scene' in which, as his dead mother, he commits the first murder we witness on the screen. In fact, Hitchcock's film is a particularly appropriate intertext because Robert Bloch's novel, on which the film is based, is itself a reworking of the Ed Glein case, a murderer who ate his victims. However, it is the allusion to the scene at the end of Hitchcock's film which perhaps has the most relevance for Carter's book, serving to highlight the elusive nature of the novel.

The details of the episode in which Honeybuzzard learns of Ghislaine's release – his face slipping for a moment into 'a mask of nothing' and the reference to the buzzing fly in the silence – are redolent of a scene at the end of *Psycho*. Bates sits alone in a police cell while a psychiatrist provides a long and unconvincing explanation for the murders which Bates has committed as his mother. The camera focuses on a fly which Bates, believing himself to be watched, refuses to swot so as to give the impression that he would not harm a fly. For a split second his face changes to that of a skeleton. At one level, this shot suggests a blank void, an amoral nothingness, which cannot be easily rationalised or summarised – the kind of indifference exhibited by Honeybuzzard. As one of a number of camera shots that throughout the film appear to look into and behind Bates's eyes to discover only an unfathomable darkness, it also suggests, in contradistinction to the psychiatrist's narrative, that the human psyche is itself unknowable. The different intertextual references which Carter employs in describing Honeybuzzard suggest that, like Norman Bates, he, too, cannot be easily pinned down: we learn, for example, that his 'high-held androgynous face was hard and fine and inhuman; Medusa, marble, terrible'; but he is also 'the beautiful, terrible Angel of the Annunciation'; and he appears to be 'a spectre, a madman, a vampire' (p. 136).

Honeybuzzard, as the duality of his name indicates, seems to embody the contradictory fears at the heart of the Gothic tradition: distrust of the ego – like the protagonist in the European romance, he appears 'possessed by some personal devil' (p. 136) – and fear of the id, the buried darkness from which it emerged and to which it must eventually return. The latter is signified most explicitly in the novel by the cellar of the house in which Honeybuzzard murders Ghislaine: 'It smelt most terrible – of damp, of rot, of excrement, of mice, of rats, of garbage, of age, of hopelessness, of uncleanness . . . of human physical corruption' (p. 133). However, Honeybuzzard, as 'Honey' and 'Buzzard', is also typical of the particular way in which the Janus nature of reality is configured in the Euro-American Gothic. This configuration is evident, for example, in Melville's *Moby Dick* in the image of the sphinx. As originally described by Carlyle – 'There is in her celestial beauty – which means celestial order, pliancy to wisdom; but there is also a darkness, a ferocity, a totality which are infernal' – this particular image takes pride of place in the novel. In *Shadow Dance*, this configuration is evident not only in the face worn by Honeybuzzard, half Cherub and half devil, but the disfigured Ghislaine: ' When she laughed, half her face was that of a happy baby and the other half, crinkled up, did not look like a face at all' (p. 153).

*Shadow Dance* also appears to follow American Gothic in suggesting that to deny one side of the mask is to risk destroying the whole.We learn from the later novel, *Love* (1971), in which Honeybuzzard is split to reappear as Honey and Buzz, that in describing the cherubic aspect of Honey, Carter had Melville's story *Billy Budd* in mind, where a man is doomed because he is too perfect. Like Melville, Carter incorporates the other into her novel against which American Gothic is defined – transcendentalism, belief in an idealised 'reality' immanent in or beyond the ordinary appearances of the world. Developed under the influence of German idealism and English romanticism, transcendentalism became the corner-stone of a New England movement from approximately 1830 to 1860. One of its basic tenets is evident in Morris's description of the fishmonger's window which presents 'a transcendental vision of mystical ecstasy' : 'all held some numinous significance, ideal forms from a universe where dead women walked and the past could run back on itself and there was palpable, tangible joy in the air' (p. 161). As in Melville's writing, such transcendental idealism, however, fails at the level of the individual. Morris tries to shut Ghislaine, and what Ghislaine represents, out of his mind:

> And she walked into his empty mind again and sat down. Ignore her, don't think of her – Ghislaine. Think of pretty things, instead; think of white cats and black waistcoats and cheerful Hallowe'en feet. (p. 79)

At one point in *Shadow Dance*, Morris squeezes too hard on a pimple so that blood and pus flow together. Such an image in the American Gothic configuration of the world would warn of the dangers of expelling pus at the expense of the blood. Carter would seem to have this and her earlier image in mind when Morris warns Oscar: 'You want to know all sorts of lovely, gory details and you think you can squeeze them out of me' (p. 33). However, Carter's work challenges the Janus configuration of the American Gothic. Blood and pus may coexist in the American Gothic, but they are distinct. The subsequent issue in American Gothic is the incorporation of a Janus configuration of reality into a worldview which is not in itself disabling. Hawthorne's novel, *The Scarlet Letter*, for example, opens by acknowledging that the founders of Boston needed a cemetery and a prison. The issue is to find a worldview in which idealism is not threatened by the presence of death and transgression. In *Shadow Dance*, however, the boundaries between blood and pus are themselves blurred.

Like Dostoevsky's Golyadkin in *The Double*, Morris appears to project deeds he dare not commit onto his 'double', in this case Honeybuzzard. The 'double' haunts nineteenth-century European literature from the tales of Theodore Hoffmann to Robert Louis Stevenson's *Dr Jekyll and Mr Hyde*. Initially, it was a device for expressing the reflected self and the split personality. But, as Elizabeth MacAndrews (1979) points out, it eventually came to be concerned, as in Hoffmann's story 'The Doubles', with two identities that are not separated halves of one personality but two quite separate people (p. 210). Following Hoffmann's legacy, Carter's novels employ the 'double' in her fiction as separate people, but in ways that also betray the influence of Dostoevsky, according to Peter Conradi (1988), 'the greatest writer to have addressed himself so wholeheartedly to the theme of the "double" ' (p. 4). In *Shadow Dance*, the Russian novelist's influence is evident in the way in which Morris is conceived as a 'double' for Golyadkin. In *The Double*, for example, Golyadkin becomes increasingly irrational as he keeps running into his evil, wish-fulfilling double. Honeybuzzard could be seen as Morris's wish-fulfilling double and, of course, Morris himself becomes increasingly distraught and irrational after Honeybuzzard re-enters his life.

The 'double' functions, however, as a more complicated and ambivalent trope in Carter's writing than in the work of either Melville or Dostoevsky, even though she was influenced by them. At one level, the 'double' in Carter's fiction is employed to suggest the immutability of patriarchal society. However, at another level, it suggests the plural and shifting nature of identities. At even a third level, it provides a means of challenging the kind of binary thinking which distinguishes – too rigidly Carter suggests – between reality and imagination, masculine and feminine, legitimate and illegitimate, good and evil, or custom and taboo.

The 'double' trope in *Shadow Dance* is developed within a framework drawn partly from American Gothic fiction and partly from twentieth-century psychoanalytical theory. In *Two Essays on Analytical Psychology*, Jung used the word 'shadow' to refer to negative aspects of the psyche. Whilst Jung believed, like Freud, that the personal unconscious is developed during the individual's life time, Jung argued for the existence of a collective unconscious which presents itself in the conscious mind. According to Jung, the personal unconscious incorporates two sets of attributes from the collective unconscious, one positive and the other negative. In order to express negative qualities that would be too dangerous to articulate directly, we project them on others. Carter was clearly familiar with this concept of the 'shadow' and directly or indirectly with the way in which it became the linchpin of the school of psychoanalytic thought known as 'object relations' theory. This branch of psychoanalytic theory provides an appropriate framework in which to read the novels written in the 1960s because of the importance which they attach to 'projection' as Gothic texts. As MacAndrew (1979) maintains, the monsters in Gothic tales 'are the shapes into which our fears are projected' (p. 8).

According to leading twentieth-century psychoanalysts such as Melanie Klein, projection and the internalising of our projections is crucial in the formation of our identities. The infant learns to keep good and bad apart in a process of dividing one from the other which continues into adulthood. This process involves absorbing aspects of another which are perceived as positive, but getting rid of negative aspects of the self by projecting them into others. However, in what Klein calls 'the paranoid-schizoid' state, one-dimensional, single-characteristic part-objects are created as a solution to internal conflict. From her study of fairy tales, Carter would have been familiar with such part-objects in, for example, wicked stepmothers and fairy godmothers. They also occur in nineteenth-century novels such as *Dr Jekyll and Mr Hyde*, with which Carter was of course also familiar.

In *Shadow Dance*, the character most obviously regarded as a part-object by another character is Ghislaine. Before she is disfigured by Honeybuzzard, Morris sees Ghislaine as an idealised phantasy: 'She used to look like the sort of young girl one cannot imagine sitting on the lavatory or shaving her armpits or picking her nose' (p. 2). After the disfigurement, he projects into her his guilt and horror at what Honeybuzzard has done. He sees her as 'the bride of Frankenstin' while his dislike of the pretentiousness of her name becomes a focus for what he now sees as her phoniness (p. 4). Morris's wife, Edna, also, sees Morris as a part-object. We learn that according to whom she is talking, she would describe Morris as either an antique dealer or a painter. These little pretensions are projections of her anxieties into him as he projected his own, far more serious, anxieties into Ghislaine. The appropriateness of a Kleinian framework is evident also in the way in which Morris's idealisation of Ghislaine is a defence, as Kleinian theory suggests, against persecutory phantasies. Indeed, one of the reasons why Morris wanted Honeybuzzard to teach Ghislaine a lesson was the way in which she seemed to challenge men, and himself in particular:

> She would say: 'I lost my virginity when I was thirteen', conversationally, as she lit a cigarette, or she would complain of the performance of her last partner, or she would ask you if your wife satisfied you sexually. . . . Or she would describe her menstrual pains; and he [Morris] remembered the graphic recital of a course of treatment for a vaginal discharge. (pp. 9–10)

Moreover, in trying to theorise violence within the psyche, Klein focused on the phantasies a child has of mutilating its parents. Morris's guilt over what has happened to Ghislaine, even though he did not specifically tell Honeybuzzard to disfigure her, is similar to that which bedevils the child in Kleinian theory who believes that thinking something can make it happen. When a bottle is thrown at Morris in the street from a passing car, he concludes 'there was a dimension, surely, in the outer nebulae, maybe, where intentions were always executed' (p. 11).


IV


In eighteenth- and nineteenth-century German Romance, the man of sorrows is closely aligned with the demonic protagonist, unable to sleep because of a troubled conscience, and driven by guilt. As a study of a traumatised individual, Morris is the product of this particular Gothic literary tradition; he is pursued by Ghislaine both literally and in his fantasies. Here Carter may be inverting Fiedler's (1960) description of the Gothic Shadow, to which I referred earlier, as 'the villain who pursues the Maiden' (p. 125). However, in developing this aspect of Euro-American Gothic, Carter blurs the distinction between the pursued and the pursuer. The text asks: Who is the Shadow? In the dream in which Morris cuts Ghislaine's face with jagged glass their bloods significantly flow together. Tormented by guilt and traumatised by what Honeybuzzard has done to Ghislaine, Morris ceases to exist as an autonomous psychic identity: 'he ran out of himself at every pore and the black sleep ran into him' (p. 18). This psychic and physical dissembling demonstrates Kristeva's point that meaning, identity, system and order collapse when confronted with 'what does not respect borders, positions, rules' (1982, p. 4). It raises questions about Morris's autonomy. Where, the novel asks, are the boundaries to be drawn between Morris and Honeybuzzard? To what extent are individuals, both male and female, complicit in acts of intimidation, degradation and violence in which they are not directly involved?

Dostoevsky's *The Double*, to which I referred earlier, suggests the doubleness and sickness of all personality. Carter develops this thesis in *Shadow Dance*, suggesting that Morris's 'doubleness' is the result of the social construction of masculinity. She may, once again, also be taking her lead from Fiedler who, in his account of the Gothic Shadow, points out that 'there is a sense in which the evil principle is mythically male' and that 'it is the Shadow projected as male which most impresses itself upon the imagination' (p. 125). Morris's instruction to Honeybuzzard to teach Ghislaine a lesson is the product, then, of particular social discourses which sanction male dominance over women and legitimate men's right to abuse women. Although Honeybuzzard mutilated Ghislaine by himself, in 'the outer nebulae' Morris is present as well. It is a significant detail that Ghislaine was naked beneath a shiny black raincoat. But this piece of information is learned at one of the points of the novel where fact and Morris's phantasies become indistinguishable. Ghislaine is described as if she were an object of male, and in particular Morris's, fetishistic phantasy. Morris's sense of complicity with Honeybuzzard specifically and with society's way of seeing women generally is reinforced by the black cat which emerges from the bushes and spits at him. As a witch's familiar, the black cat reminds us of how the persecution of women as witches provided a means of controlling and punishing women's sexuality. Morris, like Desiderio, in the later novel, *The Infernal Desire Machines of Doctor Hoffman*, is forced to confront his complicity in the dehumanisation of the objects of his desire.

The influence of social discourses in constructing Morris's perceptions is evident in his reading of one of the cards on the tobacconist's notice board: '15-year-old girl seeks riding lessons, own jodhpurs' (p. 22). Morris reads the card as if it were a cryptic advertisement for 'personal services' in a pornographic magazine. Here Carter includes pornography in the novel which at its point of entry into the text ceases to be pornography as such and becomes one of the novel's tropes. Whilst two years ago a real fifteen-year-old put the card on the notice board, in Morris's phantasy she becomes an icon for a young woman, not necessarily fifteen, but on the cusp of childhood and adulthood. She becomes a part-object, 'a panting, wet-lipped nymphet with jutting nubile breasts'. Unlike the real fifteen-year-old who has got older – the card has begun to brown – the part-object phantasy is outside of time. The real card and the phantasy card occupy different spaces in which the words 'riding lessons' and 'own jodhpurs' acquire different connotations. But in *Shadow Dance*, Carter is interested in the space in which these two sets of meanings collide.

The way in which Morris sees Ghislaine as a part-object is the product of both his individual psyche and the way in which society perceives women as part-objects. Baudrillard (1976) argues that every kind of body is articulated in terms of, and is a version of, a negative 'ideal' type on which it is based (p. 114). Although the notion of a 'negative ideal' may seem contradictory at first, the concept itself is interesting and relevant to Carter's work. For example, Baudrillard argues that in medicine, the 'negative ideal' type in terms of which the sick body is spoken is the corpse. In religion, concerned with human spirituality and the transcendence of body, it is the animal full of instincts and appetites. In *Shadow Dance*, Morris's imagining of his sick wife as dead flesh reduces her to the phantasm of the corpse on which medical discourse about the body is based. At one level, Emily is the ideal housewife. Virtually her first act on arriving at Morris's shop is to wash all the sheets, linen and clothing she can find in strong soap. As such, however, she is reduced to the phantasm of the robot, the 'negative ideal' type on which the housewife in cultural discourse is based. She is actually said to behave like 'a well-trained house-robot' and to perform her services with 'the competent impersonality of a cafeteria attendant' (p. 101).

The familiar virgin and whore phantasms to which male

representations reduce women are literally realised in Ghislaine's disfigured face. Initially in Morris's focalisation, she has a personality which is a kaleidoscope of different emotions and motivations. However, he thinks of her increasingly in terms of a binarism: as a young picture book girl or as a shocking, rude woman. The one image, like the one side of her face is soft and compliant, while the other is disturbing and embarrassing. Her Janus face forces Morris to confront a contradiction which is within both himself and the masculinised realisation of women as social objects.

If the novel presents us with any kind of realist narrative, it is one that is haunted like the main character by what is repressed. The aspect of Morris's psyche, albeit socially determined, which makes him an accomplice in Ghislaine's disfigurement is revealed through his dreams and phantasies:

> He dreamed he was cutting her face with a jagged shard of broken glass. . . . There was a gallery of people watching them, and applauding sporadically, like the audience at a cricket match; among them he made out Honeybuzzard and Edna, both smiling and nodding their heads. And then he and Ghislaine were in his own bed and her head rolled on the pillows . . . and then it was Edna he saw that he was slicing open and there was blood everywhere.  (p. 18)

This particular scene is a fictional elaboration of a point that Carter makes in *The Sadeian Woman*:

> What are the butcherly delights of meat? These are not sensual but analytical. . . . A clinical pleasure in the precision with which the process of reducing the living, moving, vivid object to the dead status of thing is accomplished. The pleasure of watching the spectacle of the slaughter that derives from the knowledge one is dissociated from the spectacle; the bloody excitation of the audience in the abattoir.  (p. 138)

The passage in *Shadow Dance* begins with Morris dissociated from Ghislaine as are those who watch and applaud. She is reduced by his shard of broken glass to a thing. If he takes any pleasure in what is happening, it is in the act of cutting. However, in the second half of the passage, he is no longer distanced from her. Meat has become human flesh. The process described in the extract from *The Sadeian Woman* is reversed. Ghislaine is changed from 'the dead status of thing' to a 'living, moving, vivid object'. Morris is not dissociated from what Honeybuzzard has done and is implicated through male objectification of women in turning women into 'the dead status of thing'.

As a Gothic protagonist, Morris has his origins in Carter's reading of American Gothic literature which was once again mediated by Fiedler (1960). Fiedler, in a discussion of the Gothic protagonist, suggests: 'But if we walk in our sleep, we also run in our dreams' (p. 149). One of the unusual features of *Shadow Dance* is that although it is narrated in the third person from Morris's point of view, we sometimes find ourselves in one of Morris's phantasies that run parallel to the events in the third person narrative. This slippage from one focalisation to another is evident in the account of the conversation between Morris and Ghislaine so that it becomes difficult to distinguish between the two perspectives:

> Oh, the lingering voice on the long vowel, like an intimate caress. A caress from a witch-woman.
>
> 'The sap's rising,' he said. His voice shook. Now, he wondered, why did I say 'The sap's rising' to her? What will she think I mean?
>
> She glanced at him over the rim of her glass, sharing sly secrets, and laughed her personalized, patented laugh – she must be the only girl, anywhere, who could laugh like that. The shimmery, constricted yet irrepressible giggle of a naughty little girl, such a young, lovely and wicked giggle. (p. 6)

The dialectic between representative codes and codes of fantasy to which I referred earlier is evident here in the language where 'naughty' and 'wicked' have different meanings when applied to a real girl from its application by men to women who are perceived as 'girls'.

## V

Like *Shadow Dance*, *Several Perceptions* (1968), written between March and December 1967, is a third-person retrospective narrative. Again the focalisation is through the consciousness of a single, male character, Joseph Harker, who, like Morris, is prey to dreams and phantasies. He is haunted like Morris, but by death rather than a woman. Whilst Morris contemplates suicide in the first chapter of *Shadow Dance*, Joseph attempts it. The narrative charts his recovery, culminating in a miraculous party at the end of the novel.

Joseph, like Morris, is an adaptation of the 'man of sorrows' from the work of Herman Melville and German Romantic literature. At times, he appears even to himself like 'a big, fat, soft, stupid, paper Valentine heart squeezing out a soggy tear at the sorrows of the world' (p. 5). His occupation as a hospital orderly brings him even more than Morris's antique business into proximity with death and abjection, 'cleaning up shit and amputations' (p. 98). Yet as for Morris and Melville's Bartleby, it is the personal effects of the deceased which arouse melancholy:

> On the other hand, false teeth, spectacles and watches were scrupulously returned to the bereaved of the deceased; when Joseph asked what happened to glass eyes, they were peremptory with him, as though he had committed a breach of taste. (p. 12)

Like Morris, Joseph has a melancholic's identification with suffering and death. As is characteristic of Euro-American Gothic, the affect that they have on him is contrasted with the response of a friend who is less affected, in this case Viv. Unlike Joseph, Viv is resigned to mortality, to the sufferings of the old, and to the horrors of the Viet Nam War. Like Morris, too, such is Joseph's melancholy that he is unable to develop his imaginary and symbolic capacities. Indeed, after Charlotte has left him, he sets fire to books in the public library. The intertextual references to T. S. Eliot's poem, *The Wasteland* – the novel contains references to the burial of the dead, the London pub and the hanging man of the tarot cards – are obviously significant here since the failure of the imagination to rejuvenate the wasteland is one of its main themes. Indeed, Carter's description of Joseph's parents' living room appears at one level as a piece of realist writing, a window on a living room furnished in a style characteristic of the 1960s. But at another level, it appears informed by the kind of disillusionment which characterises the depictions of tacky, twentieth-century materialism in Eliot's poem, albeit with stronger suggestions of violence:

At home he sat in an uneasy chair urging the plaster ducks to try and fly across the wall. There was a tooled leather *TV Times* cover and a brass Dutch girl concealing fire-irons in the hollow of her back. These things seemed wholly threatening; the leathercover was a ravenous mouth smacking brown lips and the Dutch girl must use her little brushes and shovels as cruel weapons since there was no other use for them. (p. 7)

Of particular significance is Mrs Boulder's identification of Joseph with the hanging man of the Tarot cards (pp. 108–9). The hanged man is the card which Madame Sostris in 'The Burial of the Dead' is unable to find, reinforcing the aridity of the wasteland since in Eliot's poem it signifies Christ or the hanged god from Fraser's *The Golden Bough*. In this context, it is ironic that Joseph is unable to satisfy Mrs Boulder sexually who then reminds him of the Tarot card.

Like Morris, Joseph also tends – as in his descriptions of the elderly – to translate life into death:

Everywhere Joseph looked, he saw old people with sticks and bulging veins in their legs and skulls from which the flesh of their faces hung in tattered webs; they advanced slowly as if this might be their very last walk. A man with a metal hook instead of a hand passed by and then a hunchbacked woman. (p. 9)

While this passage describes physical features usually associated with ageing, in Joseph's mind they seem to be exaggerated. It is as if being over aware of these physical characteristics, he then projects them into the people he is observing so as to turn them into part-objects, strongly suggesting Baudrillard's 'negative ideal' of the corpse to which I referred earlier.

Like the other two novels in the 'Bristol trilogy', *Several Perceptions* invites reading from a realist perspective, but also conflates the factual and the fantastic. In fact, it is less reliant than the other two novels on realist techniques. As O'Day (1994) argues, developing Lorna Sage's point that the novel is constructed like a strip cartoon, actions and interactions are not linked by cause and effect. Time in the novel seems like that which we find in fairy tale, myth and dream. More so than in *Shadow Dance,* the nature of the narrative mimics the condition of the central male consciousness. The desultory, shiftless social world of the novel reflects the depressive, disillusioned and slippery nature of Joseph's mind. In many respects, Joseph exemplifies what Julia Kristeva (1987) describes as the typical melancholia's condition. For, as she explains, there is no object for the melancholic only 'an ersatz of an object to which he attaches himself', a vague 'light without representation' (p. 22).

The dreams in the novel are a displacement of the 'shadow' of Joseph's psyche. More specifically than in *Shadow Dance*, they are related to how the central protagonist has sought to deal with the negative aspects of his subconscious. At one point, in a narrative redolent of 'Red Riding Hood', Joseph dreams he is a child walking home from the 'Wolf Cubs'. Here Carter wittily gives a Gothic twist to a social institution of the time, for the werewolf was one of the means by which Gothic writing sought to explore the intrusion of negative aspects of the collective unconscious into the personal subconscious. The maniac who follows Joseph with a knife, recalling Honeybuzzard from *Shadow Dance*, would seem to represent the suppressed parts of his own psyche. The street through which he walks is exaggeratedly neat and clean; 'privet hedges and clean milk bottles' (p. 5). It may be signifies that the conscious mind denies the existence of polluting objects – represented by the maniac and the wolf. In the dream, 'mad for sanctuary, Joseph the child burst through a front gate and beat his fists on the nearest door' (ibid.). Here, the child would seem to represent an innocence that Joseph would like to reclaim.

The way in which the suppressed, such as Joseph's childhood fears, can re-emerge and destabilise the conscious mind is mirrored in the novel in the way in which dreams – usually incorporated as metanarratives within the main narrative – and fantasy disrupt and destabilise the realist mode of narration which relies on coherence and closure. According to Catherine Belsey (1980), the realist novel is predicated on a 'declarative text' which imparts ' "knowledge" to a reader whose position is thereby stabilised, through a privileged discourse which is to varying degrees invisible' (pp. 90ff). Her reference to 'invisible' here reminds us that the realist novel purports to hold a mirror up to the world and, as readers, we tend to accept this, overlooking the ways in which the novel has constructed what we are looking at. However, within the realist text, we also encounter metanarratives, or embedded narratives, which have a different mode of address. While the dominant, declarative text suggests coherence, closure and stability, the latter are marked by conflict, indeterminacy and instability. We are presented with questions to which we are encouraged to find answers, while being made aware of the difficulties in doing so.

In *Several Perceptions*, the dreams invite the reader, who has been cast in the mode of a reader of a realist text, to consider them both in relation to the main narrative and to each other. They are part of a larger interplay within the narrative which undermines the stability and coherence which we normally look for in a realist novel. They also invite the reader to occupy a psychoanalytic position. At one level, the interconnection between the dreams appear to offer the reader some degree of satisfaction such as insight into Joseph's character. The garden dream, for example, like the Wolf Club dream, ends with Joseph looking into his own face. Both dreams bring Joseph's childhood to the fore. Joseph enters both dreams as a violent, murderous adult. Both dreams suggest, through their sexual connotations, that this figure may be the repressed father and that the dreams articulate Joseph's own, subconscious identification with him but also his fear and hatred of him. However, both dreams resist any over neat interpretation. The man in both dreams, for example, is additionally associated with time. In the garden dream, he destroys both children and spring flowers, while in the second dream his progress is as 'relentless as the clock'. While in the second dream, the maniac in pursuit, in Freudian terms, conjures up the child's fear of castration, in the garden dream he destroys the heads of the flowers and the children.

The difficulty of achieving a clear-cut interpretation of these dreams is an irony at the centre of the novel for Joseph's biblical namesake is an interpreter of dreams. However, the irony is even more complex because the dreams, as a reflection of Joseph's psyche, betray the influence of twentieth-century psychoanalytic thought in which Carter was interested but of which she was sceptical. As symbolic narratives, the dreams lend themselves too obviously to analysis. Moreover, Joseph's surname is Harker – the name of the narrator of Bram Stoker's *Dracula*. This complicates matters further; for dreams in this novel are part of a literary as well as a character's psychic history. The two become confused as, for example, in the way in which Charlotte is recreated in Joseph's dreams as one of the vampires in Dracula's castle:

A picture of Charlotte was tacked over the gas fire. . . . Her blonde hair blew over her face which did not in the least resemble the face he remembered, since that face reincarnated in fantasy after fantasy, recreated nightly in dreams for months after she left, had become transformed in his mind to a Gothic mask, huge eyeballs hooded with lids of stone, cheekbones sharp as steel, lips of treacherous vampire redness and a wet mouth which was a mantrap of ivory fangs. Witch woman. Incubus.  (p. 15)

That *Several Perceptions* should invite the reader to occupy the position of analyst but offer no guarantee of satisfaction should not surprise us given the novel's epigraph: 'The mind is a kind of theatre, where several perceptions successively make their appearance, pass, re-pass, glide away and mingle in an infinite variety of postures and situations.' In the course of the novel, Joseph's own state of consciousness is directly associated with Hume's concept of the mind. For example, when Kay and Joseph break into the zoo to free the badger, the reader is told: 'These thoughts flashed on to various screens in small sideshows of [Joseph's] mind but the main theatre was so busy with the escape itself' (p. 58).

The impossibility of the analyst's position is parodied in the comic relationship between Joseph and his psychiatrist, Ransome, who pointedly admits that, as neither a Freudian nor a shaman, he does not interpret dreams (p. 84). The weariness in Ransome's physical appearance – 'his colourless eyes hung in nets of tired lines, like trawled fish' – is mirrored in his diagnosis of Joseph's problems: 'you use [the tragedy of war] as a symbol for your rejection of a world to which you cannot relate. Perhaps because of your immaturity' (p. 64). The diagnosis is based on a narrative that has a coherence and closure not available to Joseph. When threatening to jump, Joseph opens a window, disturbing the psychiatrist's papers. Significantly, Ransome's response is to reassemble them. His solution is to write Joseph a prescription for more tranquillisers and recommend that he get plenty of fresh air. Joseph's lateral response to being labelled immature is to send excrement to President Lyndon Johnson as a protest against the war in Viet Nam.

Joseph's destruction of the books in the library draws attention to what he does read as much as what he does not. His room is filled with books, newspapers cuttings and scrapbooks about the Viet Nam War. As the first war which Americans witnessed in the media, it brought home – literally – the trauma of military conflict where there was no clearly defined front line. It was a war for which American combatants were psychologically unprepared and with which many tried to cope by taking hallucinatory drugs. In the confusion of fact and fantasy through the elision of propaganda and reportage, the Viet Nam War became a theatre – which Coppola encapsulated in both the content and style of his film *Apocalypse Now* – mirroring the theatre of the mind described in the novel's epigraph.

At the heart of the novel, as I suggested in the Introduction, there is a sense of loss which can be interpreted in psychoanalytic as well as historical/cultural terms. At one level, it is the sense of cultural loss which resulted from the decline of Britain as an industrial and colonial power that became increasingly obvious after the Second World War. It is alluded to, for example, when Joseph regrets the loss of 'military great coats of the elegant past' (p. 123) and also informs the description of the Down:

> It was a once-handsome, now decayed district with a few relics of former affluence (such as the coffee shop, a suave place) but now mostly given over to old people who had come down in the world, who lived in basements and ground floor backs, and students and beatniks who nested in attics. (p. 9)

However, this sense of historical/cultural loss is elided at the individual level with a psychoanalytical sense of lack. Kay's mansion, for example, is a mausoleum created by his dying mother – 'a footlights favourite of the 1930s, the world she knew was shot down in flames in 1940' (p. 11). Nearly all the characters in the novel have experienced a personal loss: Joseph has lost his partner six months prior to the date when his narrative begins; Anne Blossom has lost her child and may also have lost her father in the war; Old Sunny the music hall violinist has lost his violin; Mrs Boulder has lost her lover. But, as I suggested in the Introduction, Carter's fiction presents us with the experience of loss as also the experience of a frightening presence. As in the other two novels in the 'Bristol trilogy', the void in *Several Perceptions* is filled with what is sinister and violent – evident, for example, in the poster of the child murderer and the reaction it provokes; the violence in the pub; the references to the Boston Strangler; and even in the dog – 'built like a fur tank, about half the whole size of Sunny' (p. 8) – which steals Sunny's cap.

In some respects, the conclusion of the novel appears to present the reader with innocence regained. For unlike *Shadow Dance* and *Love*, the novel has a carnivalesque ending that anticipates Carter's interest in carnivalesque in the later novel, *Nights at the Circus*. Almost like a benevolent puppet master, the androgynous Kay presides over a miraculous carnival – in contrast to the puppet master, Uncle Philip in *The Magic Toyshop* published the previous year. Here Anne Blossom who has been mysteriously crippled is able to walk, Mrs. Boulder is reunited with her lover, and Old Sunny has a violin again. Even Joseph's cat has snow white kittens. Carter appears to conclude with a metaphor for the collective, utopian future envisaged in 1960s hippie counterculture. Typically, however, all this is also ambiguous. The reader is left wondering how much of it is illusion rather than miracle. With hands trembling so much that he spills his drink and cannot roll a cigarette easily, Kay insists:

> [Anne] had hysterical paralysis . . . Anybody could have cured her, anybody who said to her in a firm enough voice, "Nonsense, you don't really limp at all". Not a miracle. No miracle. It wasn't a miracle. Was it?   (p. 145)

Although the question mark here may introduce a counter sense of doubt, even more devastating is Kay's admission that he doesn't really care about her and the way in which the decaying atmosphere of his mother's mansion is consuming him so that he appears desiccated.

The miraculous party which concludes the novel is in sharp contrast to the earlier carnival site in the novel, the pub, or more specifically, the public bar. The description of the bar places it outside conventional realist narrative: 'things were happening without a sequence, there was no flow or pattern to events' (p. 52). There is a theatrical element epitomised in the fandango dancer and Kay Kyte's role as 'the demon king'. However, it is an ambiguous social space. The boy who plays the fruit machine wears jeans and a leather jacket with 'Drag City' on the back – the uniform of rebellious youth. There is an atmosphere of repressed violence created by the knife scars on the leather benches and the fandango danced by the black-eyed girl: 'It was a mating dance display and yet it had the freezing menace of a dance in an Elizabethan tragedy performed by disguised assassins concealing knives' (p. 51). But if the public bar provides a counter culture to the lounge bar, it is also defined, and even contained, by it. It may be a place with 'a jagged atmosphere' where 'violence seemed suspended in the air', but it is also the place where Kay pleads in a pained voice: 'I've never made trouble in this pub or acted in an anti-social way' (p. 52). The youth may wear what he believes to be the uniform of non-conformity yet paradoxically he is conforming to a definition of non-conformity – one of the paradoxes of 1950s and 1960s counterculture. In the enthusiasm for the 1960s, freedom of choice was not often distinguished from the illusion of choice. Two central images in this scene are the fruit machine and the juke box. Apart from the fact that both may be seen as icons of an increasingly widespread, bland Anglo-American uniformity, the juke box offers choice only from a predetermined and limited selection. Both machines pander to subversive activities: the fruit machine to gambling, and the juke box to rock-and-roll. Yet both are the product of a capitalist system which exploits those who appropriate them as sites of ostensibly subversive activities. Capitalism grows rich on the proceeds of both.

The public bar is not an alternative to the lounge bar but, to employ Baudrillard's terms, its 'negative ideal': 'The public bar was quite different to the lounge bar; it was far larger, far colder, no snug carpet underfoot but chilly, clinking tiles' (p. 50). The empty grate holds only squashed cigarette packets and 'a fresh gob of sputum' (ibid.). The word 'gob' is slang for a clot of spittle and for a worked out seam in a mine. Significantly, the public bar is where two old people sit – under capitalism, the old are literally surplus to requirements. In capitalist society, the most precious commodity is time; time is literally money. The public bar with fruit machine and juke box is a site where time, in capitalist terms, is wasted.

The narrative voice in the scene directs the reader's response. There is regret that there is no fire in the pub's grate. The metaphorical meaning of lack of fire extends to the boy with the pink tie who has 'taxidermy eyes like a dead, stuffed deer' (p. 51). But even more significant is the narrator's intrusion: 'if you looked long enough into his eyes, you would start screaming'. The narrator obviously wants a site of genuine carnival. There is hope here – in the possibility of sudden transformation, of the kind of sudden change which Joseph witnesses when he emerges from the lavatory.

But even this is ambiguous for the source of the change – the fandango dancer – is acting a part.

In the 'play within the play' in Shakespeare's *A Midsummer Night's Dream*, Bottom is distressed at the idea of presenting death to the audience. He insists on the inclusion of a prologue making it clear that Pyramus is not actually dead and that it is not in fact Pyramus at all but Bottom the weaver. In other words, realism intrudes and all but destroys the illusion of the play they are planning. At the end of *Several Perceptions*, illusion intrudes to subvert the 'realism' of loss, pain and suffering. Shakespeare's play is recalled at Kay's departure:

> He wavered as he walked as if he were a piece of trick photography and might suddenly disappear altogether, so discreetly the air would not even be disturbed by his passage. As if his goodnight act were to cast sleep upon them, both Joseph and Anne lay down and closed their eyes as soon as he was out of the room, both, in their different ways, perfectly content; already this marvellous happening seemed quite natural, like the existence of Sunny's violin, incorporated into the actuality of the house. (p. 146)

However, in reading the final pages of *Several Perceptions*, we might also think of those plays by Shakespeare, such as *The Winter's Tale*, in which the world itself is turned into a theatre. Towards the end of the miraculous party in *Several Perceptions*, as towards the end of Shakespeare's last plays, the reader is made aware of the theatricality of the event, which like Kay himself, appears to be like 'a piece of trick photography'. Realism as the dominant mode of the text dissolves and threatens to disappear altogether. Between them, Anne and Sunny identify two key elements of realist writing dispensed with at this stage in the novel. Sunny is to throw away his book of facts and Anne identifies 'time' as the enemy (p. 140). The party which closes the novel, is more than just a carnivalesque conclusion. It returns us to the David Hume epigraph and the notion of the theatricality of the mind. The incorporation of Sunny's violin into the 'actuality of the house' destabilises the distinction between fact and imagination, as does Kay's hypothesis that Anne's lameness was in her mind. The ending of the novel is meant to appear theatrical and contrived; a fitting conclusion to a text which from its very epigraph deliberately confounds illusion and reality.


## VI


Although *Love* was published in 1971, it was written in 1969. Unusually, a revised edition was published in 1987 containing an afterword written by Carter herself. Originally, she had intended to reveal her own opinions of the novel nearly twenty years after writing it, but she tells us that she chose instead to write some more of the original text. In fact, she tells us what has happened to the characters subsequent to the original narrative. At the outset, however, she pinpoints three criticisms which she would now have of the novel: 'its almost sinister feat of male impersonation, its icy treatment of the mad girl and its penetrating aroma of unhappiness' (p. 113). In drawing attention to the male ventriloquism in the novel, Carter would appear to be in accord with some of the critics I mentioned in the previous chapter. But, perhaps her views should not be taken at face value. As in some of her later novels, it would require considerable insensitivity not to be critical of the male protagonists whose views appear to be given priority. As a novelist, Carter invariably liked to work backwards, beginning by articulating positions and perspectives which are subsequently exposed, challenged and unravelled as the narrative itself unfurls.

The novel is concerned with a love–hate triangle of two half-brothers, Lee and Buzz, and Annabel, a middle-class drop-out, in sixties bohemia. There are a number of additional cameo roles, to which Carter in the afterword admits she now wished she had given more depth. Lee and Buzz share the same mother who went mad in spectacular fashion, running naked down the high street declaring that she was the whore of Babylon, and, painted all over her body with cabalistic signs, bursting into her children's school playground. However, they have different fathers. Lee's father was a railwayman killed in the course of duty, while Buzz, born during a period when his mother worked as a prostitute after her husband's death, is the illegitimate son of an American serviceman whom he believes to be an American Indian.

Brought up in south London by an aunt with strong left-wing

sympathies, Lee and Buzz move to Bristol during 1963–4 when Lee gains a place, like Angela Carter herself, at Bristol University. Annabel, whom Buzz discovers has joined his half-brother in the flat when he returns from the 1960s north Africa hippie trail, is another cliché of the period, a middle-class girl from a sheltered, conventional background who drops into bohemia as an art student. Later she emulates Buzz's lifestyle, adopting his drifter's working pattern and stealing.

As Lorna Sage (1994b) points out, the prose of *Love* is characterised by 'a glowing patina of craft and indifference . . . that exactly fits the artificial 'nature' of the people' (p. 20). However, the novel is not solely a retrospective satire on the 1960s – on 'young people seduced by the heady climate of the revolution . . . and licensing in the communal setting whatever private violence was haunting them' – as Bayley (1992) has suggested. The novel is a disturbing fusion of the Gothic and the avant-garde which may have been suggested to Carter by Fiedler (1960) who, in describing how Beatniks 'mock the "squares" of San Fransisco with the monstrous disorder of life', explains that 'the gothic is an avant-garde genre, perhaps the first avant-garde art in the modern sense of the term' (p. 127).

Buzz as the illegitimate son, as in Renaissance drama, is an important destabilising element in the text where an important trope is the significance of what is repressed or denied. In many ways, *Love* looks back to Carter's first novel. Honeybuzzard is divided and reappears partly as Buzz and partly as the beautiful Lee, 'Honey' – an aspect which, as I suggest in the discussion of *Shadow Dance*, is indebted to the influence of Melville's Billy Budd. Lee, who took this version of his name from a Western movie, is conventionally attractive with blond hair and blue eyes. Although he has entered the middle class via a university education and a teaching post in a grammar school, his working-class origins are revealed in moments of extreme emotion. Like Paul Morel in D. H. Lawrence's *Sons and Lovers,* on such occasions he lapses into working-class speech. Buzz is Lee's 'shadow'; the Indian to Lee's cowboy. In many ways, the Indian can be seen as the repressed subconscious of white America. However, Buzz is also the 'shadow' of the kind of society which Lee has been able to enter. Unlike Lee, he went to a secondary modern school so that between them the brothers reflect the kind of social schizophrenia that the eleven-plus system imposed on the country, dividing children into an able, academic élite and a less able, vocational underclass. Buzz is also the 'shadow' of middle-class, bohemian rebellion. His father left behind a finger ring with a skull and crossbones – a symbol of piracy adopted as a sign of rebellion in the 1960s by working-class subculture. Buzz also signifies a further 'shadow', the homoerotic element in the complex relationship between the two half-brothers. At a party they dance together; when Annabel has sex with Lee she is dressed in Buzz's clothes; and when Buzz is thrown out of the flat, he asks his brother: 'Going straight?' (p. 65). Lee replies: 'I'm not divorcing you, for God's sake' (p. 66). In fact, this is an aspect of their relationship about which Carter is a little more explicit in her afterword:

The brothers are no longer in communication. . . . Nevertheless, Lee is the only human being his brother ever felt one scrap for and he admits to himself, and occasionally to startled companions, that if there is one thing he would like to do before he dies, it is to fuck him. There is as much menace as desire in this wish.
(p. 117)

The middle section of *Love* is given over to an analysis of the *ménage à trois* in interviews between Lee and Annabel's psychiatrist. Here Carter employs a more concentrated version of the scenes between Joseph and Ransome in *Several Perceptions* for a similar purpose. There is a comparable tension between the complexity and intensity with which Lee perceives things and the occasionally curt responses of the psychiatrist. At one point, not unsympathetically, she pronounces that his brother 'does not seem entirely normal' (p. 59); at another, she shrugs enigmatically; and at still another she laughs long and hard at what he says. As in *Several Perceptions*, the scenes with the psychiatrist are ones of black comedy; here Lee falls in love with her. In a sequence which he might have imagined or one that might have happened and resulted in him being kicked, Lee finds himself on the floor at her feet, exploring her knees, thighs and eventually between her legs.

In her afterword to the novel, Carter calls this character, 'the peroxided psychiatrist' (p. 115). The account of her life over the next twenty years provides a commentary upon both the 1980s and her behaviour with Lee. After Annabel's death, she seems to have no more concern for him as an individual than she displayed in the earlier interviews; he is prescribed tranquillisers which turn him into 'a virtual zombie'. She goes on to work in those areas which prove the most lucrative, becoming a director of a chain of extremely expensive detoxification centres for very rich junkies and the director of three pharmaceutical companies. With a Porsche, a successful radio programme and a best-seller under her belt, she epitomises the yuppie culture of the 1980s. However, she also serves to highlight the commodification of mental health and the confusion of professionalisation and commercialisation during this period, together with the way in which people have been seduced into becoming dependent upon prescribed drugs.

## VII

In her afterword, Carter maintains that she first obtained the idea of *Love* from a nineteenth-century novel, *Adolphe*: 'I was seized with the desire to write a kind of modern-day demotic version of *Adolphe*, although I doubt anybody could spot the resemblance after I'd macerated the whole thing in triple-distilled essence of English provincial life' (p. 113). Carter's admission that the idea 'first' came from *Adolphe* suggests, of course, that there were other sources for the idea of *Love*. One of the most important of these, I would suggest, was the work of Edgar Allan Poe. Buzz, for example, looks as if he is fresh from a visit to the tomb of Edgar Allan Poe (p. 36) and is later compared with Poe's Raven. Not only has Carter split the name 'Honeybuzzard' drawn from her first novel, but the name 'Annabel Lee' in Poe's poem is also divided to provide the names of two of the leading protagonists.

The intertextual references in *Love* to Poe's 'Annabel Lee' highlights the novel's concern with a subject on which Carter, according to Elaine Jordan (1992), is particularly convincing and insightful: 'narcissistic desire, self-preoccupied fantasies which interfere in the possibility of relation between people who are "other" in themselves, not just projections of each other's desires' (p. 121). In fact, in exploring what Jordan calls 'narcissistic desire', Carter has taken up two of the major themes of Poe's poetry: the dangers in withdrawing too far into an imaginary world and the negative aspects of the human psyche. Unlike in the case of Buzz who appears to have inherited numerous fears about women from his mother, particularly that of the *vagina denata* (p. 94), little explanation is offered as to why Annabel is as she is. There is a hint, however, that Annabel is severely repressed by her parents. As an only daughter, she is brought up, and caught up, in a classic Oedipal triangle. Within this particular family unit, she can be nothing but the (only) daughter. The visit of her parents, which subsequently results in Annabel being forced to marry Lee, provides us with a glimpse into the introverted nature of Annabel's childhood and adolescence, suggesting that she has not been able to achieve a fully developed adult identity.

If the use of the names 'Annabel' and 'Lee' suggest that Carter had Poe's poem in mind when writing *Love*, it is clear that *Adolphe* sowed the seeds of the narrative idea that took her to Poe's work. Written by Benjamin Constant [Henri Benjamin Constant de Rebecque] (1767–1830), *Adolphe* (1815) is the story of a man who falls in love with Eleanor, the wife of Count P. —. Unable to terminate the relationship through guilt, he is devastated when she dies. The poem, 'Annabel Lee', is concerned with the union of two souls, that of the narrative 'I' and Annabel Lee, which cannot be separated:

> But our love it was stronger by far than the love
>   Of those who were older than we –
>   Of many far wiser than we –
> And neither the angels in heaven above,
>   Nor the demons down under the sea,
> Can ever dissever my soul from the soul
>   Of the beautiful ANNABEL LEE:
>
> For the moon never beams, without bringing me dreams
>   Of the beautiful ANNABEL LEE:
> And the stars never rise, but I feel the bright eyes
>   Of the beautiful ANNABEL LEE:
> And so, all the night-tide, I lie down by the side
> Of my darling – my darling – my life and my bride,
>   In the sepulchre there by the sea –
>   In her tomb by the sounding sea.

However, the real subject of the poem is the perils of what in Poe's day, *pace* Coleridge, was known as the 'secondary imagination'. In particular, Poe explores how this creative faculty, in reshaping the world inwardly according to its subjective awareness of life, death, time and space, can lead to an unhealthy solipsism. In the poem, each stanza through repetition coils back on and appears to absorb its predecessor.

When the reader first meets Annabel at the beginning of *Love*, she occupies a world where the boundaries between fantasy and illusion have become blurred:

> All she apprehended through her senses she took only as objects for interpretation in the expressionist style and she saw, in everyday things, a world of mythic, fearful shapes. (pp. 3–4)

Narcissistic desire is perhaps an ironic subject to choose for a novel. Normally we think of a novel as ' a meeting point between the individual and the general, bridging the isolated subjectivity and peopled world' (Connor, 1996, p. 1). Carter's Annabel has 'a capacity for changing the appearance of the real world . . . which is the price paid by those who take too subjective a view of it' (p. 3). An interest in this kind of excessive subjectivity inspired Poe – as evidenced in 'The Raven' – to write about the progression toward an 'imaginative madness'. In 'The Raven', for example, the protagonist moves from the known or 'real' world of time and dimension to a chaotic, fictive world. Here only the imagination and its morbid phantasies exist. Similarly, it is the inward subjectivity of Annabel, which eventually gives way to an 'imaginative madness' *pace* Poe, that is stressed at the outset of *Love*. In her afterword, even with hindsight, Carter is of the opinion that 'even the women's movement would have been no help to her and alternative psychiatry would have only made things, if possible, worse' (p. 113).

Annabel is a version of the Gothic 'doomed beloved' whom Fiedler (1960) says 'bears the stigmata of a tabooed figure' and is marked as 'the carrier of madness and death' (p. 385). 'One of the first images that the reader encounters in *Love*, is of a 'once harmonious artificial wilderness' having become dishevelled over time (p. 1). It is an image of the shift which occurs in Annabel's own mind from a perilously maintained balance of her faculties to their total disruption. In the park, Annabel is seeking the Gothic north, the 'shadow' of the Mediterranean south which bores her with its serenity. It is evidenced in a symbol – 'an ivy-covered tower with leaded ogive windows' (p. 2) that anticipates Annabel's subsequent withdrawal into herself. As in *Several Perceptions*, the mind is envisaged as a theatre; here the pillared portico and Gothic tower transform the park into 'a premeditated theatre where the romantic imagination could act out any performance it chose' (ibid.). The park itself seems like a metaphor for a more tumultuous version of the 'theatre of the mind' described in the epigraph to *Several Perceptions*: 'At times, all seemed nothing but a playground for the winds and, at others, an immense drain for all the rain the heavens could pour forth' (p. 2). Almost a parody of a Gothic protagonist – 'a mad girl plastered in fear and trembling' (p. 3) – Annabel is prone to visitations of 'anguish' and suffers from nightmares too terrible to be revealed.

In *Love*, Carter suggests that 'indifference', which she explored in her first novel, may be a symptom of too introverted a subjectivity. Indeed, Carter frequently uses the adverb 'indifferently' to describe Annabel's actions and responses. For example, we are told that she 'indifferently stirred the paper with her toes' (p. 8), she answers Lee 'indifferently' and, when they make love, she submits indifferently (p. 32). In the pornographic photographs given her by Buzz, Annabel is attracted to the bland, indifferent, motionless face of the model and the stark, cold juxtaposition of genitalia. She lies for hours on the cold boards 'as if she were on a slab in a morgue' (p. 19). Lee's relationship with her stands in contrast to the affairs he has with the philosopher's wife, with Carolyn and with Joanne, his fifteen-year-old school pupil. Interestingly, as O'Day (1994) points out, most of the verbal dialogue in the novel takes place in these encounters rather than within the triangle of Annabel, Lee and Buzz (p. 51).

Annabel is possessed, like Melville's Bartleby, and like Morris, with an infinite sense of sorrow: 'she had impressed her sorrow so deeply on the essential wood and brick of the place she knew for certain nobody could ever be happy there again' (p. 71). However, *Love*, more so than *Shadow Dance*, develops the condition of extreme withdrawal into which Melville's Bartleby has fallen. Annabel, like Bartleby, becomes increasingly detached from the immediate world around her, spending more and more time gazing into space (p. 71). Bartleby turns his desk to a blank wall; Annabel boards up her window and is drawn to Buzz's room where the window faces a blank wall (p. 31) However, once again, the influence of Edgar Allan Poe proves important. The apartment, like the enclosures in which many of Poe's protagonists in his tales find themselves, becomes a place of exclusion, where an individual is isolated from the world of time, reason and physical fact, creating what Carter calls in the afterword to *Love*, 'its penetrating aroma of unhappiness' (p. 113).

Even Lee associates Annabel's other worldliness with death, accusing her of going out at night to trample in graves (p. 7). Unwittingly, and ironically, in cautioning her about wandering on the hillside at night in barefeet, Lee anticipates the ultimate consequence of her introversion: 'Oh, my duck, you'll catch your death' (ibid.). In *Shadow Dance*, Morris is unable to transform his awareness of suffering and death through art. Annabel's paintings also fail because they are life denying. The tree of life she paints is like the Uppas tree of Java which casts a poisoned shade (p. 32).

In exploring 'the price paid by those who take too subjective a view' of the world, Carter rewrites that aspect of the Gothic genre in which women are usually presented as preyed on by men. Annabel's decision to have Lee tattooed in, significantly, Gothic script and circled by a heart is a rewriting of Hester Prynne's punishment in Hawthorne's nineteenth-century American Gothic novel, *The Scarlet Letter*. The Puritan elders make her wear the letter 'A' embroidered on her gown as a punishment for adultery. There are a number of parallels between the two episodes. When Hester Prynne passes young women in the street, the scarlet letter which she wears is said to give a throb of recognition. Lee's tattoo similarly seems to 'throb and burn him' (p. 70). However, once again this trace of an earlier text opens up different possible readings of Carter's novel. Carter not only rewrites the patriarchal bias of Hawthorne's novel, but develops its interest in revenge and the way revenge can affect both its victim and its perpetrator.When the tattooist creates the heart on Lee's chest, Annabel looks on with a cold, almost sadistic, sense of satisfaction reminiscent of the revengeful gaze of Roger Chillingworth in *The Scarlet Letter* as well as other cold-hearted observers such as Ethan Brand and Miles Coverdale of which there are a prefiguration in Hawthorne's work. Here Carter is exploiting the potential of the horror story for the exegesis of guilt. The victim, in this case the wronged Annabel, becomes a cold-hearted monster which must be destroyed. However, the allusions to Hawthorne's *The Scarlet Letter*, invite the reader to see Annabel through Hawthorne's moral framework. From this perspective, Annabel appears particularly disturbing because she unwittingly devises 'a revenge which required a knowledge of human feeling to perfect it' (p. 70). It is very likely that Carter had in mind the way in which this aspect of Annabel is represented when she referred to the novel's 'icy treatment of the mad girl' (p. 113).

In *Love*, Carter once again works creatively within and between different frames of reference. The concepts of excessive subjectivity and 'narcissistic desire' are developed not only with reference to paradigms from nineteenth-century American writers and her own earlier work, but twentieth-century psychoanalysis. Again, object relations theory provides an appropriate framework within which to discuss Carter's work. When he makes love to her, Lee has to undress Annabel as if she were once again a child and she regresses to the nursery. As the trope of regression suggests, Annabel, like Melanie in *The Magic Toyshop*, has not developed an autonomous sense of self. Like a child, she reconstructs the world according to her whims and populates it with imaginary elements. Even chess pieces, especially knights and castles, are phantasy objects which she introjects, falling into reverie, eyes fixed blankly on the chess board. She also, of course, projects her phantasies on Lee, imagining him paradoxically as a herbivorous lion or a unicorn devouring meat. The latter is a particularly important projection because it highlights that he is being destroyed by her. In Kleinian theory, the projection phantasy destroys the object. Annabel comes to see Lee as an incubus and as dissolving in his own sperm (p. 35). Here there is a contrast between Annabel and Joanne. For when Joanne eventually has sex with Lee she is able to distinguish the reality of the married man from the teacher on whom she had a schoolgirl crush. In her afterword, Carter stresses Joanne's intelligence and common-sense for more than the other characters she seems capable of taking control of her own life: she is said to have 'had too much brute sense of self-preservation to have anything more to do with Lee after she found out what had happened' (p. 115).

Jacqueline Rose (1993) has pointed out that psychoanalytic theory has tended to concentrate upon the relationship between the over-controlling ego and the disruptive force of desire. It has paid less attention to 'the more difficult antagonism between the superego and the unconscious, where what is hidden is aggression as much as sexuality, and the agent of repression is as ferocious as what it is trying to control' (p. 143). *Love* is concerned with the 'difficult antagonism' of which Rose speaks, but particularly with what happens when negativity enters the psychic structure. Carter appears to have found in Poe's poem, 'Annabel Lee', a stimulus for thinking about the connection between the expression of love and 'destruction' or 'negativity' (*Nachfolge*) which Freud saw as linked to 'destruction' (*Destruktionstriels*). As such *Love* embarks upon a difficult area of exploration for, as Rose maintains, thinking about negativity and its outer boundaries calls into question the very existence of boundaries (p. 164). Carter's novel suggests that when we allow for 'negativity' within our model of the psyche, we can no longer rely on the conventional boundaries between, for example, 'love' and 'destruction' or 'care' and 'the infliction of pain'; nor assign to logic and sequence their traditional priority in an explication of human behaviour.

## VIII

It is plausible, then, to read *Shadow Dance*, *Several Perceptions* and *Love* as a trilogy based on a fictional mediation of bohemian life at various points in 1960s Bristol which invites reading from a realist perspective. However, it is no coincidence that when Joanne takes Lee home to her bed in *Love*, they pass through the wrought iron gates of the park which 'neither permitted nor denied access' and seemed to negate a moral problem 'by declaring it improperly phrased' (pp. 110–11). Throughout each of the three novels, Carter is concerned with the significance of how things are 'phrased', that is conceptualised. A range of different frameworks provide different ways of approaching and pursuing issues as the hybrid nature of the novels and the myriad of intertextual references provide different pointers as to how they should perhaps be read. Realism in these novels, as in all Carter's work, offers one way of looking at things but it is disrupted by, and in turn destabilises, a combination of American Gothic and Freudian, Jungian and even object relations psychology.

   Although these novels do not have the characteristics often associated with 'magic realism' that we find in the later novels – although as I suggested in the introduction this label is not unproblematic – they demonstrate Carter's interest in the fiction-ality of realism and of much that we regard as non-fiction. In each novel, the boundaries between reality and illusion and between fact and fiction become blurred. Although each novel is a third-person narrative, they are identified, especially in the case of *Shadow Dance* and *Several Perceptions*, with a specific male consciousness. It is impossible to accept this consciousness as that of the author. And even if we accept it as a construction, it is invariably a slippery, incoherent fiction which is difficult to map adequately. Carter appears to have become interested in these novels in the different means which have been available at different times for mapping the mind. The reader soon becomes aware that ways of conceptualising the mind have a literary as well as a psychoanalytic history. In these early novels they are dehistoricised – perhaps because, as *Several Perceptions* illustrates, Carter is interested in the collage, a non-linear way of constructing fictions. Joseph's wall is covered with photo-graphs of different periods:

> There were some pictures tacked to the wall. Lee Harvey Oswald, handcuffed between policemen, about to be shot, wild as a badger. A colour photograph, from *Paris Match*, of a square of elegant houses and, within these pleasant boundaries, a living sunset, a Buddhist monk whose saffron robes turned red as he burned alive. Also a calendar of the previous year advertising a brand of soft drinks by means of a picture of a laughing girl in a white, sleeveless, polo-neck sweater sucking this soft drink through a straw. And a huge dewy pin-up of Marilyn Monroe. (p. 15)

In Joseph's room, these photographs exist in new spatial and temporal relationships with each other. The pictures of the monk and of the houses from the French magazine, for example, have been lifted out of the framework in which the reader would nor-mally encounter them, creating a new context in which the viewer might now 'read' both differently. In other words, conventional ways of 'phrasing' these events have been challenged. The ahistorical arrangement of these photographs is echoed in the early novels in Carter's use of intertextuality. For example, in *Love*, we are told that Lee 'looked like Billy Budd, or a worker hero of the Soviets, or a boy in a book by Jack London' (p. 12). Here Carter juxtaposes three pieces of representation which readers may not have thought of connecting in such a concentrated way for themselves. Lifted out of their usual cultural, geographical and temporal frameworks, and placed in this new spatial and temporal sequence, these references pose a problem for the reader. Which of these references is to be privileged over the others? To give priority to one rather than another may take our reading of Lee in a different direction from that suggested by the others. The association of Lee with Billy Budd would more than likely emphasise the feminine nature of his beauty and lead the reader to consider the ambivalence in the representation of Lee's relationship with his brother. On the other hand, placing Lee in context with idealised portraits of Soviet workers would invariably lead the reader to consider the importance to the narrative of the left-wing aunt with whom he was brought up; his own working-class origins and how they are betrayed (probably in both senses of the word); and how he represents himself in class terms, including his relationships with Carolyn and Joanne and his marriage.

The intertextuality in the Bristol trilogy may involve us in studying specific allusions, in tracing particular refrences and in comparing sources. At another level, it may encourage us to think in more general terms – recalling characters, plots, images and conventions from literary traditions which in the novels are appropriated, challenged or transformed. Thus through their intertextuality, the novels may transform the way in which we think about intellectual frameworks – encouraging us to be more aware of, and open in, how we read, think and conceptualise within frameworks; and in the way in which we consciously and unconsciously police boundaries between fiction and non-fiction.

In the next chapter, I discuss two novels in which the intertexts allude to the totality of particular literary traditions such as the fairy story and the post-apocalyptic novel. Many studies of narrative have been concerned with the way in which key narrative modes have been determined by 'real life', or rather the way in which real life has been perceived in terms of linearity, coherence and closure. Carter, however, is interested in the way in which human thought and behaviour have been structured by literary and non-literary cultural forms such as myth, folk lore, fairy stories, superstition, proverbs. As Judie Newman (1990) has pointed out, 'human experience may generate literature – but such experience has already been filtered through forms of artistic organisation' (p. 114).

# 3

# Pain and Exclusion

## *The Magic Toyshop* (1967) and *Heroes and Villains* (1969)

I

As I pointed out at the beginning of the previous chapter, *The Magic Toyshop* (1967) and *Heroes and Villains* (1969) were Carter's second and fourth novels respectively. In some respects, they recall the Bristol trilogy. For example, Lorna Sage (1994b) has pointed out that *Heroes and Villains* mocks the cultural landscape of the 1960s such as the glamour of underground, countercultural movements; the siege of university campuses; the rebirth of dandyism; and the power acquired by intellectual gurus such as Timothy Leary who is parodied in Donally (p. 18). However, they are different from the other novels written in the 1960s in ways which anticipate the later fiction. Indeed, both novels may be seen as transitional works, bridging the gap between the Bristol trilogy and the less realistic mode of the post-1970 novels.

While there are good reasons for discussing *The Magic Toyshop* and *Heroes and Villains* in a separate chapter from the Bristol trilogy, there is also a valid case to be made for considering the two novels in tandem. Ostensibly, they appear to be very different works. *The Magic Toyshop*, drawing on elements of fairy tale, is concerned with a middle-class young girl, Melanie, and her brother and sister, who are forced to move to London to live with their uncle and aunt in a flat above their toyshop. *Heroes and Villains* is a futuristic, post-cataclysmic fantasy in which a young girl, Marianne, leaves the security of what remains of established society to join a nomadic tribe of so-called 'Barbarians' who exist outside.

Despite the obvious differences between them, however, the two novels have much in common. Both belong to the period before Angela Carter travelled to Japan (1969–72), which Sage (1994b) has described as 'her rite of passage' (p. 18). Both novels are in fact 'rite of passage' narratives – for Carter herself as well as for Melanie and Marianne. Both novels employ pre-novelistic strategies. *The Magic Toyshop* adapts narrative conventions borrowed from fairy tales. It also contains many allusions to theatre, not only through Uncle Philip's puppet theatre, but in the references to masks – Aunt Margaret, for example, assumes the 'tragic mask' of a mother who has sent all her sons to war (p. 135) – to opera, Renaissance drama and, in the account of the overgrown private park, to street theatre and carnival. Whilst at one level, *Heroes and Villains* is post-apocalyptic or decline-of-civilisation fiction, it, too, employs a pre-novelistic form of writing – the wandering serial formula of picaresque narrative. It also draws on motifs from European Romance fiction in, for example, the use of wilderness and the demon lover. There are also clear fairy tale elements, including an orphaned central protagonist who, as in *The Magic Toyshop*, crosses a threshold from one world to another.

Although both *The Magic Toyshop* and *Heroes and Villains* are third-person narratives, their focalisation is through the consciousness of an adolescent girl who has lost one or both of her parents after an act of transgression on her part. In what appear to be acts of surrogate self-mutilation, both Melanie and Marianne respond initially to the trauma of the deaths violently; Melanie breaks up her bedroom while Marianne cuts off her hair. In both novels, the acts of transgression and the deaths of the parents initiate a period of exclusion for the protagonists. Melanie is forced to go and live in London, where she is an outsider in the Flowers family; and Marianne chooses to flee from the community of 'Professors' as it is called.

In both novels, there is a problematic relationship based on a combination of attraction and repulsion – Melanie and Finn in *The Magic Toyshop* and Marianne and Jewel in *Heroes and Villains*. Both young women are raped, Melanie symbolically – as I shall discuss – and Marianne literally. Whilst *The Magic Toyshop* is more obviously a critique of patriarchy, both heroines have to contend with a dominant male – Uncle Philip in *The Magic Toyshop* and Donally in *Heroes and Villains*. As Paulina Palmer (1987) says, typical of women in a patriarchal society, they are 'pressured to seek refuge from one man in the arms of another' (p. 187). In both novels, she argues, 'the contradiction between the romantic images of femininity reproduced in culture and art, and the facts of sexual violence' are highlighted (p. 184). In particular, the violence of the myths which have sustained patriarchy is signified in the recurrent images of mutilation and castration, such as Melanie's phantasy of the severed hand. However, the severed hand may also suggest the psychic severance women experience in patriarchal society.

Both Melanie and Marianne, as Palmer says, are from a different social class from the people with whom they become involved, but this is more complicated than Palmer suggests. The social differences between Marianne and Jewel, for example, are elided by the fact that he is better educated than she expected and between Melanie and Finn by his artistic sensibility, evident in his engagement with music. In Marianne's case, her view of Jewel is mediated, as I shall discuss, through the stories circulating in her community about the Barbarians while Melanie's view of Finn is influenced by her middle-class English upbringing. Each novel is concerned with the ways in which notions of self and identity, especially female identity, are constructed through language and mythology.

II

Although *The Magic Toyshop*, is not a fairy tale as such, then, it reclaims a number of elements from the genre. The word 'reclaim' is used deliberately here, for the fairy tale has been marginalised as a literary form, relegated to the non-serious world of children's fiction. In *The Magic Toyshop*, Carter rediscovers its imaginative potential, especially for the feminist writer. The storyline of the novel itself is reminiscent of a fairy story. Its heroine, Melanie, her brother Jonathan and sister Victoria are orphaned; the death of their parents in a plane crash is linked in Melanie's mind to an act of transgression – Melanie secretly trying on her mother's wedding dress one night – and the children are forced to live with a relative they hardly know who turns out to be an ogre. The stock fairy tale motifs adapted by Carter include: the arduous journey – the children travel from their comfortable home in the country to their uncle's toyshop in south London; the dumb mute – their aunt in London has been struck dumb on her wedding day; meta-morphoses – Uncle Philip's evil is revealed gradually in the course of the narrative; and even the winged creature – in the form of the swan puppet which Philip makes for the show in which Melanie takes part.

Traditional fairy tales, rewritten by male writers, became vehicles for the socialisation of young women producing a subgenre of 'warning tales'. As Jack Zipes (1988) points out:

> Almost all critics who have studied the emergence of the literary fairy tale in Europe agree that educated writers purposely appropriated the oral folk tale and converted it into a literary discourse about mores, values and manners so that children would become civilised according to the social code of that time.  (p. 3)

The stories acquired a moral which often arose out of a young girl being punished or brought to 'wisdom' through realising the foolishness of transgression. In a discussion of Perrault, whose tales Carter translated, Zipes points out that such stories do not warn 'against the dangers of predators in forests', but warns girls 'against their own natural desires which they must tame' (p. 29). In other words, Carter, like many feminist critics, recognises fairy tales as a reactionary form that inscribed a misogynistic ideology. However, critics have not always questioned, as Makinen (1992) has pointed out, whether women readers would necessarily identify with the female figures (p. 4). Carter's attempts to re-vision fairy tales in, for example, *The Bloody Chamber and Other Stories* (1979), have been the subject of much debate among critics. Some critics, following Anthea Dworkin (1981), have suggested that Carter has not adequately re-visioned the fairy tale form, working within the strait-jacket of their original structures, so that her attempts to create an active female erotic are badly compromised. Makinen takes issue with this view, arguing that 'it is the critics who cannot see beyond the sexist binary opposition' (ibid.). They have tended to assume that the fairy tale is a universal, unchangeable given. Although all narrative genres clearly do inscribe ideologies, as Makinen argues, later rewritings of a genre do not necessarily encode the same ideological assumptions.

Although *The Magic Toyshop* is not a fairy story as such, it anticipates how in her later collection, *The Bloody Chamber and Other Stories*, Carter adapted the form to criticise the inscribed ideology and to incorporate new assumptions. The novel incorporates the reactionary element of the fairy story in the consequences which befall Melanie borrowing her mother's wedding dress. However, it also undermines this inscribed ideology by emphasising what the misogynistic fairy stories suppressed, an adolescent girl's excitement about her body and the discovery of her emerging sexuality:

> she would follow with her finger the elegant structure of her rib-cage, where the heart fluttered under the flesh like a bird under a blanket, and she would draw down the long line from breast-bone to navel (which was a mysterious cavern or grotto), and she would rasp her palms against her bud-wing shoulder-blades. (p. 1)

Carter appropriates a Renaissance convention whereby the continent of America (of discovery and enjoyment) serves as a metaphor for the body: 'The summer she was fifteen, Melanie discovered she was made of flesh and blood. O, my America, my new found land' (ibid.). However, as Richard Brown (1994) points out, the implied male colonial explorer is now a young woman – an index in the text of female self-possession (p.92). As I said in the Introduction, Fredric Jameson has suggested that one of the most potentially disruptive elements in narrative, and especially 'magic realist' narrative, is the appearance of the body. While I would not describe *The Magic Toyshop* as a 'magic realist' narrative for the reservations which I expressed earlier, the novel has more in common with 'magic realism' than 'realism'. As Jameson suggests, the body, in this case Melanie's, in *The Magic Toyshop* diverts the narrative in a number of directions. According to Jameson, in the realist novel, the disruption is resolved through fetishising the body as image. In *The Magic Toyshop*, this is clearly not the case. Indeed, the disruption is not only sustained, but thematised in the narrative. Through her phantasies enacted before her mirror, Melanie begins to explore her different potential identities and the contradictory roles that make up the female subject in art and society such as a Pre-Raphaelite, a Lautrec model with her hair 'dragged sluttishly across her face', and a Cranach Venus. She indulges in secret acts of transgression, gift-wrapping herself for a phantom bridegroom and, after reading *Lady Chatterley's Lover*, sticking forget-me-knots in her pubic hair.

The novel's concerns here with the female body and sexuality are typical of Anglo-American feminist art and literature of the late 1960s and early 1970s and it is important to place the zeal of such work, which from a later feminist perspective may appear intellectually a little crude, in the context of the times. Feminist artists and writers of the day were mounting a challenge to the way in which women's bodies were rendered invisible in art and culture other than as idealised objects in works produced by men within the tradition of the classic female nude. The focus of their challenge was this Western tradition's denial of women's experiences of their own bodies. In other words, they attacked the mythical sense of the integrity of the body and its boundaries in the representation of the female nude and drew attention to the internal bodily changes or bodily fluids which regularly crossed those boundaries and subverted the body's sense of closure. As Lynda Nead (1992) points out, artists such as Judy Chicago, for example, were claiming, 'that vaginal and vulvic forms were an innate and natural language for female artistic expression' (p. 65). The notoriety which works such as Chicago's *Red Flag* (1971), depicting the removal of a bloody tampon, achieved was a result of the sanitised way in which the female body had hitherto been perceived in art. Much of the feminist artistic space now taken for granted had not been won at that time. As Nead (1992) argues:

> The feminist claim of the 1970s to 'our bodies, our selves' put the issues of control and identity at the centre of the movement's political agenda . . . art that focuses on images and aspects of the female body, was one attempt within the sphere of culture to create a different kind of visibility for women.  (p. 64)

The episode in *The Magic Toyshop* in which Melanie enters the garden at night wearing her mother's wedding dress begins with a description of Melanie's anxieties about tree-climbing since she began menstruating. As if to reinforce what culture had so long denied, the novel mentions periods, pregnancy, embryo, gestation and miscarriage within one short paragraph (p. 20). Although this may seem like straining for effect to contemporary readers, Carter is following the feminist concerns of her day to challenge, and work against, traditions which reified the cosmetically finished surface of the female body and denied the abject matter of its interior. Ironically in London, Uncle Philip tries to turn Melanie into a fetishised object as spectacle, a wooden marionette. The image of the puppet, as Palmer (1987) points out, suggests the coded manne-quin metaphor employed by the French psychoanalytic literary critic, Julia Kristeva, to represent the robotic state to which human beings are reduced by a process of psychic repression (p. 180).

The way in which the wedding dress episode is structured appears to suggest a young girl's first experience of sex and the anxieties around it. In *The Interpretation of Dreams* (1965), Freud observes that climbing in a dream signifies vaginal intercourse (p. 401) The purring cat at the centre of the tree she is about to climb gives Melanie the confidence to step out of the wedding dress and become naked. In her nakedness, she feels vulnerable, pulling her hair around her for protection. The cat unexpectedly hurts her, the dress which she had parcelled up and placed in the tree is symbolically ripped and there is now blood on the hem. Melanie now feels 'a new and final kind of nakedness, as if she had taken even her own skin off' (p. 21). Moreover, the season is the end of the summer – the end of childhood and 'innocence' – and the moon, the female symbol to which menstruation is linked, is 'beginning to slide down the sky'.

At this point in the novel, Carter rewrites the myth of the Garden of Eden of which we are reminded by the tree itself, clearly the Tree of Knowledge, by the reference to the shower of apples, and by an allusion to Eve's realisation of her nakedness after eating the forbidden fruit – Melanie is 'horribly conscious of her own exposed nakedness'. However, if the biblical imagery reminds us of Genesis, there are counter elements drawn from witchcraft, paganism and superstition – the cat is a well-known witch's familiar, Melanie crosses her fingers, and there are references to blackness, the night, blood and nakedness. They remind us of elements absent from the biblical version of the Adam and Eve story and the novel seems to be challenging a myth which endorses the inferiority of women to men.

III

An important aspect of the novel's re-vision of the Adam and Eve story is the female focalisation, or point of view, which stresses not only a developing sexuality, but the excitement, fears and phantasies to which sexuality gives rise and through which it not only finds expression but is explored and developed. The emphasis eventually falls upon anxiety, pain and disillusionment.The initial reference to the domestic in this episode promises reassurance – the cat purrs as if someone had lit a small fire for it – but it proves to be unstable and cruel. The purring cat turns out to have paws 'tipped with curved, cunning meat hooks' (p. 21). Melanie's experience of nude tree-climbing leads to injury and, quite literally, agony. Here the novel may be prefiguring more than what is in store for Melanie as a consequence of her parents' death and her enforced move to London. It may also be giving expression to a centuries old fear of women: that their husband's may turn out to be monsters and wedded bliss prove a nightmare. Ironically, while much of the passage suggests the irretrievable loss of childhood – Melanie has started her periods, decided to grow her hair long and has stopped wearing shorts – Melanie emotionally regresses to childhood: 'Please, God, let me get safe back to my own bed again.' Particularly important to the novel's concern at this point with Melanie explicitly and all women implicitly is the tension between desire and restraint which causes a scream to swell up in Melanie's throat. The unexpressed scream, of course, becomes a symbol of the condition in which Melanie, and perhaps many women, will come to live:

> Once a branch broke with a groan under the trusting sole of her foot and she hung in agony by her hands, strung up between earth and heaven, kicking blindly for a safe, solid thing in a world all shifting leaves and shadows. (p. 21)

Zipes (1988), drawing on Freud's theory of the uncanny, suggests that fairy stories have remained popular because they are concerned with the quest for an idealised notion of home which has been suppressed in the adult consciousness. In discussing the liberating power of feminist fairy tales, Zipes suggests that they present us with a means by which the idealised home may be reclaimed. These include the ways in which the opposed protagonists learn to free themselves from 'parasitical creatures'. For Zipes, the latter are allegorical representations of the sociopsychological conflicts which have prevented the opposed protagonists from having a psychic realisation of home. They are also the conflicts which, in Zipes's psychoanalytic approach to fairy stories, the reader, in a similar position to the opposed protagonist, needs to revisit.

Zipes's argument is particularly relevant to Carter's fiction where a number of characters are motivated by a desire to realise the ideal of home. Desiderio in *The Infernal Desire Machines of Doctor Hoffman*, for example, temporarily realises the ideal of home among the River People and even more fleetingly with Albertina, the object of his desire, among the Centaurs. However, Zipes's work is especially applicable to *The Magic Toyshop* and *Heroes and Villains* where for Melanie and Marianne, as for so many of Carter's characters, their early home life is severely disrupted by trauma. After being raped by Jewel, on whom she projected her erotic phantasies, Marianne wants to escape, 'as if somewhere there was still the idea of a home' (p. 52). The description of the flat in London in *The Magic Toyshop* is in the third person, but the focalisation is Melanie's. The contrast between the new home and the one she has left opens up a new space in which Melanie imagines, locates and develops an ideal:

> Porcelain gleamed pink and the soft, fluffy towels and the toilet paper were pink to match. Steaming water gushed plentifully from the dolphin shaped taps and jars of bath essence and toilet water and after-shave glowed like jewellery; and the low lavatory tactfully flushed with no noise at all. It was a temple to cleanness. Mother loved nice bathrooms. (pp. 56–7)

She is cast as an opposed protagonist. Even though Aunt Margaret, Francie and Finn love each other, making Melanie feel 'bitterly lonely and unloved', the Flowers family become the parasitical creatures of fairy stories. Finn, for example, is described as 'a tawny lion poised for the kill'. Melanie does consciously what Zipes argues all readers of fairy stories do unwittingly. She translates the parasitical creatures of fairy stories into the sociopsychological conflicts which separate her, and will continue to separate her, from the psychic ideal of the home. Finn comes to represent an 'insolent, off-hand, terrifying maleness' and the threat that he poses is suggested when, in order to comb out her hair, he 'ground out his cigarette on the window-ledge and laughed' (p. 45). For all the differences between Finn and his uncle, the laugh and grounding gesture at this point blur the boundary between them.

From the outset, *The Magic Toyshop* is concerned not only with the importance of phantasy but of ego disturbances within the psyche. These are often brought about by what Lorna Sage (1994b) has described as 'the bad magic of mythologies' (p. 18). In the novel, the psyche is perceived as constructed within a wide system of relationships including familial, social, cultural and political forces. Some of these – such as nature and sex – we tend to 'mythologise' and regard as if they are 'outside' of history and a particular social milieu. Desire and phantasy, especially, we tend to regard as 'universal' or 'archetypal', ignoring the way in which these, too, are socially constructed. Many teenagers, for example, may identify with the lyrics of chart-topping pop songs because they appear to reflect their emotions, anxieties and frustrations, without realising that these songs as part of popular culture contribute to the social construction of emotional identity, of gendered behaviour within relationships, and of desire itself. In her exploration of the different social roles and subjectivities available to women, Melanie not only challenges the notion of a singular female identity, but demonstrates how women have to negotiate a myriad of received assumptions and social conventions.

One approach to *The Magic Toyshop*, then, would be to consider Melanie's acquisition of an autonomous identity in the context of the circumstances which befall her. In this respect, the text poses a challenge to conventional psychoanalysis which has tended to be based on relationships within the kind of comfortable bourgeois family which for Melanie collapses. As Jennifer Fitzgerald (1993) has pointed out in a critical essay on the African-American writer, Toni Morrison, psychoanalysis has traditionally pathologised non-normative families such as the one to which Melanie moves. However, it is not really the function of literary criticism to examine characters as if they were people. As Fitzgerald goes on to argue, it is the purpose of literary criticism to analyse discourses not psyches. This seems particularly appropriate to Carter's novel which is sceptical of many of the discourses, such as the Adam and Eve story, which circulates through it. This does not mean that we should not bring a psychoanalytic discourse to bear on a discussion of Melanie within the novel. It means that we should recognise that psychoanalysis is only one of a number of discourses, such as female identity, patriarchy and the family, circulating in this text, and that one discourse is always articulated within other discourses. In the account of the relationship between Melanie and Finn, for example, there is a wide variety of allusions. There are references, for example, to Romeo and Juliet, Tristan and Isolde, loveknots, and lovers in New Wave films. Any one of these might trigger a different reading of what happens between them.

Since Melanie's normative family life is disrupted, classical psychoanalysis based on the traditional bourgeois family norm is not the most appropriate framework within which to explore what happens to her in the toyshop. A more sympathetic model is provided by the psychoanalytic school of thought known as object relations theory to which I referred earlier. In contradistinction to classical psychoanalysis, it recognises the range of relationships, including those within the family, which can influence the psyche. According to object relations theory as developed by Melanie Klein, an infant experiences complex and contradictory emotions which are projected into objects, including people, with which it comes into contact. These objects, subsequently transformed into positive or negative phantasy objects, or 'imagos', are 'introjected' back into the child's psyche. Eventually, the child forges a sense of its own identity out of these experiences and phantasies and begins to recognise others as separate individuals rather than 'imagos'. Clearly, one of the most powerful, negative 'imagos' in Melanie's childhood is the jack-in-the-box with a grotesque caricature of her own face which Uncle Philip, whom she had never met, sent her one Christmas and which turned the uncle himself into an 'imago'. The face is mocking and cruel, mirroring the way in which the father, according to Freudian psychology, imposes on the girl-child a sense of lack. Uncle Philip epitomises the intrusion of patriarchy: how the male will come between a young girl and her relationship with her mother and will seek to silence and control the female.

The novel's brief account of Melanie's childhood emphasises her reclusive nature, her privileged upbringing and a range of likely and unlikely 'imagos'. Inscribed almost exclusively in terms of projection and introjection, it is clear that Melanie's privileged and limited childhood has prevented the full development of a sense of her own identity. This is exacerbated by the trauma of her parents' deaths. She is unable to recognise that other factors which had nothing to do with her were responsible which results in a form of self-loathing. In her own mind, she becomes the kind of part-object which I suggested in the discussion of *Shadow Dance* are characteristic of fairy stories: 'The girl who killed her mother' (p. 24). Unable to expel this imago – initially by vomiting – she projects it on her mirror image which she tries, unsuccessfully, to destroy. Ironically, she kills her parents a second time by destroying their photograph. However, the imago into which she has projected her guilt now consumes her so that she becomes inhuman: 'She neither saw nor heard anything but wrecked like an automaton. Feathers stuck in the tears and grease on her cheeks' (p. 25). Of course, this description of her anticipates the puppet which Uncle Philip tries to make of her. The distinction between her own intense subjectivity and external objects becomes blurred – for example, she refrains from cutting her hair short because it grew while her parents were alive. Although Mrs Rundle moves on to another family, Melanie continues to cling to her in her memories. Significantly, Mrs Rundle has created for herself an independent sense of self; although not married, she has chosen to be called 'Mrs' since it makes it easier for her to be 'acceptable' in a society geared towards men and married women. In the course of the novel, Melanie has to seek her own autonomous identity.

In London, Melanie's reactions to the people she meets is regressive. She projects her emotions into them as external objects, introjecting the resultant 'imagos' as part of herself. This is partly the consequence of the intensity with which Melanie sees things, as suggested in the image of Aunt Margaret's coal fire which is 'rendered more fierce by the confines of the small, black-leaded grate' (p. 41) In Melanie's case, the confines are those of Uncle Philip's flat and the guilt she feels over her parents' deaths. At the flat above the toyshop, the people she meets and the objects she encounters are rendered more fierce by these confines. Although, for example, it is the third-person narrative which introduces the fallen puppet – 'Lying face-downwards in a tangle of strings was a puppet fully five feet high, a *sylphide* in a fountain of white tulle, fallen flat down as if someone got tired of her in the middle of playing with her' – the focalisation is Melanie's: '"It is too much", said Melanie, agitated. "There is too much"' (p. 67).

In terms of Kleinian theory, the processes of identification and projection are particularly intense in Melanie's case. Regressively, she clings to the imago of a lover which she has derived from children's books and poems. While it is difficult for the reader to separate the reality of Finn from Melanie's perceptions of him and her projections into him, he at least draws her away from her past. Eventually, her idealised lover crumples 'like the paper he was made of before this insolent, off-hand, terrifying maleness, filling the room with its reek. She hated it. But she could not take her eyes of him' (p. 45).

As the jack-in-the-box demonstrates, Melanie also becomes an object into which others, whom we may suspect of not having forged an adequate sense of their own identity, project their own phantasies and desires. Not only does Finn insist on combing her hair differently almost as soon as she arrives, but he paints her secretly through a hole in her bedroom wall. Uncle Philip sees her as a nymph covered with daisies. This is, of course, how in her regressive state she has tended to see herself. At one level, the toy shop is a parody of patriarchy, under which women are silenced. It is significant, albeit rather crudely, that Aunt Margaret is struck dumb on her wedding day and only regains her voice when Philip discovers her locked in an embrace with Francie.

As Nicole Ward Jouve (1994) points out, father figures in Carter's work are 'attacked, deconstructed, shown to be hollow or vulnerable' (p. 155). Uncle Philip's need to control, and manipulate others – on the poster advertising his puppet show he is depicted holding the ball of the world in his hand – is evident in one of his favourite creations – the 'Surprise Rose Bowl'. The shepherdess which appears from a simulacra of a rose made out of stiffened card or wood shavings performs a perfectly poised pirouette. But Philip is so obsessive and violent – worryingly evident in the way he 'attacks' the Christmas goose with the carving knife – that he appears to have serious and deep-rooted psychological problems. He seems driven by a repressed and violently tinged sexuality – in manipulating Melanie in his version of *Leda and the Swan*, he appears to be performing a surrogate rape. The narrative makes him an even more disturbing personality by comparing him with the Nazis, especially bearing in mind how he is shown on the poster. Having attacked Finn because he has ruined the 'Grand Performance', we are told that Philip shoves the body aside 'with the casual brutality of Nazi soldiers moving corpses in films of concentration camps'

(p. 132). Here Carter is introducing a popular connection between private sadism and the public brutality of totalitarian regimes. She is not necessarily arguing for the link, and indeed in the course of the novel it is not really developed. However, in the novel's more general exploration of private and socially sanctioned domination of one group by another, it is introduced as one position that can be, and has been, struck. Particularly ominous is Finn's blood-streaked vomit, a harbinger of the violence to come. The extent of Philip's callousness is reinforced by the way in which he laments the damaged puppet as a dead friend or sibling might be mourned in a Renaissance tragedy: 'Poor old Bothwell! All his wires gone!' But even more disturbing are the changes which occur in him. In the wake of the disastrous show, his language becomes increasingly crude and violent – Finn is accused of 'buggering me Bothwell' and the family are told to 'piss off' (p. 133). An especially chilling development is the way in which he becomes a parody of the wicked, incestuous uncle. In insisting that Melanie now acts with his puppets, 'He rubbed his hands with satisfaction. 'What's your name, girly? Speak up' (ibid.). Particularly disturbing, he addresses her as if he does not know who she is. The word 'girly', robs Melanie of her identity as his niece, reinforces her vulnerability and confirms his power over her.

In contrast to Philip's favourite toy, the movements of Finn's own creation of a yellow bear with a bow tie around its neck riding a bicycle are erratic. They permit an unpredictability which has no place in Uncle Philip's universe, and the toy itself is witty. In fact, Melanie's reaction to the toy is different from her response to the objects which filled her bedroom as imagos at the beginning of the novel. In making her laugh, the toy and Melanie remain distant from each other so that it is able to represent the wit and perspective which Melanie needs to acquire in order to achieve a confident, autonomous self-identity.

At the end of the novel, Melannie and Finn escape from the toyshop, like Adam and Eve from the Garden of Eden, returning the reader to the biblical myth which is employed in the earlier description of Melanie's sexual awakening. In fact, Carter herself has said that she saw the novel in terms of the 'Fortunate Fall': 'I took the Fortunate Fall as meaning that it was a good thing to get out of that place. The intention was that the toyshop itself should be a secularized Eden (Haffenden, 1985, p. 80). The 'Fortunate

Fall' is not only from the toyshop but the cultural myths which have contributed to women's intellectual, emotional and sexual oppression.

The theme of a new Eden and the human race reduced to an elemental pair was common in science fiction of the 1950s and 1960s. Carter's adaption of it is ambiguous and possibly influenced by the art of the time, especially collage work that suggested that desire, as Thomas Crow (1996) maintains, is 'held hostage' by the Adam and Eve myth (p. 47). In Richard Hamilton's collage, *Just what is it that makes today's homes so different, so appealing?* (1956), for example, Charles Atlas, the model body-builder of comic-book back pages is the naked Adam and the pulp pin-up is Eve. In Hamilton's collaborative contribution, the same year, to the installation art exhibition, *This is Tomorrow*, the primal male is the robot from *Forbidden Planet* who holds a Jane-like figure in his arms. Next to him is Marilyn Monroe in a still from the pavement grating scene in Billy Wilder's film, *The Seven Year Itch* (1955). The latter, in which a married man has a fling with the girl up stairs, suggests through a series of dream sequences that desire is structured by the dominant fictions in society. At the end of *The Magic Toyshop*, Carter appears to imply, as she said, that the Fall was fortunate, but also that Melanie and Finn are trapped by the Genesis myth. It is ironic that in the fire 'everything is gone' but that the myth remains: 'At night, in the garden, they faced each other in a wild surmise' (p. 200).

## IV

The agency which Melanie needs to acquire in her own life is evident in the early part of *The Magic Toyshop* in acts of transgression – Melanie trying on her mother's wedding dress and stealing her brother's books in order to raise the money to buy false eyelashes. Ironically, whilst, at one level, her desire for false eyelashes is a sign of her independence, at another, it is a symbol of the way in which her identity as a young woman is defined by discourses outside herself. Inevitably these discourses take from her control over her own body. Even at fifteen, Melanie is beginning to feel a failure because she has not yet married or had sex. In *Heroes and Villains*, which like *The Magic Toyshop* has a female focalisation, Marianne's acts of independence are similarly acts of transgression.

*Heroes and Villains* is a version of the post-apocalyptic novel which was popular in the Cold War 1950s. As Roz Kaveney (1994) has pointed out, it draws upon an older decline-of-civilisation genre which can be traced back to Mary Shelley's *The Last Man* (1826) and Richard Jefferies's *After London* (1885). More specifically, *Heroes and Villains* is based on tropes, especially that of living among the ruins, familiar in British and American post-apocalyptic science fiction written by women in the 1970s. As Nan Albinski (1988) reminds us, in the 1970s and 1980s, 'women writers increasingly foresee the destruction of the cities, with groups of survivors (sometimes groups composed solely of women) living in the ruins, scavenging the left-overs' (p. 133).

In *Heroes and Villains*, a nuclear war has transformed a mundane environment into a Gothic fantasy. Although there are numerous post-cataclysmic, science fiction fantasies, Carter's novel is one of the few to highlight the effects on people and the landscape. Marianne, from whose perspective the novel is told, runs away from what remains of civilisation, orderly communities based on farming and craftwork and guarded by soldiers who rule over them with the Professors, between whom there is little respect. She enters the outside, Gothic world of ruins and forests inhabited by the Barbarians, by whom she is taken captive, and by mutants who are the products of radiation. However, despite similarities between Carter's novel and post-apocalyptic science fiction written by women, it is unlikely that Carter had read much of it in any detail, if at all. Rather as Kaveney (1994) maintains, it is likely 'that she was interested in those aspects of the culture where ideas from SF were liable to make their mark' (p. 182).

Although a sense of loss pervades the novel at a number of levels – civilisation has all but been destroyed and Melanie loses her parents – Carter's novel avoids focusing on the decline itself. On a cursory reading, Carter appears to establish a clear polarisation between the two societies. The community of the Professors and soldiers is rigidly hierarchical, totalitarian, militaristic and sexually repressive. The society of the Barbarians is more strongly linked to the natural world, has a quasi-tribal structure and regards the community as a family. However, Carter does not establish, as the conventional post-apocalyptic novel would have done, a rigid binarism between the Professors/soldiers and the Barbarians or pursue the tensions between the soldiers and the intellectuals. The post-apocalyptic fantasy becomes a narrative space in which Carter explores the blurring of conventional boundaries and binarisms and the ways in which such artificial boundaries are maintained.

In playing 'Soldiers and Barbarians' with the son of the Professor of Mathematics, Marianne refuses to accept that she should always have the part of the Barbarian, the villain, and that, as the hero, he should always shoot her. The Professor's son thinks within a rigid, binary structure which he never questions and which has its external equivalent in the stout wall around the village, manned with machine guns and topped with barbed wire. The word 'manned' is significant for within the compound life is structured, as the game of 'Soldiers and Barbarians' indicates, according to male rules and male logic. Even Marianne's own mother prefers her brother to her. In tripping up the Professor's son, Marianne disrupts the male symbolic structure. Overturned by this sudden act of violence, the boy loses command of language and is reduced to 'yowling' in the dust. Marianne, like Melanie, learns that in order to achieve an autonomous sense of self she has to disrupt the symbolic structures which have taken away from her control of her own language and of her sense of self and identity.

Marianne, we are told, is a child who 'broke things to see what they were like inside' (p. 4). This might serve as a summary not only of Marianne but of Carter herself. Certainly, *Heroes and Villains* displays a similar scepticism about mythologies as *The Magic Toyshop*. Both societies in the novel employ mythology and folk tales to maintain their geographical, cultural and intellectual boundaries including those which define the 'otherness' of outsiders. The 'warning tales' told by Marianne's nurse that the Barbarians slit the bellies of women after they have raped them and sew cats up inside them (p. 10) and that the Barbarians wrap little girls in clay and bake them (p. 2) are echoed by the stories of the Barbarians themselves who believe the Professors kill and bake Barbarians in their ovens (p. 35). When Marianne first meets Donally, he alludes parodically to the Barbarians' belief that women in the society of the Professors have sharp teeth in their vaginas in order to bite off the Barbarians' genitalia (p. 49). Of course, like the European 'warning tales' of the seventeenth century discussed by Zipes (1988), the stories Marianne is told warn children, especially girls, 'against their own natural desires which must be tamed' rather than against the Barbarians in the forest.

Marianne, like Melanie in *The Magic Toyshop*, comes to realise that identity is produced in the perception of others and rendered real through linguistic mechanisms. As Baudrillard (1993) points out:

> the progress of Humanity and Culture are simply the chain of discriminations with which to brand 'Others' with inhumanity, and therefore with nullity. For the savages who call themselves 'men', the others are something else. (p. 125)

This is evident not only in the way in which folk tales and games are used in the society of Professors, but in the mythologising of death – her brother is said to have 'gone to the ruins' – which Marianne is able to contrast with her own witnessing of his killing. Marianne realises that not only is the self located in the word, but when the word changes so does the concept of self. Increasingly, the ostensibly stable wor(l)d in the community of Professors is exposed through the soldiers slack use of language. On returning home, having committed an act of transgression by going into the ruins, Marianne discovers that her nurse has killed her father with an axe and then poisoned herself. The Colonel, her uncle, offers only the explanation that she was 'seriously maladjusted' (p. 15), which Marianne cannot equate with the love which the woman had shown them. This loose connection between fact and interpretation characterises the soldiers' discourse. The complex relationship between cause and effect, event and consequence, is frequently elided as in the Colonel's response to the (symbolic) killing of the Professor of Psychology which he believes to be justified because he, like Marianne's nurse, was 'maladjusted' (p. 17). Here Carter may well be parodying the way in which military language in the late twentieth century, employing evasive terms such as 'conflict management', has become increasingly diffuse.

A key text which the two societies in *Heroes and Villains* share, and which is tattooed on Jewel's back, is the myth of Adam and Eve. Encapsulating the story of Adam bewitched by Eve's smile, the tattoo signifies the ideologies through which Jewel's view of Marianne is mediated. Like *Shadow Dance*, *Heroes and Villains* places misogynism within a larger ideological and cultural context. Jewel's fear of Marianne is given as his explanation for raping her. However, his fear of her is also a product and reflection of the way patriarchal societies more generally fear the loss of control to women. Significantly, Jewel is happiest with Marianne in those moments when she has been subdued.

One of the most innovative aspects of *Heroes and Villains* is the way in which the confusion created by nuclear war, explored at the level of plot and theme in the conventional post-apocalyptic, futuristic novel, is pursued at the level of semiotics. The relationship between language and meaning is learned and arbitrary – as in the relationship between a word and the object to which it refers – and is always subject to change. However, meaning is conveyed through language because words relate to each other as part of a linguistic system. The wedding ceremony in the novel draws elements from so many different cultures and linguistic systems that they are unable to relate in any coherent way. Whilst Marianne wears a second-hand, white dress, Jewel wears a stiff, scarlet coat interwoven with gold thread that may have once belonged to a Bishop. Donally who performs the ceremony is robed from head to foot in a garment woven from bird feathers and wears a painted mask carved from wood. Although Donally reads from the *Book of Common Prayer*, the centre piece of the ceremony is taken from North American Indian culture, the cutting of the bride and groom's wrists and the mixing of their bloods. The semiotic confusion here is also an index of a greater confusion over identity created when traditional boundaries are crossed or blurred. Stepping outside the world which has been named and defined is exciting as Marianne realises near the end of the novel; on the seashore, she discovers how losing the names of things is 'a process of uncreation' (p. 136). However, the novel also suggests that without naming, everything reverts to chaos, to things 'existing only to themselves in an unstructured world'.

## V

Towards the end of *Heroes and Villains*, a sick and slightly drugged Marianne admits: 'When I was a little girl, we played at heroes and villains but now I don't know which is which any more, nor who is who, and what can I trust if not appearances?' (p. 125). As in *The*

*Magic Toyshop*, shifting frames of reference are used in *Heroes and Villains* to disrupt and deconstruct mythologies which have gone unchallenged for many years. Two of the most obvious are connected with post-Enlightenment European thinking. The novel confounds the conventional binarism in post-apocalyptic novels between 'civilised' and 'barbarian'. Jewel, for example, turns out to be an educated thinker. When he first meets Marianne, he quotes from Tennyson: 'It's the same everywhere you look, it's red in tooth and claw' (p. 18) and, much to Marianne's surprise, knows the zoological name for the adder which bites her (p. 28). This combination of encyclopaedic knowledge and primitive lore – he treats her with a folk remedy for snake bite, for example – is an index of the way in which Carter has created a 'third space' in her narrative about the Barbarians which defies analysis along the lines of conventional binarisms. Marianne's father makes the mistake of associating the Barbarians only with instinct – a view of which she is disabused shortly after meeting Jewel. Whilst her father and the other Professors believed that the painted faces of the Barbarians was an indication of how they had 'reverted to beasthood' (p. 24), she discovers that their masks are worn for a reason, it makes them look more frightening to their enemies in battle. The social structure of the Barbarians also challenges Rousseau's myth of the noble savage which is provocatively invoked at the outset of the novel. Whilst Rousseau envisaged natural man as an isolate, in the novel Marianne – the product of civilisation – is the outsider while the 'natural' people are social with a highly valued family structure.

*Heroes and Villains* also challenges the European Romantic notion of suffering, which has its origins in the Christian contemplative tradition and which valorises suffering as a pivotal experience whereby an individual becomes human. Post-apocalyptic narrative inevitably provides a space in which suffering as a means to full human subjectivity at the individual level can be expanded into the public realm where there is an obvious communal need to make sense of suffering as part of the human condition. However, the way in which the soldiers reductively attribute acts of violence and human breakdowns to 'maladjustment' suggests the difficulty of doing so. The death of the Professor of Psychology suggests that a means of explaining the bizarre instances of suffering which pervades the opening of the novel has been lost to the Professors of Mathematical Sciences. It may be difficult in terms of psychology to discuss fully, for example, the actions of the worker who 'went mad' and burned his wife and three children to death before killing himself. However, it is even more difficult to do so within a metaphysical framework which attempts to valorise human suffering.

In *Heroes and Villains,* suffering makes one less real rather than brings one to full subjectivity. This is evident in Jewel's whipping of his brother in which Precious swings under the blows 'like a carpet being beaten' (p. 113) and Jewel himself becomes 'mechanical' and 'a man no longer'. Jewel's muscle movements animate the tattoo on his back whereby Eve offers Adam the apple in 'an uncompleted series of actions with no conclusion', suggesting that violence holds one prisoner within actions which cannot move beyond themselves or to any sense of completion. Indeed, pain and suffering in the novel frequently take away the power of language in which a sense of self and identity are located – Precious grunts in 'a mechanical repetition of sounds' (p. 113). Through the suffering inflicted on him by Donally, the boy which Marianne first sees chained is regressed to pre-language, 'to a babbling murmur' (pp. 12–13). Indeed, extreme violence of any sort frequently has the same effect. Jewel 'howls' in fury before he strikes Marianne (p. 20) while his brothers, tearing at their meal of meat, issue screeches and foul abuse (p. 46).

The tattoo on Jewel's back is a permanent reminder of oppression and of the infliction of cruelty upon others; Jewel admits that when Donally tattooed him he was delirious and that only Mrs Green's care saved him from blood poisoning. It is also a reminder that suffering does not valorise pain but repeats the circumstances in which the suffering originated. Whilst Jewel believes that the tattoo on his back is impressive, Marianne is only reminded of the pain which it must have caused. For her, there is no question of the tattoo's beauty transcending Jewel's suffering even though pain is eroticised. Asking Jewel why he allowed Donally to 'attack him' with the needles (p. 86), she wants to know how much it hurt him (p. 96). Indeed, Marianne is preoccupied with the imposition of pain upon one person by another. Carter's own retrospective essay, 'People as Pictures', in *Nothing Sacred,* on the subject of Japanese tattooing, 'irezumi', provides a gloss on what Donally has done to Jewel. Irezumi, Carter maintains, 'transforms its victim into a genre masterpiece' (p. 33), but the technique employed is particularly painful. Indeed, Carter observes that the novelist, Junichiro

Tanizaki, describes one particular tattoo artist as a sadist: 'His pleasure lay in the agony men felt . . . The louder they screamed, the keener was Seikichi's strange delight' (p. 35). Donally's art is similarly sadistic – an extension of the abuse he inflicts on his own child. Significantly, he tattooed Jewel when he was a young and made most use of green – according to Carter's own essay one of the most painful colours to use. He was also responsible for the death of the little girl who died as he tried to turn her into a 'tiger lady'. Eschewing romantic valorisation of suffering enables Carter to explore the extent to which men are trapped within codes of violence and aggression which sometimes eroticise suffering, and the extent to which violence and pain are used to dominate women.

## VI

In the lives of both Melanie and Marianne an older woman – Mrs Rundle and Aunt Margaret in *The Magic Toyshop* and Mrs Green, Jewel's foster mother, in *Heroes and Villains* – proves to be important. The relationships which Melanie establishes with Mrs Rundle and Aunt Margaret are much closer and less ambiguous than the relationship between Marianne and Mrs Green. As is evident when Melanie gives Margaret her dress and lends her her mother's pearls, Melanie comes to see Margaret as a surrogate mother. At another level, however, their relationship suggests that women might establish among themselves an alternative community to the male-dominated social structure represented by Uncle Philip (a concept of which Carter is explicitly critical, though, in *The Passion of New Eve*). When Margaret tells Melanie that Philip does not allow her any money, Carter describes 'an ancient, female look' that passes between them:

> 'I understand', said Melanie. An ancient, female look passed between them; they were poor women pensioners, planets round a male sun. In the end, Francie gave Melanie a pound note from his fiddling money. He slipped it into the pocket of her skirt and she hardly knew how to thank him. (p. 140)

The look that passes between them is evidence of a deeper female bond. At the puppet show, Margaret pushes a toffee into Melanie's hands, a compensatory gesture between two females. However, the word 'bond' is double-edged; the women are also brought together by their shared economic dependency upon men. Even though Finn helps Melanie, the basic problem reminds the same – she is still a planet circulating around a male sun. Although Mrs Rundle has cared for the children, she is powerless to stop them from having to go to London if she wanted to, and she has had to change her own title to that of a married woman to survive in a patriarchal society. Margaret may offer Melanie a toffee to console her, but she is unable to rescue them from the oppression of their uncle. Moreover, at one level, both Mrs Rundle and Margaret are complicit in their own and Melanie's oppression. The message which Margaret has written on the toffee paper reads: 'Look as though you're enjoying it, for my sake and Finn's' (p. 128). The toffee suggests the kind of consolation that a mother would give to a child. This in turn suggests that one of the risks in valorising the mother/daughter relationship as an alternative to the male line, as critics such as Kristeva have done, is that it can locate the daughter in a state of childlike dependency.

The theme of women being complicit in their own oppression is developed further in *Heroes and Villains* where Marianne is regarded with suspicion by the other women of the tribe who believe that she is possessed of dangerous powers and separated from them by her social background. Like Margaret, Mrs Green is dependent on the goodwill of the men. However, unlike Margaret, she identifies with the men, encouraging Marianne to do likewise, although there are moments when she sympathises and tries to be supportive of Marianne. As Palmer (1987) points out, 'in a patriarchal society, contact between women is frequently ambiguous. They help to arrange each other's hair and make each other beautiful not for their own pleasure and satisfaction, but in order to attract men' (p. 192). Maintaining that often the only gift women can bestow on each other is 'tears, images of suffering and pity', Palmer draws attention to the fleeting moment of closeness between Marianne and her cousin, Annie:

> Annie shrank away but she was as much afraid of Jewel's displeasure as she was of Marianne and he had perversely ceased to give her signals. Marianne saw the baby's bleared, red face pressed against a breast from which it was too ill to suck and

helplessly she began to cry. Her tears splashed on Annie's cheek. Annie touched them with her finger and then licked her finger to see if they were salt enough. Marianne slid down to her knees, sobbing as if her heart was breaking. Annie pushed the girl away and turned her back on her with a sigh.  (p. 104)

However, the passage is even more ambiguous than Palmer suggests; Marianne is ordered by her husband to kiss Annie and she does so unwillingly – afraid that she will pick up an infection from Annie's baby. Although Marianne is moved to tears by Annie's baby, Annie is suspicious of her tears – she has to test the level of humanity, the salt, in them. Marianne can fall on her knees sobbing, but Annie, who has responsibility for the child, pushes Marianne away and turns her back on her – as if tears were an indulgence that, in different social circumstances from Marianne, she can not afford herself.

As in Melanie's case in *The Magic Toyshop*, Marianne's lack of an adequately defined, autonomous sense of self is evident in the intensity of her processes of projection and introjection. Like Melanie at the outset of the novel, her close identification with her possessions are important to her sense of self and identity: 'She marked all her possessions with her name, even her toothbrush, and never lost anything' (p. 3). From the moment when Marianne sees Jewel killing her brother, she projects on him the phantasy of the *homme fatale*. Although Jewel has killed her brother instead of his own, she perceives the tattoo on his back as the mark of Cain, a figure she then eroticises. The idealised nature of the phantasy which she projects on Jewel is evident in the appeal that even the word 'barbarian' – 'the wild, quatrosyllabic lilt of the word' (p. 4) – has for her.

The emphasis in the novel, through its focalisation in the consciousness of a female character, presents us with an erotic objectification of men. However, Marianne's eroticising of Jewel is a product of the way in which her own feelings are strange and unknown to her. As Carter herself maintained in a letter to Elaine Jordan: 'she *is* very much a stranger to her own desire, which is why her desire finds its embodiment as a stranger' (Jordan, 1994, p. 198). The occasion during which, without the light of the moon, Marianne explores Jewel's face with her hands, is a discovery of her desire as much as his body. The strangeness of his face to her is expressed in geographical metaphors so that it becomes a 'landscape' which is also the terrain of her sexual feelings. Once again, we are reminded of Jameson's (1986) argument, that this kind of manifestation of the body is what remains in a culture where larger perspectives have lost their validity and older narratives have been neutralised (p. 321). And also that in this type of non-realist narrative, as in *The Magic Toyshop*, such a manifestation of the body diverts the narrative logic of the unfolding story in new directions.

Forced to wear a second-hand wedding dress, Marianne becomes, in terms reminiscent of Melanie, ' a mute furious doll' (p. 69). Again this reminds us of Aunt Margaret and of the scream that swells in Melanie's throat during the tree-climbing episode. Like many women, Marianne has been rendered mute, but her enforced silence is accompanied by a swelling rage. At one level, the dress suggests that there is a universal element to women's experiences, occurring as it does in both novels and located in two societies which have similar expectations of women. At the same time, the wedding dress, occurring in different circumstances in each novel, reminds us of the difficulties of, and dangers in, attempting to essentialise women's experiences.

The wedding dress which Marianne is made to wear has sweat stains left by the previous bride, reminding her of her own sexuality and her own desire to which she is a stranger. However, as the bride, she is also a sacrificial victim. In fact, the way in which she is handed over to the male is linked to cannibalism. When Mrs Green adjusts Marianne's wedding dress, she brings with her 'the sharp smell of burned fat and roasting meat' (p. 69). The bodice of the dress itself is said to have 'crackled and snapped' – like roasting meat. In the chapel, the congregation are turned out like animals, in rags and fur, reminding us that their leader Donally has his teeth filed to points – a detail which links him tellingly to Dracula. In Bram Stoker's Gothic tale, where the victim becomes predator, the subjects in question, as in Carter's novel, are sexuality and desire.

In the relationship between Marianne and Jewel, Carter also rewrites a further traditional story, that of the demon-lover, of whom Jewel has many of the characteristics – he is powerful, mysterious, supernatural; and he can be cruel, vindictive and hostile. However, in her depiction of him, Carter challenges the male–female binarism which ascribes so-called 'masculine' qualities to men and 'feminine' characteristics to women. In discovering the nature of her own desire, Marianne finds that male–female attributes exist within each individual. The demon-lover is also reconfigured as part of her eroticisation of the male 'other'. So Marianne is surprised, in exploring Jewel's face when he is asleep, to discover tears. Marianne, too, is not entirely the traditional victim of the demon-lover. Normally, she is persuaded to leave home and travel to unknown places, but in *Heroes and Villains* it is Marianne who makes the decision to do so of her own volition. In fact, Marianne is far from as malleable as the conventional victim. Normally the demon-lover returns to remind his victim of a bond from the past, but in *Heroes and Villains* it is Marianne who reminds the demon-lover of the bond – in this case the bond that developed between herself and Jewel when he killed her brother.

The way in which the initiative in *Heroes and Villains* is shifted from the demon-lover to the so-called victim, and the way in which Marianne subverts the role of the female in traditional demon-lover stories, is an index of the power which is ascribed to the novel's female focalisation. Melanie responds to her symbolic rape and Marianne to her literal rape with anger and indignation. As Palmer (1987) points out, Carter highlights a distinction between the young women's physical vulnerability and the strength of their independence of spirit (p. 188). After marrying Jewel, Marianne gradually turns from victim to predator, surmounts rape and humiliation, and takes Jewel's place as leader. Nevertheless, even this is ambiguous. She says to Donally's son: 'I'll be the tiger lady and rule them with a rod of iron' (p. 150). The phrase 'tiger lady' associates her with what Donally was trying to create from the little girl he killed. Whilst she seems unaware of the irony in talking to Donally's son who has suffered so much abuse at his father's hands of rods of iron, there is the strong suggestion that one tyranny will be replaced with another.

## VII

In conclusion, then, the focalisation of both *The Magic Toyshop* and *Heroes and Villains* gives priority to a female consciousness. However, readers will probably find themselves assuming a complex, if not ambivalent, attitude towards the key female protagonist. These are novels where nothing can be taken for granted. The allusions to key literary traditions, such as the fairy story and the post-apocalyptic novel, are designed to call into question some of the grand narratives – such as the Western romantic view of suffering – which we have tended to accept unquestionably. But they also alert us to ways in which human action is shaped by literary and other cultural forms. Hence the reclamation of the fairy story as an appropriate genre for serious writers in *The Magic Toyshop* is also a deconstruction of some of the ways in which the genre was used to regulate female sexuality. And in *Heroes and Villains,* Carter appears interested in the ways in which the societies of the Professors and soldiers and of the Barbarians, both construct and police their boundaries through myth and folklore.

There is a sharper focus in these two novels than in those discussed in the previous chapter on how identity is produced in the process of other people's perceptions and rendered 'real' through linguistic and other symbolic mechanisms. *The Magic Toyshop*, for example, explores some of the consequences of the Genesis account of creation, especially its role in the construction of female subjectivity and sexuality within twentieth-century psycho-analytical thought – a topic pursued in the later novel, *The Passion of New Eve.* In both the novels discussed in this chapter, some of the more important of the linguistic and symbolic mechanisms, as in the scene where Melanie tries on a number of different female roles, are presented in ways which alienate the reader from them. In other words, the text defamiliarises them. This is in turn evidence of the way in which Carter was beginning to see her culture as 'foreign', without may be realising the full implications of this position, even before her visit to Japan.

In *The Magic Toyshop* and *Heroes and Villains,* the processes of demythologising and defamiliarisation emerge as two sides of the same coin. Within this twin process, intertextuality plays an important part. A further difference between these novels and those discussed in the previous chapter is that whereas the other novels proceed intertextually, *The Magic Toyshop* and *Heroes and Villains* turn intertextuality into a theme. They are concerned with the role of intertextuality in the social construction of women's identities. The casting of Melanie as a puppet for the wicked puppet master, her uncle, provides a means to explore a number of the key facets of women's lives within patriarchal societies: the female as rendered passive, controlled and silenced; the denial of many aspects of female sexual identity; the idealisation of the female form yet debasement of women as Woman; and the way in which women are exposed to prurient commercial exploitation. Through the inter-text of Marianne as the victim of a demon lover, *Heroes and Villains* explores some of the challenges, difficulties and barriers women face under patriarchy in trying to achieve a sense of agency in their own lives and an autonomous sense of self. The interconnection between the processes of cultural defamiliarisation and thematising inter-textuality in the fiction itself is especially obvious in *The Infernal Desire Machines of Doctor Hoffman*, which was completed while Carter had her award to travel to Japan, and *The Passion of New Eve* which she wrote subsequently. The way in which these novels thematise intertextuality in a much bolder way, probably, as a result of the defamiliarisation process Carter experienced in Japan, is discussed in the next chapter.

# 4

# The Last Days

## *The Infernal Desire Machines of Doctor Hoffman* (1972) and *The Passion of New Eve* (1977)

Although there are parallels between *Heroes and Villains* and the novels to be discussed in this chapter, all three might be described as 'last days' narratives, there are important differences between them. As Elaine Jordan (1990) points out: '*The Infernal Desire Machines of Doctor Hoffman* draws on 'pornography, the Gothic, fairy tales, horror films, boy's imperial adventure stories, anthropological idylls according to Rousseau or Levi-Strauss, and the fantasies of philosophy, the world as Will and Idea' (p. 34). It also has some of the characteristics of the quest narrative.

Whilst *Heroes and Villains* focuses on the binarism between two types of community, *The Infernal Desire Machines of Doctor Hoffman* and *The Passion of New Eve* feature a number of differently organised social structures. Whilst Melanie in *The Magic Toyshop* and Marianne in *Heroes and Villains* have to acquire power in order to achieve a fuller sense of their own subjectivity, the protagonists of *The Infernal Desire Machines of Doctor Hoffman* and of *The Passion of New Eve* have to lose power in order to do so. Unlike Melanie and Marianne, they have to assume in serial fashion a number of different identities. Desiderio, for example, is forced to take refuge among the River People as Kiku, is driven to join a travelling circus as its peep show proprietor's nephew, becomes a companion to a sadistic Count who takes him to a Sadeian Brothel peopled with androids and automata, falls among a tribe of cannibals, becomes involved with the masochistic religion of the Centaurs and ends up in the Gothic castle of the Doctor himself. And as Roz Kaveney (1994) observes, the changes through which the protagonists are put 'are remorseless, one might almost say sadistic in their intensity' (p. 172).

Both *The Infernal Desire Machines of Doctor Hoffman* and *The Passion of New Eve* are intensely philosophical novels concerned with, in Jordan's words, 'the deliberate construction of communal myths' (1994, p. 207). Each novel focuses upon communities or societies that want 'to make belief, value and reality the same for everyone'. However, their narrators, who come from a future world locked in ideological as much as political conflict, are outside the conventional boundaries of the societies in which they live. Desiderio, the son of a European prostitute and an unknown Indian father, is a young man of mixed blood while Evelyn/Eve is a transexual. *The Infernal Desire Machines of Dr Hoffman*, is a retrospective narration of a war between the Reality Principle and the Pleasure Principle; in *The Passion of New Eve* society is breaking down into sects, movements and guerrilla bands.

In *The Infernal Desire Machines of Doctor Hoffman*, Desiderio, a former confidential secretary to the Minister of Determination, has been instructed to write down his memories of the Great War. While working for the Minister of Determination, Desiderio respected him for his stand against Dr Hoffman, who represents an opposing mode of apprehending 'reality'. The Minister of Determination represents the positivist laws of science while the poet-physicist, Dr Hoffman, represents their subversion. While the one stands for reason, law, structure, restraint and philosophy; the other represents imagination, freedom, desire and anarchy. Carter appears to be recalling Plato's *Republic* – Hoffman is after all a poet – and the banishment of the poets from the Athenian city-state. In Plato's *Republic*, the poets compete with the philosopher-king as Hoffman competes with the Minister of Determination; threatening the stability of the state by appealing to the irrational desires and the unruly appetites.

The narrator of *The Passion of New Eve*, Evelyn, describes his movement from London to New York and from there to the desert. That his journey ends up in the desert, traditionally associated in Euro-American literature with sterility and death, seems particularly ironic – a parodic reversal of the myth of America as the land of opportunity and possibility. In the desert, Evelyn is captured by a band of feminist guerrillas controlled by Mother, who transforms him biologically into a woman but who does not have time to complete the psychosurgery before he escapes. Fleeing from her, he is captured once more, this time by a male tyrant called Zero who, like Evelyn, is obsessed with a film star called Tristessa de St Ange. But, unlike Evelyn, Zero believes that Tristessa telepathically emasculated him during a showing of one of her films.

In the novel, linear time is often associated with the male and the onward drive of modernity, evidenced in technology, wars, cities and 'the space race' while cyclical or recurrent time is associated with the female. However, such an essentialist binarism, even though it is not fully endorsed in the narrative, becomes irrelevant to the novel's delineation of a postmodern Euro-America. At the centre of the novel, Tristessa's house of glass, an illusion sustained by light and a vast rotating apparatus of reproduction, signifies the postmodernist cycle of self-construction and self-replication which America, once signifying the European dream of spiritual greatness, has become.

Up to a point, what Desiderio, too, experiences in the meaningless plurality produced by Hoffman's ghosts is the postmodern, consumer-oriented world dominated by media images. However, it is also more than that. People, objects, landscapes and even time are subject to the whims of the desire machines. Generating erotoenergy, a force in opposition to rational knowledge, the machines disrupt reality making epistemological certainty an impossibility.

Neither of these novels can be fully understood without reference to their intertexts. *The Infernal Desire Machines of Doctor Hoffman* is a rewriting of the Oedipus story. Desiderio sets out with instructions from his stern father to destroy Hoffman, but commensurate with the quest narrative is seduced by a woman, in this case Hoffman's daughter. Like Oedipus, Desiderio eventually rids the city of its pollution but has to pay a price for his victory and his new-found knowledge. However, the most important intertext in both novels is the work of twentieth-century linguistic philosophers such as Ferdinand de Saussure. Of particular relevance is his argument that all linguistic signs have two aspects: the 'signifier' (an actual word, printed or spoken) and the 'signified' (the thing the word describes or the meanings associated with a word) which were arbitrarily linked. In the Minister's world, in *The Infernal Desire Machines of*

*Doctor Hoffman*, there is no 'shadow' or slippage between a word and the object to which it refers; boundaries, rules and hierarchies are clearly defined and observed without ambiguity or ambivalence. Hoffman's world is one of simulacra where signifier and signified bear only the most arbitrary relationship to each other. Boundaries are blurred and 'everything that is possible to imagine can also exist' (p. 97). Yet this binary distinction between the two worlds proves to be an illusion itself. Like Donally in *Heroes and Villains*, who tries to construct a social mythology for the Barbarians, and Mother in *The Passion of New Eve*, the Minister of Determination and Dr Hoffman in *The Infernal Desire Machines of Doctor Hoffman* try to impose a particular set of perspectives on their societies. While Hoffman offers a surreal, liberating opposition to what the Minister represents, he is also the embodiment of capitalist control of desire through media technology.

Truth in classic realist fiction, as Steven Connor (1996) argues is 'a matter not of correspondence to facts but of perspective' (p. 53). As a result, what is important in the realist novel is the establishment of a vantage point from which disparate issues and widely separated experiences can be grasped. In *The Infernal Desire Machines of Doctor Hoffman*, Carter focuses not so much on the experiences of the protagonists as on the difficulty of establishing vantage points.

II

The opening lines of Desiderio's account of the Great War give us reason to doubt at least some of the narrative that follows for he claims to have remembered everything perfectly. Although Desiderio emerges as a war hero, he has failed to find his master/ father figure or the object of his desire since he has had to kill both. His heroic status is further undermined by his complicity in domination and exploitation. Ostensibly, Desiderio's focalisation derives from his commitment to rationality. But we soon discover that he is sceptical of rationality, of his Minister and of the Determination Police. Moreover, not only does he appear critical of rationality, but his own behaviour is much less rational than he thinks. It is no coincidence that Carter writes of the Minister's denial of shadows, employing the term which Jung used to refer to the negative aspects of the collective unconscious that enter the personal consciousness. For the emphasis upon rationality denies not only the importance of the irrational but the fact that what we perceive as rational behaviour, even in ourselves, may not be as rational as we might believe.

Once again Carter appears to be challenging a basic assumption of the classic realist novel which as Connor (1996) says, is normally regarded as a meeting point between reality and desire (p. 1). The realist novel can be seen as a concentrated fusion of how the world is, or appears to be, and the shaping force of imagination and/or fantasy. Desiderio's name actually means 'desire' in Italian and, of course, he falls in love with his phantasy version of Dr Hoffman's daughter, Albertina, modelled on Proust's androgynous Albertine in 'The Captive' from *Remembrance of Things Past*. Albertina awakens passion and desire in Desiderio, who until then has been merely a passive observer of Hoffman's phantasies. Indeed, the history is dedicated to her with all his 'insatiable tears' (p. 14). So whilst he denounces the mirages created by Dr Hoffman, Desiderio spends much of his life chasing one. Even after her death, Desiderio cannot rid himself of his obsession with her and hers is the final image of his memoirs. Albertina, of course, does not appear as a character in her own right in this novel – only as a creation, or projection, of Desiderio's phantasies. As Sally Robinson (1991) points out, women in this novel, as in the quest story, are objects, 'put into circulation according to the logic of male desire' (p. 101). They function as fetish, foil or exotic/erotic objects.

Desiderio, who did not have a proper relationship with his mother, a prostitute, and never knew his father, whose genetic imprint he carries in the colour of his skin, was brought up after his mother's death by nuns. The perpetual presence of a sense of loss in the psyche of individuals who do not experience a close, fulfilling relationship with their mothers is a recurring trope in the novel. Mamie Buckskin, the 'phallic paradox', always wears a picture of her dead, alcoholic mother between her breasts which themselves remind Desiderio of the 'bosom of a nursing mother' (p. 108). The way in which Desiderio interprets his time with the River People, too, suggests that he is impelled in a Freudian sense, like Melanie in *The Magic Toyshop*, to discover a sense of home as an ideal in his own psyche: 'If I murdered Desiderio and became Kiku for ever, I need fear nothing in my life ever, any more. I need not fear loneliness or boredom or lack of love' (p. 80). Here Desiderio lists three of the forces which disrupt the psyche. He wishes to eradicate all desire except for that associated with the pre-Oedipal. Indeed, there is a significant difference between the sound of the name 'Desiderio' and the sound of 'Kiku' which is much closer to the kind of sound that an infant would make at its mother's breast. But Desiderio is not only returning to his absent mother but his unknown father. For although the River people's society is theoretically matrilineal, in practice all decisions are devolved to the males.

Similarly Desiderio's idealisd account of his and Albertina's life among the Centaurs reflects his own deep-rooted need to discover an ideal psychic home. His memoirs note how Albertina's skin responded well to the sun, how 'she would come home in the golden evenings, wreathed with corn like a pagan deity in a pastoral and naked as a stone' (p. 187). They also betray his masculinist bias; he is uncritical, for example, of the way in which the females have to work in the fields, while the men have a more leisurely lifestyle.

Another disturbing feature of Desiderio's account of life among the Centaurs is how the recreation of a pastoral innocence-cum-naïve primitivism is linked to his perception of his relationship with Albertina as a loving one between a brother and sister. At one level, this is regressive on his part, an attempt to reclaim the ideal of the home. But the reader cannot forget that relationships between brothers and sisters often involve repressed desires as, of course, does the pastoral itself. Indeed, incest is a recurring trope in Carter's work. Moreover, Desiderio's account sublimates within his phantasies about sibling relationships the trauma which Albertina experiences and that even when her physical wounds following the rape are healed, she will not let him touch her.

Desiderio, however, is not wholly blinkered. He witnesses cracks appearing in a mode of awareness which has dominated Western thinking since the Enlightenment: 'But I think I must have been one of the first people in the city to notice how the shadows began to fall subtly awry and a curious sense of strangeness invaded everything' (p. 15). Although at the outset of his memoirs, Desiderio describes physical changes that appear to be happening in the city, such as the sudden erection of cloud palaces, his real anxiety concerns the emergence of a new way of looking at 'reality'. It is not simply that 'reality' has changed but that the conventional assumptions about the relationship between language and external

referent have proved false and shown to be illusory: 'Hardly anything remained the same for more than one second and the city was
no longer the conscious production of humanity; it had become the
arbitrary realm of dream' (p. 18).

From the post-Enlightenment emphasis on rationalism, denying
the acceptability of beliefs founded on anything but experience,
reasoning and deduction, developed the mode of awareness in
literature and art normally referred to as 'realism'. In the Middle
Ages, literature concerned itself with a world of ideals rooted in
cosmologies which suggested that the human world was divinely
ordained, ordered and controlled. However, in post-Renaissance
England, this centre of gravity shifted. The new worldview was
rooted in scientific and rational notions of comprehending the
world, with real human experience at the centre of it. In *The Infernal
Desire Machines of Doctor Hoffman*, the centre of gravity is shifting
again; on this occasion away from the rigid hierarchies and
classifications of the rationalism in which Desiderio has been
educated. The fruits which begin to appear in the market stalls are
'remarkable' because they defy boundaries: they are pineapples but
have the colour and texture of strawberries and taste of caramel.
They literally and metaphorically occupy a space between the rigid
classification of fruit into, for example, oranges and apples while at
the same time subverting conventional definitions.

The way in which Desiderio expresses his criticisms of the
Minister of Determination – 'He was the hardest thing that ever
existed and never the flicker of a mirage distorted for so much as a
fleeting second the austere and intransigent objectivity of his face'
(p. 22) – suggests he is sceptical of the familiar post-Enlightenment
myth that through reason human beings become most positively
human. Moreover, the way in which reason and social progress have
been habitually linked in Western thought is debunked by the
description of the Determination Police. Desiderio, the first person
to recognise that shadows are beginning to fall 'awry', has enough
imagination to link the Police with the German SS of the 1930s and
1940s: 'They looked as if they had been recruited wholesale from a
Jewish nightmare' (p. 22). The reference to the Holocaust here also
reminds us, as the appearance of the police reminds Desiderio, that
rationality played a key role in the design of the Holocaust, of
the concentration camps and of the gas chambers. This post-
Enlightenment myth of an inextricable connection between reason

and the progress of civilisation is also undermined by the concept of Reality Testing and the irony that even though the Minister had a 'a battery of technological devices' at his disposal, he had to resort to 'the methods of the medieval witch-hunter' (p. 22).

Carter's novel also disabuses us of any inevitable correlation between technological development and the betterment of humanity. Apart from the fact that technology may unwittingly have dire consequences for humanity, it has been employed in the creation of ever more imaginative ways of inflicting pain and torture on human beings. In the course of the novel, it becomes clear that rationality and imagination, although they are perceived as binary opposites, have come together in history to further rather than abolish the means by which one individual is abused by another. In a world governed by rationality, efficiency – as in the speedy despatch of undesirables by the Third Reich – becomes a kind of morality. This is something that Desiderio observes but does not fully appreciate. He is quick to point out that the Minister of Trade, who later tellingly became the Minister of Determination, was 'always the model of efficiency' and that when he helped the Minister with the crossword puzzle he admired the speed with which Desiderio completed the squares. Significantly, Desiderio, without realising the implications, describes the Minister as a 'thing'. The suggestion is that a degree of imagination is necessary for human beings to empathise with each other while an overemphasis upon rationality leads to tyranny.


III


The focalisation of *The Infernal Desire Machines of Doctor Hoffman* is male. However, the reader is not easily seduced into identification with this male point-of-view. As Sally Robinson (1991) points out, the novel presents 'an epistemological revolution . . . in which culture's master narratives are losing the power and authority to order experience' (p. 78). The exception is the 'Oedipal narrative that places man in the position of questing, speaking subject, and woman in the non-position of object who is *subject* to male regula-tion, exploitation and violence' (ibid.). Initially, neither Desiderio in *The Infernal Desire Machines of Doctor Hoffman* nor Eveyn/Eve in

*The Passion of New Eve* are able to see the inequality in which they are both complicit. When the reader first encounters Desiderio, he lives and works in a city which according to him, is 'thickly, obtusely masculine' (p. 15). In discussing the general character of cities, he employs a clichéd binarism, apparently unaware of the gendered nature of the assumptions underpinning it: 'Some cities are women and must be loved; others are men and can only be admired and bargained with' (ibid.). Women here are associated with love and, by implication, with the private and the domestic. Men, who, it would appear do not need love, are associated with the public realm of business and bargaining – a point reinforced when we remember that this male city 'throve on business' and is 'prosperous'. While Desiderio recognises that many of the landmarks of the South American city from which he starts out were anointed with his forefather's blood, he does not bring the same level of critical acumen to his description of his mother, only observing that 'her business, which was prostitution of the least exalted type, took her to the slums a great deal' (p. 16).

As if to remind us that sight does not always mean insight, the peep-show displays are, as Susan Suleiman (1994) points out, 'unmistakably male voyeuristic fantasies' (p. 114). In most of the societies which Desiderio visits, women are in a subordinate social position, but this is something of which he is insufficiently critical. Even though Desiderio observes, for example, that the River Women all moved in 'the same, stereotyped way, like benign automata', the only conclusion he draws is that it were possible to 'understand what had produced the prejudices of the Jesuits' (p. 73). Meanwhile, his subconscious desire to 'masculinise' women is revealed when he cannot help but approve of the practice whereby mothers of young girls manipulate their daughters' clitorises so that they approximate penises. This phantasy of 'masculinised' women renders many of his representations of women unreliable – as, for example, his portrait of Mamie Buckskin, who always has at her thigh, 'a gun, death-dealing erectile tissue' (p. 108). She treasures, 'lovingly fingering', the weapons of dead male outlaws – Billy the Kid, Doc Holliday and John Wesley Hardin – from the American West which was itself a masculine imaginary. We are also told that for shooting a man, she was 'imprisoned in the far West' (ibid.). Ironically, this may also be taken to refer to the way in which she is entrapped in an essentially masculine phantasy.

The initial privileged positions which Desiderio and Evelyn/Eve enjoy are reversed in the course of the narratives. Once at the centre of all systems of representation, man has become decentred and with him traditional notions of patriarchal authority. Both suffer pain and humiliation and in doing so discover what women have to endure. The most obvious example is Desiderio's rape by the Moroccan acrobats which makes him realise what Albertina endured when she was raped by the Centaurs while he, as a male, was able to study in relative ease: 'The pain was terrible. I was most intimately ravaged I do not know how many times. I wept, bled, slobbered and pleaded but nothing would appease a rapacity as remorseless and indifferent as the storm which raged outside' (p. 117). Initially, as Jordan (1994) says, Albertina cannot accept that she was raped, convinced that though every male Centaur has carnal knowledge of her, the beasts were only emanations of her desires (p. 208). But the account that we have of the rape and how it has affected her, which seems to preclude any possibility of trauma, is Desiderio's. A compounding irony is that when the Centaurs realise that Albertina is Desiderio's 'mate' – that is his property – they apologise for raping her. And he accepts the apology!

Part of Desiderio's problem is that he does not understand the feminine even within himself. Throughout his memoirs, women are castrating Amazons, mutilated bodies or erotic toys. His 'otherising' of Albertina is as inhibiting to the development of a fully reciprocal relationship as Marianne's projection of her phantasies on Jewel in *Heroes and Villains*. At that moment among the Centaurs when Desiderio cannot understand why Albertina does not want him to touch her, she is more the 'other' in his imagination than at any other time. She becomes most erotic to him when she becomes most exotic – 'brown as an Indian' and 'wreathed with corn like a pagan deity' (p. 187). Her Mongolian skin is tangible; it places her in a specific part of the globe and gives her an identity and history. But in eroticising her, Desiderio also makes her abstract. She acquires a body 'naked as a stone', a face that 'fell into the the carven lines of the statue of a philosopher' and eyes 'which sometimes held a dark, blasting lightening' (ibid.). The effect of this for Albertina, as the object of Desiderio's projection, is betrayed when he remembers how he would gaze at her for hours, 'feeding on her eyes'. In other words, his projections are devouring her. The effect for him is betrayed through a piece of linguistic play typical of Carter; he admits that 'her difference almost withered me'.

The explanation offered in the novel for Desiderio's attitude towards women is that, as in Buzz's case in *Love*, he has been adversely influenced by his childhood experiences. Like Buzz, he has grown up with a sense of fear which he projects into women: 'I had been afraid when I was a child, when I would lie awake at night and hear my mother panting and grunting like a tiger in the darkness beyond the curtain and I thought she had changed into a beast' (p. 30). His fears are most vividly revealed in a dream in which, like Melannie in *The Magic Toyshop*, he is threatened by a swan. At one level, the black swan signifies the horror of nothing which is central to much of Herman Melville's work which influenced Carter's early writing: ' a black as intense as the negation of light, black the colour of the extinction of consciousness' (ibid.). At another level, it makes Desiderio's fear of women explicit for it is both a swan and female, turning eventually into Albertina.

In *The Infernal Desire Machines of Doctor Hoffman*, as in *The Passion of New Eve*, Carter in effect reminds us that a notion of eradicating violence has been important to the idea of 'human progress'. Both novels, however, encourage us to ponder why attempts to do so have failed – and in the twentieth century failed so spectacularly. Although Desiderio experiences different types of human community, with different social structures and at different stages of technological development, pain is employed within all of them as a means of social control. Both the Chief whom Desiderio encounters in the African coast and Zero in *The Passion of New Eve* surround themselves with women rather than men. The chief controls his army of women by circumcision; the clitoris of every girl child born to the tribe is removed as soon as she reaches puberty, as are those of his wives and concubines brought from other tribes.

Within this framework, the inclusion of a parody of the Marquis de Sade's *The 120 Days of Sodom* in *The Infernal Desire Machines of Doctor Hoffman* opens up further possible readings of the novel around debates pertaining to the supposed 'progress' of human civilisations. The Marquis de Sade's unfinished 'novel' was written in 1786, while he was a prisoner in the Bastille, although it was not published until 1904. It is a pre-novelistic work with the same structure as *The Decameron*. Four libertines – a duke, a bishop, a judge and a school friend of the Duke's – shut themselves away with four brothel madames, a crowd of young men and women and their own wives for one hundred and twenty days. During that time they recount the details of every sexual perversion they have encountered and the libertines try to perform them. *The 120 Days of Sodom* is a work of the imagination which, in subverting traditional moral codes, seeks to push sexual phantasy to the point of creating 'evil' – the phantasy becomes divorced from sexual pleasure.

As Gasiorek (1995) points out: 'While Albertina hints at the benign effects of Hoffman's worldview, the Count discloses its malignant consequences' (p. 130). The Count and his servant, Lafleur, are modelled on the Marquis de Sade and his valet, Latour – in fact, he is a fusion of de Sade and Dracula. In the Count's case, the liberation of desire leads to an endless search for increasingly perverse manifestations to satisfy an insatiable and increasingly sadistic appetite. Initially, as Robinson (1991) says, the Doctor is attractive in 'his ability to think beyond binary oppositions, to read the world in ways not wholly dependent on a logic which would repress the unconscious in a hegemony of logocentrism' (p. 99). However, his desire gives way, and free reign, to exploitation and domination.

Equally disturbing, the Sadeian brothel scene elides masculinitiy, sexuality and violence. When they enter the brothel, the Count and Desiderio are dressed for the occasion in special costumes which hide their faces – signifying their identity and individuality – but which leaves their genitals exposed: 'the garb grossly emphasised our manhoods while utterly denying our humanity' (p. 30). The Bestial Room to which they are led takes up where *The 120 Days of Sodom* leaves off, eliding Doctor Hoffman's Marcusean principle that 'everything it is possible to imagine can also exist' with the perversity of de Sade's imaginative liberty. de Sade only completed thirty of his hundred and twenty days, leaving sketches for the rest which included the criminal passions and others which combined the comic with sheer cruelty. When they enter the room, the Count and Desiderio are confronted by monkeys turned into living candelabra and animals turned by a taxidermist into living furniture. Then they notice the prostitutes kept in cages redolent of Victorian drawing-room birdcages. They are not women but 'sinister, abominable, inverted mutations, part clockwork, part vegetable and part brute' (p. 132). If all this were not horrific enough, Desiderio is shocked by the way in which the Count is aroused by it all.

Here, as in parts of *The Passion of New Eve*, Carter parodies the principal tradition of pornographic writing. As she explains in *The Sadeian Woman* (1979), since pornography is 'produced in the main by men for an all-male clientele' it has 'certain analogies with a male brothel' (p. 15). Desiderio is the author of a narrative which, as Robinson (1991) says, 'enlists an array of misogynist sentiment and fantasy' (p. 102). However, here Carter as a female author is appropriating a male consciousness to expose how women are trapped, like the woman reader of this novel, in a male imaginary. Moreover, the narrative technique of ventriloquism – a female author speaking in a male voice – is employed to create not just pornography but an especially sadistic version of it. Hence as a parody of pornography, Desiderio's account positions the (male) reader as voyeur but does not necessarily guarantee a voyeuristic, pleasure position for him.

While *The Infernal Desire Machines of Doctor Hoffman* might take up where de Sade leaves off in its depiction of how evil can be created in the human mind, it offers an alternative understanding of evil as something which is likely to be produced when the external circumstances are congenial to it. The problem is that evil, like the subordination of women, has occurred in so many different cultures, societies and histories that generalising about those circumstances is difficult. In *The Sadeian Woman*, Carter points out that 'pornography reinforces the false universals of sexual archetypes because it denies, or doesn't have time for . . . the social context in which sexual activity takes place, that modifies the very nature of that activity' (p. 16). Throughout the novel, the creation of evil is seen as embedded in particular sociohistorical circumstances. The Count's account of himself to Desiderio, even if allowances are made for the context in which the Count relates his tales and for Desiderio's inevitable filtering of them as narrator, would suggest that he is the kind of person de Sade believed the imagination might create: 'From the cradle, I have been a blasphemous libertine, a blood-thirsty debauchee. I travel the world only to discover hitherto unknown methods of treating flesh' (p. 126). However, many of the serial atrocities he recounts betray particular contexts. But they also have much in common. Victims are people designated inferiors and marginalised – such as geisha girls in Japan, eunuchs in the Royal Court of Siam, people accused of witchcraft in Salem, Negro slaves in Alabama, a mulatto whore in New Orleans. In Salem and Alabama, the retribution is the product of a group of people afraid of losing their control and authority. While the African Chief might boast 'I am happy only in that I am a monster' (p. 161), the vicious retribution inflicted on even those suspected of harbouring critical thoughts is a means of maintaining his authority. Even the activities in the Bestial Room are dependent upon, and are the product of, a particular context created by the blackness of the room; the blood colour of the curtains; the use made of animals; and the importance of a particular type of uniform, as worn by the Count and Desiderio and the Madame. Each wears the kind of mask associated with a public executioner. The account of the executioner's mask in Carter's story 'The Executioner's Beautiful Daughter' from *Fireworks: Nine Profane Pieces* (1974) provides a gloss, redolent of the concern with flesh as meat in her early novels, upon the way in which the two men are dressed:

> This mask reveals only his blunt-lipped, dark-red mouth and the greyish flesh which surrounds it. Laid out in such an unnerving fashion, these portions of his meat in no way fulfil the expectations we derive from our common knowledge of faces. They have a quality of obscene rawness as if, in some fashion, the lower face had been flayed. He, the butcher, might be displaying himself, as if he were his own meat.
>
> Through the years, the close-fitting substance of the mask has become so entirely assimilated to the actual structure of his face that the face itself now seems to possess a parti-coloured appearance, as if by nature dual; and this face no longer pertains to that which is human as if, when he first put on the mask, he blotted out his own, original face and so defaced himself forever.
>
> (*Burning Your Boats*, p. 36)

The novel, as is typical of Carter's work, does not offer the reader a fully developed thesis. As Kaveney (1994) reminds us, Carter 'is not one for telling us what to do or what to believe' (p. 183). One proposition is introduced in opposition to, and as if to undermine, another. Even the realisation that evil behaviour arises from specific contexts stands in contradistinction to other suggestions that it is linked to the 'shadow' aspects of the psyche. The description of the Determination Police suggests that there is something fetishistic about their uniforms – the coats are of black leather and the boots 'too highly polished' – a criticism which has been made about the uniforms and regalia of the German SS. The fetishistic overtones are, in turn, linked to hints of repression in the ankle-length of the coats and in the fact that they are worn 'truculently belted' (p. 22). The atrocities committed by the Klansmen in Alabama are one thing; the fact that they ululate while watching the Negroes burn is another. Throughout the novel, a thesis that evil can only be understood in relation to specific contexts in which it emerges is countered by the horror of an evil that cannot be rationalised, signified in Desiderio's dream of the black swan whose eyes 'expressed a kind of mindless evil that was quite without glamour, though evil is usually attractive, because evil is defiant' (p. 30).

## IV

The names of two of the key protagonists in *The Passion of New Eve* seem to have arisen from the earlier novel, *Heroes and Villains*. Eve and Lilith are the two possible identities which Jewel and Donally discuss as appropriate for Marianne:

' . . . Embrace your destiny with style, that's the important thing. Pretend you're Eve at the end of the world.'
'Lilith', said Donally, pedantically. 'Call her Lilith.'
'That's a bad heredity. Besides, I always thought of Lilith as kind of mature.' (p. 124)

Although in a loose sense both novels are 'last days' narratives, *The Passion of New Eve*, as I suggested earlier, is a different type of post-apocalyptic text from *Heroes and Villains*. While *Heroes and Villains* appears to have been written with British post-apocalyptic science fiction in mind, *The Passion of New Eve* is distinctly in the American vein. In fact, as Nan Albinski (1988) points out, the novel, which is almost wholly set in the United States, is partly a satire on the work of 'American separatist writers whose women celebrate female rituals, and joyfully claim the pastoral world' (p. 134). Carter parodies a matriarchal society in the American desert – possibly thinking of the kind of society which Marianne as the 'tiger lady' would introduce – and through a black American woman ridicules the projection of gender, whether male or female, onto gods. Moreover, as Kaveney (1994) says, while Zero is 'an unholy cross between the macho litterateur and Charles Manson' (p. 181), he is also a satire on another strain of American futuristic literature, survivalist narrative. A key element in Zero's harem is the violence with which the regime is run and the novel holds up a mirror to American society which celebrates the part guns have played in its history, associating them with freedom and individual liberty. The crucial issue is the causal nature of the relationship between Zero's enthusiasm for guns, his violence and his misanthropy. Zero spends each afternoon shooting empty beer cans placed on sticks in the ground. It is quite clear that they signify people and there are two disturbing dimensions to this activity. Firstly, the choice of object suggests the contempt in which he holds people in general. Secondly, there is a thin line between shooting at an imaginative projection of a human target and attempting to kill the real thing.

*The Passion of New Eve* appears to have been written from the point of intersection of two genres: American 'last days' futuristic fantasy and the British Innocent/Englishman abroad narrative of which there is a long lineage from authors such as Charles Dickens, Evelyn Waugh, David Lodge and Malcolm Bradbury. In keeping with the expectations of the latter, the focalisation is from Evelyn/Eve as an Englishman in America. But since the Englishman abroad narrative is essentially a *Bildungsroman*, the emphasis is upon his education. This particular focalisation provides a vehicle for mounting a satire on the communities into which Evelyn/Eve comes into contact through his reactions to them and the 'shadow' which falls between what he appears to describe and what the reader perceives.

Like *The Infernal Desire Machines of Doctor Hoffman*, *The Passion of New Eve* is a retrospective picaresque, serial narrative. Both are told from a male point-of-view, but invite their readers to occupy a position outside the narrative. The male focalisation of *The Passion of New Eve* is often parodic as in Evelyn's admission, when discussing the way humiliation of men by women had become rampant, that male manhood is much more vulnerable than the male head (p. 17)! Jouve Ward, with help from her fifteen-year-old son who grasped the significance of the whip and fishnet stockings on the cover of the earlier edition, points out that the novel sets up and then frustrates a whole series of male pornographic expectations. In other words, like the account of the 'House of Anonymity' in *The Infernal Desire Machines of Doctor Hoffman*, *The Passion of New Eve* refuses to guarantee a voyeuristic subject position for its readers. Like the peep show and the brothel in *The Infernal Desire Machines of Doctor Hoffman*, the novel makes voyeurs of its readers and then subverts their voyeurism. Such is the fate also of the two narrators. Evelyn/Eve, like Desiderio, falls in love with a phantasy.

Albertina, whom Desiderio pursues in *The Infernal Desire Machines of Doctor Hoffman*, turns out to be the Doctor's puppet and agent who almost succeeds in drawing Desiderio into a cage. In *The Passion of New Eve*, Evelyn/Eve, too, discovers a Grand Unreality. At the centre of *The Passion of New Eve* is Tristessa's Grand Illusion. Living in the middle of the desert, in a glass mausoleum where she 'sculpts' enormous tears by dropping molten glass into a swimming pool, Tristessa is a man trying to preserve the illusion that he is a woman. In fact, both novels have a similar elegiac tone. As Desiderio is haunted in his phantasies by Albertina after her death, Eve is haunted by Tristessa:

> Tristessa. Enigma. Illusion. Woman? Ah!
> And all you signified was false! Your existence was only notional; you were a piece of pure mystification. (p. 6)

But the representation of Tristessa is more complicated than might appear on a first reading. Evelyn fails to make a distinction between transvestism and female masquerade. In other words, he fails to distinguish between a man dressed as a woman and a man dressed as a woman masquerading as Woman. Even when he believed Tristessa was a woman he failed to see that she was a woman masquerading as feminine. Drawing on Mary Russo's work, Robinson (1991) suggests that the female masquerade subverts all notions of a 'natural femininity' (p. 120). Tristessa, then, was both an affirmation and a denial of femininity for in her masquerade as Woman she implied that femininity was a mask that could be taken off.

Although Evelyn enjoys watching Leilah dress in the mirror, he does not seem to notice the grotesquely erotic nature of what she puts on. Self-consciously re-enacting a traditional role assigned to women, she subverts the classic opposition between male and female spectator, but also suggests the possibilities available to women as a result. A consequence of the take-it-and-leave-it female masquerade, to which Robinson (1991) draws attention, is that 'if one can both tale it and leave it, then gender becomes a performance rather than an essence' (p. 120). Leilah, of course, is literally a performer. As such, she assumes a degree of agency over her own subject position. This is evidenced in the extent to which her masquerade is an engagement with the phallic construction of femininity as in, for example, the elision of eroticism and exoticism:

> The finicking care she used to give to the creation of this edifice! Applying the rouge to her nether lips and the purple or peony or scarlet grease to her mouth and nipples; powders and unguents all the colours of the rainbow went on to the skin in the sockets of her eyes; with the manual dexterity of an assembler of precision instruments, she glued on the fringe of false eyelashes. The topiary of her hair she would sometimes thread with beads or dust with glinting bronze powder she also applied to her pubic mound. Then she sprayed herself with dark perfumes that enhanced rather than concealed the lingering odour of sexuality that was her own perfume. (p. 29)

For the reader, positioned outside the frame of Evelyn's narrative, the artificial nature of what Leilah has constructed is difficult to miss. Some of the language – 'grease', 'glued', 'sprayed', 'sockets' – is as applicable to a factory body-shop as a human body. Moreover, Leilah is seen as 'an assembler of precision instruments' and the selection of words which cross the boundary between the human and the inhuman is particularly pertinent. Leilah's make-up gives her a metallic quality, evidenced in the words 'sprayed' and 'glinting bronze'. The feminine within the masculine imaginary is exposed as grotesque. Unlike the reader alert to the artificiality of what is being presented here, Evelyn elides the constructed Woman with women. As Mendoza claimed in the previous novel 'if a thing were sufficiently artificial, it became absolutely equivalent to the genuine' (p. 102).

Both *The Infernal Desire Machines of Doctor Hoffman* and *The Passion of New Eve* emphasise the mutability of identity. Both Desiderio and Evelyn/Eve are brought to knowledge through intense, sadistic pain; although Evelyn/Eve remains surprisingly immune to a full appreciation of his own pain as well as other people's.

Both Albertina, an androgynous, shadowy and vague presence throughout *The Infernal Desire Machines of Doctor Hoffman* and Leilah, reborn as Lilith, Adam's first and unacknowledged wife, undergo transformation – metamorphosis into guerrilla leaders. Whereas Desiderio is disturbed by this projection of Albertina, Eve, as he now is, recognises the importance of Leilah's transformation from whore/victim.

V

As Gasiorek (1995) reminds us, the elegiac tone of *The Infernal Desire Machines of Doctor Hoffman* 'resists a dualistic conception of reality that can only pit philosophy and poetry against one another' (p. 131). *The Passion of New Eve* clearly challenges another duality, male and female. In a postmodernist mode, it takes on de Beauvoir's claim that one is not born, but becomes a woman. However, it does much more as well. The novel takes us into a world which is closer to Hoffman's than the Minister's. As the Czech who lives in the apartment above Evelyn observes: 'The age of reason is over' (p. 13). This is a world where, like Hoffman's, the mass media controls desire; which aspires, as Evelyn hints at the outset, to establish celluloid in a more perfect 'complicity with the phenomenon of persistence of vision' (p. 5). In this respect, *The Passion of New Eve* pursues and develops an important area of enquiry suggested in the previous novel in which Desiderio complained: 'The motion picture is usually regarded as only a kind of shadow play and few bother to probe the ontological paradoxes it represents' (p. 102). In particular, it gives priority to a thesis proposed by the peep-show proprietor in the previous novel, which Desiderio remembers when he begins to doubt some of the things he sees, as for example when he watches the riders in the travelling fair service their horses: 'It all depends on persistence of vision' (p. 109). In suggesting in *The Passion of New Eve* that gender identities are deceptions, Carter confronts the role of cultural iconography in maintaining 'the phenomenon of persistence of vision'.

In *The Infernal Desire Machines of Doctor Hoffman*, Desiderio becomes increasingly aware of the extent of the Doctor's power games. Here again *The Passion of New Eve* seems to take up where the previous novel leaves off. For behind the media-manipulated phantasies, there are elaborate power structures for which the apparent 'persistence of vision' is a shadow dance. However, there is not yet the perfect 'complicity' between celluloid and 'the persistence of vision' that Evelyn mentions. As he observes, symbols are inevitably inadequate and paradoxical.

Even when we first encounter Evelyn and Leilah together, the narrative confounds any simple definitions of who is the victim:

> She was black as my shadow and I made her lie on her back and parted her legs like a doctor in order to examine more closely the exquisite negative of her sex. Sometimes, when I was exhausted and she was not, still riven by her carnal curiosity, she would clamber on top of me in the middle of the night, the darkness in the room made flesh, and thrust my limp cock inside herself, twittering away as she did so like a distracted canary, while I came to life in my sleep. Waking just before she tore the orgasm from me, I would, in my astonishment, remember the myth of the succubus, the devils in female form who come by night to seduce the saints. Then, to punish her for scaring me so, I would tie her to the iron bed with my belt. I always left her feet free, so she could kick away the rats . . . .
>
> If she had fouled the bed, I would untie her and use my belt to beat her. And she would foul the bed again, or bite my hand. So these games perpetrated themselves and grew, I suppose, more vicious by almost imperceptible degrees. (pp. 27–8).

The way in which pain and violence are used to control women is as central to *The Passion of New Eve* as *The Infernal Desire Machines of Doctor Hoffman*. Evelyn is an arch-misogynist; a vicious parody of the male, objectifying gaze. In peering at Leilah as if were a doctor conducting a medical examination, Evelyn reveals his indifference and lack of empathy, with no appreciation of how humiliating such an examination is for women. Indeed, as a narrator, Evelyn is most obviously defective in describing the quality of his feelings in relation to other persons. When he finishes with Leilah, he characteristically writes: 'But soon I grew bored with her. I had enough of her, then more than enough . . . the sickness ran its course' (p. 31). Eventually, he admits: 'So I abandoned Leilah to the dying city and took to the freeway' (p. 37).

However, there is evidence in the above passage for suggesting that while Evelyn may think he is in control this may not be the case. Not only is his cock – the supposedly master signifier – limp, but Leilah 'tears' the orgasm from him. Indeed, her fouling of the bed may well signify her expulsion of Evelyn and his sperm from inside of her. The violence which develops in the sadomasochistic games between Evelyn and Leilah is clearly the product of a particular context in which one partner agrees to be tied up. But in sadomasochism, it is often the masochist who is in control.

The above passage, then, is ambiguous and contradictory. Indeed, Carter's writing on sexuality generally defies singular readings. Merja Makinen takes Patricia Duncker to task, for example, for simplistically reading *The Bloody Chamber and Other Stories* (1979) as 'all men are beasts to women' and for seeing 'the female protagonists as inevitably encting the roles of victims of male violence' (p. 12). Despite the inscribed critique of Evelyn, at another level, through the notion of consent in sadomasochistic transaction, the passage anticipates what Makinen (1992) has called 'the decolonization of feminine sexuality' in *The Bloody Chamber and Other Stories*. There Carter suggests the need to break away from the 'sadist or masochist, fuck or be fucked, victim or aggressor binarism' and, as Makinen says, argues 'for a wider incorporation of female sexuality . . . that it too contains a whole gamut of 'perversions' alongside 'normal' sex' (p. 12). However, where Carter suggests – or appears to suggest – the need to recognise a more mutual sexual transaction, critics have found her work particularly disturbing. One of the recurring complaints is that the narrative appears to manipulate the reader to sympathise with masochism. Yet, Carter's fiction is never so simplistic, exploring, often within the same context, the need for a wider view of female sexuality, male sexual objectification, the extent to which males are locked within a particular construction of sexuality, and the denigration of women. In the Evelyn–Leilah sequence, Carter appears to be aware of the irony that while there was increasing recognition in society of the violence to which women were subjected, the definition of violence was being withdrawn from areas such as consensual sado- masochistic sex. The Evelyn–Leilah relationship raises a number of questions including: Are patriarchal relationships over women such that they are frequently coerced into subordination? Are images of women such that they are conditioned – as the women in Zero's harem – to behave in a particular way? Do we have here the fetishist's desire, as in *Shadow Dance*, to affirm but disavow the threat to his narcissism? Eve who is writing with the hindsight acquired from his experiences asks pointedly in the first chapter: 'Our external symbols must always express the life within us with absolute precision; how could they do otherwise, since that life has generated them?' (p. 6). The question, 'how could they do otherwise?' is crucial, opening up the possibility of an indefinable space between 'external symbols' and 'the life within us'. It is in this space that *Passion of New Eve* is located.

It is not immediately clear which genre we have entered with the above passage from the novel. Are we reading, for example, realist fiction, fantasy, pornography, or confessional writing? Evelyn – recalling Jung's term for the way in which negative aspects of the psyche are projected on others – describes Leilah as his shadow. But Evelyn's admission at the end of the extract that their games grew increasingly vicious brings another writer to mind. At this point, Carter is clearly intending us to recall again the Marquis de Sade's *The 120 Days of Sodom* and its concern with the development of sexual phantasy to the point where it is more violent phantasy than sexual phantasy. Evelyn phantasises about meeting Tristessa, tied stark naked to a tree. But then the narrative asks where is the boundary to be placed between this and what the Gestapo do to Baroslav and his wife. The Gestapo rape his wife and cut her into pieces while, tied to a tree, he is forced to watch. The latter is the kind of perversion left simply sketched by de Sade but into which he believed sexual phantasy would develop from the kind of phantasy Evelyn has of Tristessa.

As in the Gothic dimension of *The Infernal Desire Machines of Doctor Hoffman*, Carter is interested in the intensity of sexual passion in which the boundaries between sexuality and violence become blurred. Recalling the scene in the tenement doorway when he forces himself upon Leilah, Evelyn's explanation for his behaviour is that his passions are so intense that they are virtually uncontrollable: 'But, in the grip of such savage desire, I was unable to sustain fear as fear. I only felt it as an intensification of the desire that ravaged me' (p. 24). Here Evelyn thinks of his own sexual drive as a kind of demonic possession. If we accept Freud's account in 'Three Essays on the Theory of Sexuality' of the way in which our perceptions of sexuality have changed, then Evelyn's perspective is more akin to antiquity when stress was laid on the instinct than to later centuries which have tended to stress the object of love. Evelyn articulates, then, not only a psychological, but a historical phenomenon – a conflict between two competing conceptualisations of sexuality. However, although he abandons himself to his instincts in a demonic way redolent of German Romance literature, he pays a price for habitually doing so by only being able to relate to others in a limited way. Here, as elsewhere in Carer's work, violence affects both the perpetrator and the victim. As in *Heroes and Villains*, Carter in *The Passion of New Eve* subverts Romantic notions of pain and suffering. The violence which is imposed on the women in Zero's harem, for example, takes away their sense of self. Significantly, all the noises they make when they capture Eve are animal sounds. Confronted with Zero's violence, Tristessa can only 'babble incoherently' (p. 121). Zero, too, has given up using an extensive vocabulary and communicates through expletives.

## VI

Although, as in *Heroes and Villains,* Carter is not interested in tracing the decline of civilisation, she is interested in *The Passion of New Eve* with how cultural myths may have contributed to the disintegration of Western, or more specifically in the novel American, civilisation. The irony of the novel to which its epigraph from John Locke's *Second Treatise of Government* draws our attention – 'In the beginning all the world was America' – is that the myth of America once offered Europe an opportunity to return to a point of origin outside of European history. However, the epigraph is ambiguous, especially when read in conjunction with Eve's assertion at the end of the book that 'we start from our conclusions'. That is to say, America is the future from which late capitalist, Western society will have to begin again.

When Tristessa is discovered by Zero, Eve observes in her face, 'all the desolation of America' (p. 121). This scene is redolent of an incident in Carter's short story,' John Ford's *'Tis Pity She's a Whore'* published in *American Ghosts and Old World Wonders* (1993) in which the play by the seventeenth-century dramatist, John Ford, becomes a western. In the story, Ford's Annabella has become Annie-Belle and Giovanni has become Johnny. After their mother's death they are left alone with their father and an incestuous relationship develops between brother and sister. At one point: 'Turning from the mirror, each saw the other's face as if it were their own' (*Burning Your Boats*, p. 336). Carter is suggesting hidden aspects of Ford's play, but her story is really about America: 'The light, the unexhausted light of North America that, filtered through celluloid, will become the light by which we see *North* America looking at itself' (p. 338). Just as America was a step beyond the Old World, Carter has stepped beyond John Ford's Jacobean text. While for men the American Prairie represented openness and possibility, for women it was oppressive as Carter makes clear. Annie-Belle's mother 'died of the pressure of that vast sky, that weighed down upon her and crushed her lungs' (p. 332). America, as read through Carter's story, is made problematic by the loss of the mother. As I suggested in earlier discussions of Kleinian theory, loss creates a void filled with the presence of something darker. In the case of America, the loss of the mother is also the presence of an overwhelming emptiness and intense loneliness. In Annie-Belle's case, it is filled, too, with the presence of her mother-in-law when, pregnant by Johnny, she marries the Minister's son. In the space and unimaginable freedom, Johnny becomes a further threatening presence. In trying to get away from him, we are told that Annie-Belle drove the buggy 'lickety-split' to town. (p. 345). This is a story where Carter drops in the briefest of references to other texts. At one point in a description of Annie-Belle as a 'repentant harlot', for example, we are told that 'she wore a yellow ribbon', an allusion to one of John Ford's most famous films (p. 346). 'Lickety-split' might suggest that Annie-Belle is Brer Rabbit running 'lickety-split' away from the tar baby, Johnny. Or possibly the tar baby is the American prairies.

America in 'John Ford's *'Tis Pity She's a Whore'* is riddled, like America in *The Passion of New Eve*, with confusion, pretence and illusion: in *The Passion of New Eve*, Tristessa is a woman in a man's body masquerading as Woman and Evelyn becomes a man in a woman's body; in 'John Ford's *'Tis Pity She's a Whore'*, Annie-Belle 'cross-dresses' as her brother's wife, the community believe her to be pregnant by the Minister's son and Johnny is mistakenly regarded as a shamed member of her family. At the centre of both texts, there is a void, metaphorically and literally and a concern with oppression and a claustrophobic masculinity. But it is perhaps Fiedler, whose *Love and Death in the American Novel* (1960) I suggested earlier to be an important influence on Carter's under-standing of Gothic, who provides us, and provided Carter, with the key concept which links both works. Fiedler argues that 'when the last great communal myth system begins to collapse' the individual is 'unprotected against the inruption of the id, unsure of his relationship to the ego-ideals left him by the past' (p. 109).

In *The Passion of New Eve*, America is disintegrating – California is seceding from the Union and the Siege of Harlem rages. Among the great communal myths which are collapsing in postmodern Euro-America are those pertaining to the formation of gender identity. At the beginning of *The Passion of New Eve*, Evelyn finds himself 'unprotected against the inruption of the id' as the gendered ego-ideals of the past come under attack, literally:

> As the summer grew yet more intolerable, the Women also furthered their depredations. Female sharp-shooters took to sniping from concealed windows at men who lingered too long in front of posters outside blue movie theatres. They were sup-posed to have infiltrated the hookers who paraded around Times Square in their uniforms of white boots and mini-skirts.   (p. 17)

*The Passion of New Eve* suggests that 'the great communal myths' are increasingly Hollywood projections and exposes the 'ego-ideals of the past' as grand illusions. As Laura Mulvey (1994) reminds us, 'it is not, of course, *women* who have this privileged relationship with the world's greatest illusion, but an image of feminine beauty, highly stylised by cinema's conventions, and styling them in turn' (p. 232). Tristessa is the ideal phantasy figure for an Evelyn who seems unable to establish reciprocally fulfilling relationships with women. It is telling that he cannot remember the name of the girl he took to the cinema to see Tristessa and, of course, he can only see Leilah as the object of his grotesque voyeurism. It seems as if there is a large vacuum inside Evelyn anticipating the consequences of Mother's operation!

Tristessa herself is the phantasy projection of the only woman which as a male she could find desirable. When he is captured by

Zero, the harem women make him aware of the maleness which he has never been able to accept as part of himself. They perform obscene naked dances, 'contemptuously flourishing their fringed holes at him' and 'brandishing mocking buttocks' (p. 128). But, of course, this is a parody of how men are supposed to like to see women. They show Tristessa a false, carnivalesque version of the maleness from which he has tried to separate himself. It is a version forged, as the phrase 'their fringed holes' suggests, in peepshows and pornography.

Although *The Passion of New Eve* may be a rewriting of the biblical story of Genesis, its emphasis are upon the consequences of the Garden of Eden story rather upon than the original narrative as such. Some of the narratives of twentieth-century psychoanalysis are implicated in the assumptions which have emerged from the biblical narrative where woman, as inferior to man, is created out of a bone from the man's ribcage and becomes a sexual temptress. And in which can also be found some of the subjects with which twentieth-century psychoanalysis has preoccupied itself such as forbidden knowledge and the dangers of sexuality.

In the earlier extract, from Evelyn's account of his relationship with Leilah, Evelyn clearly sees Leilah in Freudian terms. According to Freud, the child is fused with the mother in what he calls the pre-Oedipal stage, but it is in the Oedipal stage – in which it identifies with the father – that the child acquires gender identity. It is a process by which the female accepts castration and a sense of lack because she is unable to identify fully with the father and by which the male child, identifying with the father, fears castration. So the female in Freudian psychoanalysis is defined – as Evelyn defines Leilah here – by an absence or sense of lack, what Evelyn fetishises as 'the exquisite negative ' of Leilah's sex. Fetishism in Freudian terms is based on presence and absence. The fetishist acknowledges, as Evelyn does here, that the woman is castrated. But in making a fetish of her lack, the fetishist, unlike the male norm, transcends or attempts to transcend phallic value. Such a view complicates the Oedipal narrative and it is appropriate that Carter begins the story of what happens to Evelyn in this way. For, as I suggested in the introduction, very few of Carter's characters come from a prototypical family structure and *The Passion of New Eve* may be read as an undoing of gender identities as formulated in the Oedipal stage.

The Evelyn–Leilah extract may also be alluding to the ideas of the French psychoanalytic philosopher, Jacques Lacan, who drew on Freud's insights. The two stages of identity formation which Lacan detailed were the mirror stage and the entry into the symbolic order. The mirror stage refers to an infant's realisation of its separate embodiment in a world of things. It notices that its reflection in a mirror is different from the self it experiences through embodiment. Later as the child learns language, it enters what Lacan calls the 'symbolic order'. There the child discovers that division between the sense of an inner and outer self – named as the 'I' who speaks as opposed to the 'I' who is spoken about. Thus the Freudian idea of a split self is affirmed and named in language.

Lacan's work, as Carter must have been aware, has been used to show that males and females enter language differently. Lacan pointed out that language systems are constructed so that what was previously assumed to be a shared position of 'I', which could be used by both men and women, was implicitly a male 'I' position. Feminist theorists have adapted Lacan's model, suggesting that because language systems were created from a male way of looking at things, they reinforce the assumption that male experience is the norm. Thus, in 'John Ford's *'Tis Pity She's a Whore*', the implied norm is the masculinist discourse in which ideas about America and life in the American prairies are located. On learning a language women have to learn a male way of looking at things and have much of their own female experience silenced. This may well be suggested by the fact that Leilah in the above extract is tied down by the male. So the episode might be read as a description of sadomasochistic sex or as the way in which in the symbolic order represses female experience. Significantly, Leilah's feet are free so that she can still kick. Within this allegorical reading, the fact that Leilah can still kick suggests that in any language system the female which is repressed threatens to subvert the dominant male discourse.

The novel also takes up the doubt which Lacan's thesis casts on the origins of desire. As Evelyn watches Leilah dress in front of the mirror in order to dance in theatres and restaurants, he witnesses the emergence of a self from 'the not world' of the mirror. He is cast in a role which is the reverse of that of men who watch a striptease. The reversal begs the question: Where does Evelyn's desire as he watches Leilah come from? Is it from Leilah as the object of his desire, or does it originate from within himself? In the later novel,

*Nights at the Circus*, the men who visit Madame Schrek's brothel do not hire the use of the women's bodies, but 'the use of the idea' of them (p. 70).

We normally regard our phantasies as private and unique to ourselves. But are they – as Carter suggests in *Shadow Dance* – socially constructed? Or can they be traced to experiences which have been buried in our subconscious? The novel frequently hints at different possible reasons for the way characters behave but without giving credence to any particular one. The text teasingly suggests, for example, psychoanalytical reasons for Zero's behaviour. That he wishes to humiliate the women by rubbing excrement in their breasts might suggest, in addition to how patriarchy views women, that his hatred of women stems from his childhood when he may have been humiliated during toilet training. However, Zero's excessively macho behaviour hides homophobia; that his ultimate fear is homosexuality becomes clear when Tristessa is revealed as a man. Indeed, it drives his hatred of Tristessa whom he believes is a lesbian who has emasculated him. Ironically, Eve's fear that he may recognise that she is a former man leads her to exaggerate her femininity which in turn makes him suspect that she is a lesbian.

The key issue for Carter is that the biological differences between men and women are not as important in the construction of gender identities as their elaboration in complex cultural codes which lay down the appropriate or inappropriate behaviour and physical appearance for each gender. Evelyn's unquestioned assumptions about women which underpin his Freudian view of their biological sense of lack is parodied in Beulah. The name 'Beulah' is particularly ironic, of course, as a poetic name for the state of Israel in its future restored condition.

The operation which Mother performs on Evelyn is an elision of a number of male phantasies including a parody of the male fear of castration. Mother behaves in contradictory ways, sadistically ensuring that Evelyn is conscious during the operation, comforting him in a cruelly deep baritone voice, and running her finger up and down the equally cruel phallic knife. There are echoes here of Victorian sadomasochistic pornography where a male is whipped by a surrogate for the mother. Normally she is armed with a rod which like Mother's knife here is a symbolic phallus. Within this context, Mother's baritone voice is significant for in Victorian sadomasochistic pornography, as Steven Marcus (1964) says, references to masculine attributes such as muscular biceps and hairy arms suggest that behind the violent, phallic mother was the father (p. 258). Mother is in some respects a development of Mamie Buckskin who runs the fairground rifle range in *The Infernal Desire Machines of Doctor Hoffman*. She is described as 'a paradox – a fully phallic female with the bosom of a nursing mother and a gun, death-dealing erectile tissue, perpetually at her thigh' (p. 108). In the earlier sadomasochistic sequence in *The Passion of New Eve* between Evelyn and Leilah, the cultural significance assigned the phallus was debunked in the references to Evelyn's limp cock, his exhaustion and Leilah's greater energy. It is reinforced here by the way in which his genitalia – useless in themselves – are tossed to Sophia. The surgical operation performed by Mother mirrors the linguistic severance performed by the author in the separation of 'lyn' from 'Eve'. This serves to remind us that masculine and feminine are not complementary terms. The masculine, as Robinson (1991) says, has always had the power to construct itself, unlike the feminine (p. 81). In a witty reversal of his earlier patronising regard for Leilah's 'exquisite negative', Eve finds that 'where I remembered my cock was nothing. Only a void, an insistent absence, like a noisy silence' (p. 75). Here Carter is parodying what she regards in the later work of non-fiction, *The Sadeian Woman*, as 'an imaginary fact that pervades the whole of men's attitude towards women' and which 'transforms women from human beings into wounded creatures who were born to bleed' (p. 23). The possibilty of a relationship between Evelyn's fetishising of Leilah's clitoris and his violence towards her is an exploration of the argument in *The Sadeian Woman* that the myth of the bleeding wound sets the male desire to exercise domination.

The confusion which Evelyn/Eve experiences after the operation is also redolent of Victorian sadomasochistic pornography where, as Marcus (1964) says, ' the sexual identity of the figure being beaten is remarkably labile' (p. 259). Indeed, he goes on to point out that the ambiguity of sexual identity seems 'to be part of the pleasure which this fantasy yields' (ibid.). The ambiguity of Evelyn's name is also itself redolent of Victorian sadomasochistic pornography in which naming was often ambiguous.

Ironically, when Mother asks Eve after the operation how he finds himself, he replies: 'I don't find myself at all' (p. 75). At one level, this is because his identity has been so bound up with his physical anatomy. He now finds that he has become his own phantasy! At another level, his problem is that he has perceived of gender identity in strictly essentialist and binary terms, whereas the novel itself suggests that identities are imaginary and provisional rather than fixed and closed. This is evidenced in the two main characters, as I suggested earlier: Eve, a man trapped as the result of surgery in a female body, and Tristessa, a woman trapped in a man's body masquerading as Woman. Their wedding in which they are required to assume a conventional subject position as bride and groom emphasises the 'shadow' or gap, to employ terms from *The Infernal Desire Machines of Doctor Hoffman*, between socially determined subject positions and the more complex lived experiences of the individual. The marriage takes place before a congregation which includes reassembled wax figures:

> Ramon Navarro's head was perched on Jean Harlow's torso and had one arm from John Barrymore Junior, the other from Marilyn Monroe and legs from yet other donors – all assembled in haste, so they looked like picture-puzzles.  (p. 134)

Robinson (1991) points out that 'the overall effect of Carter's novels is to drive a wedge between Woman and women, between male-centred metaphysical representations of Woman and the feminine, and women's multiplicitous and heterogeneous self-representations' (p. 77). *The Passion of New Eve* is typical of Carter's work in that it resists any conventional view of the mother figure. As Ward Jouve (1994) says, in this novel, 'Carter hunted the archetype down to extinction' (p. 157). Jouve, of course, is referring to the end of the novel, in which Eve, initially accompanied by Lilith, engages in a journey back to the source; a parody of mythical journeys to the Underworld where Eve finds that 'Mother is a figure of speech, and has retired to a cave beyond consciousness' (p. 184). Carter may have had in mind here Fiedler's (1960) assertion that in the Age of Reason 'Satan has become a figure of speech' (p. 128). He argues that the Evil One is evoked by those who no longer believe in him.

Carter, however, is putting a twentieth-century psychoanalytical assumption to the test. This time it is the proposition, from French theorists such as Julia Kristeva, that before the infant child enters the world of symbolic language, it uses a pre-linguistic babble, the music of the tongue, learned at its mother's breasts. Since, the symbolic language which the child learns involves a separation of the 'I' who speaks from the 'I' that is spoken about, and the voice predominantly expresses a male point of view, rediscovering the music of the tongue is virtually a 'mothering' of the tongue. The initial awareness of the pleasant sounds and the musicality of the tongue Kristeva calls the 'semiotic'. The 'semiotic' is suppressed by the symbolic so that it exists as the 'shadow' or 'underworld', capable of disrupting the symbolic (masculine) order.

The rediscovery of the 'semiotic' has been the linchpin of a great deal of feminist theoretical writing since the 1970s, as has the importance attached to the matrilineal line. As I noted in the discussion of *The Magic Toyshop*, a line of communication from mother to daughter has been posited as an alternative to male, symbolic communication, which has tended to repress or exclude the female and the semiotic. For many women writers, the presence of the mother figure has served as a muse. However, the daughter needs both to identify with, and to achieve independence from, her mother. Against the grain, Carter, as Ward Jouve says, 'never writes from the vantage point of the mother. Always that of the daughter' (p. 160). In her work, she regularly rebuts the mother. That the mother at the end of *The Passion of New Eve* has now become a figure of speech is ambiguous and might suggest Carter's scepticism about the reclamation of the mother in contemporary French theory. That it is an argument which might trap women in motherhood – as distinct from mothering. On the other hand, Carter's daughters always behave in unconventional ways and take on non- stereotypical roles, denying the mother may be a phallocratic act; a denial of what should be empowering. So that instead of giving the mother a phallic weapon, may be the solution is Irigaray's: 'if mother's could be women, there would be a whole mode of a relationship of desiring speech between daughter and mother, son and mother' (1991, p. 52).

After managing to escape from Mother's programme before becoming a Virgin Mother produced out of her/himself, Eve is forced to experience a condensed and fantastic version of a woman's life in Zero's harem. In this respect, Eve's observation that '[Zero] was the first man I met when I became a woman' (p. 86) seems an appropriate retribution for the humiliation which, as Evelyn, he heaped on Leilah. Although Mother performs an operation that transforms Evelyn biologically, it is the subsequent experiences which transform Evelyn into Eve. Significantly, Eve is not the agent in what happens to her – which, of course, is the position for many women.

Zero, a one-eyed, one-legged monomaniac, seems to be an exaggerated version of what some women have to endure and probably an understatement of what others have to put up with from men. He is physically repulsive and Eve loses her virginity in a parody of the way many men have taken women. But the irony is that Zero is an exaggerated version of the young Evelyn. He treats the women in his harem in an exaggerated version of the way in which Evelyn treated Leilah. As Eve herself realises: he 'forced me to know myself as a former violator at the moment of my own violation' (p. 102). I suggested earlier that Zero's fear of lesbianism and the humiliations which he heaps onto his harem may be projections of his fear of the feminine side of himself. In this respect, too, he may be an older version of, and a commentary upon, Evelyn. In tying up Leilah and beating her, Evelyn suggests that he, too, may be afraid of the feminine. Significantly, when he phantasises about meeting the real Tristessa, he imagines her tied to a tree.

One of the most important distinctions between *The Infernal Desire Machines of Doctor Hoffman* and *The Passion of New Eve* and the two novels discussed in the previous chapter, then, is the greater degree of irony with which the focalisation in the novels is presented. Carter's interests in the social processes and the cultural mythologising which determine gender identity and which turn women into Woman are pursued in much bolder and theatrical ways, especially in *The Passion of New Eve*. Whereas realist fiction is written from a perspective through which different issues and widely disparate experiences cohere, these novels are more overtly concerned with the difficulty of assuming a vantage point from which to write. At the same time, they engage with diverse debates of the 1970s such as the extent to which gender identity is based on biological difference, the masculinist bias in Freudian psychoanalysis, separatist feminist movements, actuality as the product of media-generated images, and the ability of Western nations to survive as stable entities.

# 5

# Illegitimate Power, Carnival and Theatre

*Nights at the Circus* (1984) and
*Wise Children* (1991)

I

Merja Makinen (1992) has drawn a distinction between 'the disquietingly savage analyses of patriarchy' in the novels of the 1960s and 1970s – *The Magic Toyshop*, *Heroes and Villains* and *The Passion of New Eve* – and the 'exuberant' last two novels, *Nights at the Circus* and *Wise Children*:

> This is not to argue that the latter novels are not also feminist, but their strategy is different. The violence in the events depicted in the earlier novels (the rapes, the physical and mental abuse of women ) and the aggression implicit in the representations, are no longer foregrounded. While similar events may occur in these last two texts, the focus is on mocking and exploding the constrictive cultural stereotypes and in celebrating the sheer ability of the female protagonists to survive, unscathed by the sexist ideologies.  (p. 3)

'Exuberant' is certainly an appropriate adjective to describe the last two novels. Their narrative voices appear to be a development, as several critics have noticed, of Puss in 'Puss-in-Boots' from the fourth story of *The Bloody Chamber and Other Stories* (1979). There love, sex and desire are demythologised, as Makinen says, 'in a

lighthearted *commedia dell' arte* rendition' (p. 11). For Margaret
Atwood (1994), too, the 'humour and gusto' of the earlier story
anticipates that of the last novel:

> ['Puss-in-Boots' ] is above all a hymn to here-and-now common
> sensual pleasure, to ordinary human love, to slap-and-tickle
> delight – not as an object to be won, achieved or stolen, nor to
> be reserved by the rich and privileged for themselves, as in de
> Sade, but available to all, tabby cats as well as young lads and
> lasses. In spirit it anticipates *Wise Children*, with its rollicking
> cockney narrative voice; it's *The Marriage of Figaro* rather than *Don
> Giovanni:* it's no accident that the clever valet Puss is himself
> named Figaro. It is, in a word, Carter thumbing her nose at de
> Sade.  (pp. 126–7)

The controlling consciousness of both *Nights at the Circus* and *Wise
Children* is female. The female narrator of each novel assumes a
position of authority, taking control of her own story-history and
asserting herself as the author of her own words and actions. As
Magali Michael (1994) points out, 'the customary association of
authorship and activeness with the male is here reversed' (p. 500).
In *Wise Children*, Dora Chance is writing her autobiography on her
seventy-fifth birthday. The narrative has the impact of her speaking
voice, and, as Kate Webb (1994) says, appears to transcend the word
processor on which she is writing (pp. 294–5) It positions us as if
we were in the audience of a theatre listening to a stand-up
comedian: it draws attention to itself, frequently postpones the
subject and prods us into attention.

Through a narrator who is both elderly and a woman, Carter
conflates feminist appreciation of the importance of autobiography
to women and the changing values ascribed to oral histories of the
elderly from the 1970s. As Pam Morris (1993) points out, autobiography helped women discover that their emotions, circumstances,
frustrations, and desires were shared by other women (p. 60). Whilst
dwelling on the past in old age was generally seen as a sign of
regression and mental deterioration, after the 1970s 'life story
review' was seen as increasingly important as one of the ways in
which people could fulfil the need to make sense of their lives. In
*Wise Children*, Dora is energised by her past. In depicting those
aspects of women's lives which, in Morris's words, 'have been

erased, ignored, demeaned, mystified and even idealised' (ibid.), Dora's autobiography challenges the notion of history as a narrative written by men, by the young and, as I shall discuss later, by the legitimate.

In *Nights at the Circus*, Fevvers, an apparently winged-lady, tells her story to an initially sceptical American reporter, Jack Walser, a wanderer whom Carter, recalling her interest in the work of Herman Melville, describes as a latter day Ishmael, the narrator of Melville's *Moby Dick*. In the first chapter of Melville's novel, the reader discovers that Ishmael 'is tormented with an everlasting itch for things remote' and that whenever he finds himself 'growing grim about the mouth' he accounts it 'high time to get to sea as soon as possible'. In *Nights at the Circus*, we learn that Walser, too, 'subjected his life to a series of cataclysmic shocks because he loved to hear his bones rattle. That was how he knew he was alive' (p. 10). In some respects, Walser is also like the Desiderio we first encounter in *The Infernal Desire Machines of Doctor Hoffman*; for example, he, too, casts himself as an objective observer: he has 'the professional necessity to see all and believe nothing' and this 'habit of suspending belief extended even unto his own being' (ibid.). However, although Fevvers' story in *Nights at the Circus* is written up by a male, hers is the controlling voice even to the point where the male voice is emasculated. Fevvers carefully evades all attempts by Walser to try to fix her identity and, in doing so, she not only challenges male definitions of women but, as Michael (1994) argues, notions of truth and reality (p. 497). Indeed, Walser loses the ability to write because his writing is dependent, like Desiderio's, upon his masculinised view of the world.

Autobiography is one of the strategies by which women can take responsibility for their own sense of self in a restricted and restrictive environment or milieu, challenging the traditional appropriation of women's lives and histories by men. Self-making is an essential element in women's autobiography and the notion of the self as 'a subject in process' is important to both *Nights at the Circus* and *Wise Children*. In *Nights at the Circus*, for example, the brothel literally becomes the place where Fevvers is 'brought up' because during the day – in the absence of male clients – it becomes a feminist centre in which the women are active subjects rather than the sexual objects they appear to become during working hours. The female inmates and warders of Countess P's asylum – based on the

French historian, Michel Foucault's version of Bentham's panopticon – escape as an army of lovers committing themselves to a female Utopia in the taiga. Here Carter has revisited in a less cynical way the notion of a female utopia which she explored in *The Passion of New Eve*. One important difference is that whereas in the earlier novel we join the communities after they have been formed, here we share how the oppressed turn the tables on the oppressor without her realising it and are invited to experience the optimism of the women:

> They were armed and all clad in good stout greatcoats and felt boots stuffed with straw taken from the guardroom. They had food with them. The white world around them looked newly made, a blanket sheet of fresh paper on which they could inscribe whatever future they wished.
> So, taking bearings by the pale sun, they set off hand in hand, and soon started to sing, for joy. (p. 218)

Indeed, the novel is an extended metaphor – the Winged Victory come to life – and both literally and metaphorically a flight of fancy. As Morris (1993) says, Fevvers 'fully embodies the vertiginous freedom of self-making' (p. 157). As a winged-lady, she spreads her wings and defies both the law of gravity and female decorum – a point to which I will return later. As the embodiment of freedom, the winged Fevvers stands in contrast to Walser. Among the clowns of the circus whom he joins in order to observe Fevvers, he becomes 'a human chicken' – a chicken being significantly a bird without flight:

> Walser had some more fun jumping on the rolling eggs and smashing them, but not as much fun as all that. Bored, he flapped his arms, again.
> 'Cock-a-doodle-do! Cock-a-doodle-dooski!'
> When he realised the kind ladies were all gone, tears ran unhindered from his eyes. Crowing like a cock, flapping his arms up and down, he sprinted off among the trees. (p. 224)

The movement of the novel, as the extract describing the escape from the asylum illustrates, is beyond language into song – women's songs are a celebration and break the enforced silence –

and through carnivalesque into a conjure world; in Siberia, Fevvers and her companions take a train which ceases to exist as soon as they turn their backs on it. In *Revolution in Poetic Language* (1984), and in subsequent works, Julia Kristeva argues for greater recognition of the joy and physical sensation to be found in the music of language but which are not normally experienced in public utterance. This 'joy' has it origins literally in 'baby language', enunciated with the appearance of delight, and associated with the 'mother tongue' as the parent croons 'baby sound' back to the babbling infant. The women, escaping from the panopticon, reclaim, then, their 'mother tongues'. Within this context, the fact that one of the prisoners in the asylum writes her notes to a warder who befriends her in menstrual blood – conventionally seen as 'dirty' and a demarcation between men and women – proves significant. Her 'love words' to another woman are outside of the male tradition of 'love words' because they are written to another woman and because they are written, literally and metaphorically, in the womb's blood.

Both novels begin with an ending – reminding us of the ending of *The Passion of New Eve* in which Eve declares: 'We start from our conclusions' (p. 191). *Nights at the Circus* is set in the last months of the nineteenth century: 'the fag-end, the smouldering cigar-butt, of a nineteenth century which is just about to be ground out in the ashtray of history' (p. 11). It is concerned with cusps. Not only is the novel located at the peak of the nineteenth century but Fevvers is at the peak of her career. But 'cusp' is also the point where two branches of curve meet and stop. Fevvers, apparently a winged lady, is at the cusp of two physical existences – woman and bird – as well as of reality and illusion, the genuine and the fake. As half-woman and half-swan orphan, and as someone who claims to have been hatched, Fevvers, of course, was born outside of the classic Oedipal triangle in which, according to Freudian psychoanalysis, the girl child acquires a secondary and inferior sense of identity to the male child. Moreover, as 'Virgin Whore', Fevvers is at the cusp of the two polarised categories – 'virgin' and 'whore' – in which women have been categorised in Western culture. And Walser, too, is at the cusp of scepticism and belief and, later in the novel, of reason and emotion.

Both novels are located at what is seen as the cusp of a particular period for England and Europe in history. In *Nights at the Circus*,

Mignon, according to Carter herself, is 'supposed to be Europe, the unfortunate, bedraggled orphan – Europe after the war – which is why she carries such a weight of literary and musical references on her frail shoulders' (Haffenden, 1985, p. 87). *Wise Children* begins with Britain, to use Carter's own words, as 'an advanced, industrialised, post-imperialist country in decline' (Wandor, 1983, p. 73). As Dora Chance observes: 'these days, there is no such thing as a penny any more and it is as if this foggy old three-cornered island were dangling from a cloud' (p. 112). The novel associates this decline with that of the English theatre and, through the trope of the degenerating family line which Carter no doubt borrowed from Edgar Allan Poe, with the demise of the Hazards as a theatrical family. The first wife of Melchior – himself called 'Mr British Theatre' – is now in a wheelchair, while Tristram has become the 'weak but charming' host of a sadomasochistic television game show, 'Lashings of Lolly', in which Hazard himself appears and is humiliated – the 'last gasp of the imperial Hazard dynasty that bestrode the British theatre like a colossus for a century and a half' (p. 10). In America, the English colony of actors, playing Disraeli, Queen Victoria and Florence Nightingale, is a parody of Empire.

According to Dora, there are a number of indications of Britain's decline. One of them is the disappearance of the Lyons teashops. The nostalgia with which she describes them betrays that sense of cultural loss which I suggested in the introduction Carter observed in Britain though did not necessarily share herself:

> Do you remember the Lyons teashops? Thick, curly white plaster on the shopfronts, like walking into a wedding cake, and the name in gold: J. Lyons.
>   Poached eggs on toast keeping snug in little tin pigeon holes as you shuffled down the counter. The moist and fruity Bath buns with crumbs of rock candy glistening on the top, and a little pat of butter lined up alongside. The girl would pour hot water, whoosh! in a steaming column into a fat white pot and there you were, your good, hot cup of tea, with leaves left in the bottom of the cup, afterwards, to tell your fortune with. (p. 111)

The demise of the Lyons teashops is seen as part of a larger sociocultural change reflected in the London railway stations. At Waterloo and Victoria, there is 'nowhere you can get a decent cup of tea, all they give you is Harvey Wallbangers, filthy cappuccino' (p. 3). Intriguingly, they are compared with the station in *Brief Encounter* (1946), David Lean's film – based on a one-act play by Noel Coward – of a love affair between middle-aged people, a suburban housewife and a local doctor – both comfortably married to other partners – who meet in the station buffet. It is an especially pertinent allusion in a novel in which extramarital affairs is a strong trope, but in which the female protagonists emerge unscathed. Like Carter's novel, the film is a retrospective narrative as Laura sits at home with her husband listening to a recording of Rachmaninov's Second Piano Concerto enacting the reveries of her affair. It is not clear how much is based on memory and how much on phantasy.

The most obvious symbol of post-war Britain in the novel, however, is Gorgeous George – a latter day parody of the English patron saint. He is a comedian who has the map of the world tattooed on his body. But, as Dora notes, he is 'not a comic at all but an enormous statement' (p. 66). Some of the irony is of his own design; he flexes his muscles to 'God Save the King' and 'Rule Britannia'; the Cape of Good Hope is at his navel and 'the Falkland Islands disappear down the crack of his bum'(p. 67). Some of it is the product of circumstance. The tattooed map is pink, but in limelight – suggesting the way limelight has changed the way we see the British Empire – it is turned into 'a morbid raspberry colour that looked bad for his health', perhaps suggesting how the Empire has eventually proved bad for the psychological and economic health of Britain. When Dora last sees George, he is a pathetic street beggar who approaches her for a cup of tea. But there is also irony which comes unwittingly from George himself. His catch phrase is: 'Nothing queer about our George.' It suggests an anxiety about homosexuality which may be his own, but may also be part of English culture. Carter, through the narrator Dora, may be having fun with traditional concepts of English masculinity, with anal fixation – George plays Bottom in *Midsummer Night's Dream* – and with sexual violence – George carries a golf club, an object with phallic as well as chauvinistic connotations.

However, in addition to being at the cusp of a particular history, each novel is outside of history through the nature of its narrator: Fevvers, as someone who has been hatched, is outside of the normal pattern of origins, and Dora, as an illegitimate child, is someone who has been excluded from established society. The embedded stories in each novel are generally told by or about women who are oppressed by men and who are literally and metaphorically excluded from or marginalised within male versions of history. Within this context, the priority given to theatre, often associated with subversion, and to women taking control of their own story-history is very significant.

As I have suggested in previous chapters, theatre as subject or metaphor and theatricality – in the prose style and in the flamboyance of ideas – have always been important dimensions of Carter's writing, driven by her ironic self-consciousness. However, in *Nights at the Circus* (19984) and *Wise Children* (1991), theatre is a theme of the novels, as intertextuality is a theme in *The Magic Toyshop* and *Heroes and Villains,* not least because the characters in both novels are professional performers. Indeed, at the end of *Wise Chidren*, we have a list of 'Dramatis Personae (in order of appearance)' (p. 233).

Fevvers in *Nights at the Circus* is a famous trapeze artist, a friend of Toulouse-Lautrec and the toast of Europe. When we first meet her, she has signed up with a circus run by Colonel Kearney – a short, fat, cigar-chewing, bourbon-swilling cliché from Kentucky. In her career as an aerial performer, she has been a great success because of the liberty in the air which her wings have allowed her. Yet prior to this, her life has been equally unusual and eventful. She was brought up in a London brothel run by a one-eyed madame known as Nelson! She escaped from a spell put on her at the dreaded Madame Schrek's museum of women monsters and from a wealthy necromancer who was intent on having her as a human sacrifice. Her near death is echoed later in Walser's experiences; posing as a human chicken in the circus he is almost chopped to death by an insane clown! The novel has a picaresque, serial structure composed of even more events than in Carter's previous books including a great clown's lapse into madness; the defection of Monsieur Lamarck's Educated Apes; and the derailment of the train in a wilderness by a whirlwind. The inventiveness of these events are supplemented by further equally bizarre stories such as those of the girl who imitated lost ones brought from the grave by the tears of loved ones; of the House of Correction set up by a murderess; and of the Grand Duke who planned to shrink Fevvers to a miniature and imprison her in a Fabergé egg.

*Wise Children* is concerned with the tangled history of two theatrical families: the Hazard dynasty, which has dominated English (Shakespearean) theatre for one-and-a-half centuries, and its illegitimate progeny, represented by Dora and Nora Chance who had a novelty act but also worked as extras and took part in strip shows. Like so many of the pairs of characters in Carter's fiction, the one sister is the opposite of the other. While Dora is restrained, she describes herself as 'constipated', Flora is 'fluxy' and a spend-thrift. Although the action of the novel takes place in one day, which is Dora and Nora's birthday and Shakespeare's birthday – it rakes up one hundred and fifty years of family history. As Kate Webb (1994) has remarked, a roster of stars make guest appearances in the novel including Charlie Chaplin, Judy Garland, Fred Astaire and his wife Adele, Ginger Rogers, Ruby Keler, Jessie Mathews, Josephine Baker, Jack Warner, W. C. Fields. Gloria Swanson, Paul Robeson, Orson Welles, and Noel Coward (p. 296). Apart from the fact that the action takes place on Shakespeare's birthday, the novel is written around a mock Shakespearean plot involving disguises, the search for true parentage and false trails.

Theatricality, as an important part of the narrative content as well as the style of each of the last two novels, produces a sense of expansiveness which is also reflected in the geography of the texts. Both novels begin in London. After her 'conquests on the continent', Fevvers has returned home to a London where, in a description that links the world of the two novels, 'the principal industries are the music hall and the confidence trick' (p. 8). Here Fevvers and her adopted mother, Lizzie, tell her story to Walser. Dora begins her narrative with a sociological sketch of how London has changed, observing while once you could think of the city divided by the river, now 'there's been a diaspora of the affluent' (p. 1). Then through the plot device of a touring circus and touring theatre, each narrative takes us to other parts of the globe. *Nights at the Circus* is divided into three parts, each labelled in terms of a geographical location. The movement toward increasingly remote places, as Michael (1994) points out, 'is accompanied by a movement away from the stable ground of reality and toward the ever more fantastic' (p. 495). After 'London' the novel shifts to 'Petersburg', focusing on Walser's transformation into a circus clown and on the experiences of abused female performers who have been befriended by Fevvers, and then moves to 'Siberia', the most picaresque part of the novel in which various characters encounter strange people and situations. As Carter herself admitted: 'The last half of *The Nights at the Circus* gets very picaresque indeed; the middle section is very elaborately plotted, like a huge circus with the ring in the middle' (Haffenden, 1995, p. 89). In *Wise Children*, Ranulph's zeal to spread Shakespearean theatre to the farthest reaches of the globe, for example, takes him, as far afield as Canada, America, the Far East and Tasmania. However, as I shall discuss later, the most significant shift of focus in *Wise Children* is from England to America.

## II

Carter's interest in the theatre comes from a number of sources of which the most important are clearly the theatre of Japan and China; the work of Bertolt Brecht which prepared her for, and in some ways helped shaped her response to, oriental theatre; and, perhaps most important of all, Shakespeare and Renaissance drama. It is hard to believe that Carter, as a student of English at Bristol University in the 1960s, was not influenced by Brecht's essay 'Alienation Effects in Chinese Acting'. But even if she were not, Brecht's essay provides a useful theoretical framework within which to read Carter's work in relation to the theatre. Although Brecht compares the alienating effects of Chinese theatre with the realism of mainstream European theatre, the origins of his interest in alienation as a dramatic strategy is located in popular, folk traditions: 'This effort to make the incidents represented appear strange to the public can be seen in a primitive form in the theatrical and pictorial displays at the old popular fairs' (Willett, 1964, p. 91). Carter would certainly have applauded this thesis, and considering Brecht's next sentence, it probably had a direct influence on *Nights at the Circus*: 'The way the clowns speak and the way the panoramas are painted both embody an act of alienation' (ibid.). In the novel, the clowns occupy a particularly interesting ex-centric position, they are outside the privilege of established culture and as masks they are also outside themselves. One of the salient ironies of the text is that Walser himself joins the circus as a clown, finding behind the mask that he is also within the mask, and able to enjoy the newfound imaginative freedoms.

*Nights at the Circus* conflates the two key tropes of Brecht's essay, alienation and masks, locating the origins of both in carnivalesque theatre. Mikhail Bakhtin's study of Rabelais and carnival, *Rabelais and his World* (1965), placing Rabelais in the cultural context of his milieu, provides a pertinent introduction to the carnivalesque in relation to Carter's work. In effect, it is, like Carter's use of the carnivalesque, a particular way of looking at European cultural history, or more specifically the transition to modernity in Europe. The book, based on a thesis completed in 1940, applies the term 'carnivalesque' to the varied popular-festive life of the Middle Ages and the Renaissance to which Brecht refers in his essay. Although Bakhtin does not suggest that this was the only attitude to life at the time, he sees, as Simon Dentith (1995) says, 'the flowering of a gay, affirmative, and militantly anti-authoritarian attitude to life, founded upon a joyful acceptance of the materiality of the body' (p. 66). In this respect, Bakhtin's theory of the carnivalesque bears out Fredric Jameson's thesis, to which I referred earlier in this study, that the appearance of the body is a potentially disruptive element of narrative, especially when other larger narratives such as Order, Civilisation, Progress and Destiny begin to lose their authority. The appeal of the carnivalesque for Bakhtin, Brecht and Angela Carter is that it valorises the subordinate, the anti-authoritarian and the marginal. Carter's emphasis on carnivalesque in the later work reflects her shift in interest, described by Marina Warner (1994 ), from folk tales in the German Romantic mode, *Wundermarchen*, to those which she saw as connecting with 'the imaginations of the ordinary men and women whose labour created our world' (pp. 244–5). Carnivalesque writing is work which 'has taken the carnival spirit into itself and thus reproduces, within its own structures and by its own practice, the characteristic inversions, parodies and discrownings of carnival proper' (Dentith, 1965, p. 65). The circus in *Nights at the Circus* is an ambivalent symbol. On the one hand, with its hierarchy of male performers, pursuit of profit and oppression of subordinates it is a symbol of patriarchal capitalist society. The male protagonists impose on Fevvers, as Palmer (1987) says, stereotypical interpretations of femininity, invented by a patriarchal culture: 'Angel of death', 'queen of ambiguities', 'spectacle' and 'freak' (p. 199). However, it is also the focus for an alternative, carnivalesque worldview, which, like the popular fairs to which Brecht and Bakhtin allude, demystifies and debunks the established social hierarchy.

Sage (1994b, p. 17) has suggested that *Nights the Circus* and *Wise Children* develop the carnival aspect of Carter's earlier novel, *Several Perceptions* (1968). Indeed, several specific details in the later novels recall that earlier work. Madame Schrek's manservant Toussaint is lifted from *Several Perceptions* where he is the friend of the prostitute, Mrs Boulder (p. 132). Mrs Boulder herself is the source for some of the motifs developed in *Nights at the Circus* for she is the daughter of a fairground fortune teller who called herself Madame Sophia. However, the experience of creating Mamie Buckskin, the fairground rifle-range proprietor in *The Infernal Desire Machines of Doctor Hoffman*, with 'death-dealing erectile tissue' always at her thigh, may also have helped her towards the creation of Fevvers in *Nights at the Circus*.

Several critics, and Carter herself, have expressed reservations about Bakhtin's notion of the carnivalesque. Gąsiorek (1995) points out that critics of carnival have argued:

> that it is often conceived in an essentialising way, as innately oppositional and subversive; that it relies on a nostalgic notion of 'real community'; that it often reinforces existing power structures because it is a licensed form of release from social restraint; and that its transformations take place within certain kinds of discourse but are unable to challenge the hierarchy of discourses, which comfortably contains their apparent subversiveness.
>
> (p. 134)

Linda Hutcheon has been taken to task by Robinson (1991) for suggesting that Carter's carnivalesque world is simply 'the pluralized and paradoxical metaphor for a decentred world where there is only ex-centricity' (p. 127). Anticipating Gąsiorek's reservations, Robinson insists that this marginalised world exists only in relation to existing structures and centres of cultural power. Robinson has in turn been influenced by Judith Mayne (1987) who argues:

> [the] assumption that the mode of carnival is by very definition radical, posited from outside the dominant order rather than from within it. . . . obscures the extent to which the carnival may exist as a safety valve, as a controlled eruption that guarantees the maintenance of the existing order. (p. 40)

In an interview with Lorna Sage in 1992, Carter expresses reservations along similar lines to those of Mayne:

> It's interesting that Bakhtin became very fashionable in the 1980s, during the demise of the particular kind of theory that would have put all kinds of questions around the whole idea of the carnivalesque. . . . The carnival has to stop. The whole point of the feast of fools is that things went on as they did before, after it stopped. (Sage, 1992, p. 188)

Carter's reservations are evident in the way in which *Nights at the Circus*, through a woman-centred perspective, challenges some of the key features of the carnivalesque. As Palmer (1987) points out, 'the beatings and thrashings associated with carnivalistic mirth' are used to 'represent the violence which is rife in a male-dominated culture' (p. 198). This is evident in the circus, at one level, a debased carnival, in the clowns' brutal slapstick and the ape-man's beating of his woman friend, in a phrase which recalls Jewel's whipping of his brother in *Heroes and Villains*, 'as though she were a carpet' (p. 115) – that is to say she is literally reduced to, and treated as, an object.

In *Wise Children* where the spirit of the carnivalesque is embodied – literally – in the ever-expanding, Rabelaisian Perry, the carnival is stopped. He is the proverbial American sugar daddy, but also the wicked uncle who seduces Dora when she is thirteen. Toward the end of the novel, Nora reflects on her love-making with Perry when for a moment they were prepared to 'fuck the house down'; in carnivalesque terms, to overturn the social order presided over by the patriarch, Melchior:

> While we were doing it, everything seemed possible, I must say. But that is the illusion of the act. Now I remember how everything seemed possible when I was doing it, but as soon as I stopped, not, as if fucking were the origin of illusion.
>
> 'Life's a carnival', he said. He was an illusionist, remember.
>
> 'The carnival's got to stop, some time, Perry,' I said: 'You listen to the news, that'll take the smile off your face.'
>
> 'News? What news?' (p. 222)

This is not, of course, Carter's final word, but it is an indication of how the carnivalesque in her novels is a theme and not necessarily a position from which she writes. In *Wise Children*, the thematising of the carnivalesque is evident in the tension which Webb (1994) has identified at its heart between the avowed intention of the narrator, Dora Chance, to exorcise the family lies, skeletons and secrets and the obvious interest in the way in which these stories overturn the established social order.

Her work on her memoirs is linked to the dustbin being blown over, 'all the trash spills out' (p. 3). The day on which she starts the narrative is a topsy-turvy combination of wind and sunshine. This binarism can be interpreted in terms of the legitimacy and illegitimacy binary in the novel. However, interestingly, it is the wind that gets into the blood and turns a person wild. Later in the novel, it is the wind, like the skeletons in the family cupboards, that whips 'round the wings and the bare backstage corners' (p. 83). As a narrator, Dora seems determined to celebrate the carnivalesque in life as her refrain – 'What a joy it is to dance and sing' – suggests.


## III


If there is a single position from which Carter writes in *Nights at the Circus* and *Wise Children*, it is not the carnivalesque *per se* but the theatre. I have already suggested that *Several Perceptions* pursues the fictional possibilities of its epigraph by David Hume, that 'the mind is a kind of theatre', through the consciousness of the novel's central protagonist, through the way in which the structure of the book reflects that consciousness, and through the way in which several of the characters are themselves performers. And the interest in the theatre in this novel is not incompatible with its indebtedness, as I have suggested, to Gothic. As Duncker (1996) points out:

> The theatrical, indeed, melodramatic element in Gothic is crucial to the form. The narratives are linear; each confrontation, dis-covery or event is exaggerated and overplayed for its own sake, for the immediate thrill, and not for its significance in a tightly shaped and constructed plot. The form is episodic, building up to local climaxes, rather than a final catastrophe involving all the

dramatis personae. Even within the prose narratives the important unit of meaning is *the scene*. (p. 58)

In her last two novels, however, Carter seems to go even further. She appears to write from the theatre conceived as a location of illegitimate power, pursuing the creative possibilities in the way in which in the Renaissance 'illegitimacy' and 'theatre' were often linked. From this vantage point, she is able to explore different sites of the illegitimate power associated with theatre, such as the carnivalesque, the mask, the brothel, and the social margins. Indeed, the source of the carnivalesque element in *Nights at the Circus* and *Wise Children* was undoubtedly Shakespeare rather than Bakhtin, as suggested by an interview Carter gave in 1991. Here, she criticised the way in which Shakespeare's recognition as a canonical writer has led to a misrepresentation of his work:

> intellectuals . . . are still reluctant to treat him as popular culture. . . . You mention folk culture and people immediately assume you're going to talk about porridge and clog dancing, there's this William Morris and Arnold Wesker prospect, truly the bourne from which no traveller returns. Shakespeare, like Picasso, is one of the great hinge-figures that sum up the past – one of the great Janus-figures that sum up the past as well as opening all the doors toward the future. . . . I like a *Midsummer Night's Dream* almost beyond reason, because it's beautiful and funny and camp – and glamorous , and cynical. . . . English popular culture is very odd, its got some very odd and unreconstructed elements in it. There's no other country in the world where you have pantomime with men dressed as women and women dressed as men. . . . It's part of the great tradition of British art, is all that 'smut' and transvestism and so on.
>
> (Sage in Bradbury and Cooke, 1992, pp. 186–7)

Salman Rushdie (1993) has described *Wise Children* as a 'oo-er- guv, brush-up-your-Shakespeare comedy' (p. xi). A further gloss on the way in which Carter perceived Shakespeare as a source of the carnivalesque is provided by her short prose piece, 'Overture and Incidental Music for *A Midsummer Night's Dream*' from *Black Venus* (1985). Indeed, *Black Venus* as a project is very relevant to a discussion of Carter's interest in the illegitimate and its relationship to the carnivalesque in *Nights at the Circus* and *Wise Children*. It is a collection of her own short fiction written between the late 1970s and early 1980s supposedly resurrecting episodes and versions of events that have not made it into the official records. Hence 'The Cabinet of Edgar Allan Poe' inserts into the literary biography of Poe an account of the significance of the black muse, his dead mother's legacy. 'Overture and Incidental Music for *A Midsummer Night's Dream*' places the reader, Sage (1994b) says, 'behind the plot, before the curtain rises, eavesdropping on the suppressed subtext ' (p. 45). Carter suggests that the Court of Oberon and Titania has been idealised over the centuries and that the original Court was a much less sedate place. Like the wind which Dora observes whips around backstage, Carter exposes what is hidden behind the scenes: the Golden Herm is an hermaphrodite – lusted after by Oberon who sees him/her as a boy – through which Carter pursues her interest in the blurring of sexual boundaries. In a carnivalesque spirit, Carter gives us the 'reality' – the fairies all have head colds – behind the English midsummer fantasy:

> Puck is no more polymorphously perverse than all the rest of these sub-microscopic particles, his peers, yet there is something particularly rancid and offensive about his buggery and his undinism and his frotteurism and his scopophilia and his – indeed, my very paper would *blush*, go pink as an invoice, should I write down upon it some of the things Puck gets up to down in the reeds by the river, as he is distantly related to the great bad god Pan and, when in the mood, behaves in a manner uncommon in an English wood, although familiar in the English public school. (*Burning Your Boats*, p. 70)

It is important to appreciate the full implications of the relationship between the two texts which Carter encourages us to question by calling her story an 'overture and incidental music'. An 'overture' is normally an introduction, which reverses the chronological relationship between the two texts, and does not have to have a close relationship in style to the main piece of music. Carter is really saying that *Midsummer Night's Dream* is predicated on an absence. If Shakespeare's play is situated in a dream-world, the ever present absence is what the Grimm brothers realised in their 'dark necro-mantic forest'.

The spirit of the carnivalesque which we find in 'Overture and Incidental Music for *A Midsummer Night's Dream*' pervades the account of the night of the fire which destroys the Hazard Mansion – marking the end of the great tradition of the English theatre – in *Wise Children*:

> The fire had unleashed a kind of madness. . . . The tenor and me weren't the only ones who'd succumbed to nature, either. Nothing whets the appetite like a disaster. Out of the corner of my eye, I spotted Coriolanus stoutly buggering Banquo's ghost under the pergola in the snowy rose-garden whilst, beside the snow-caked sundial, a gentleman who'd come as Cleopatra was orally pleasuring another dressed as Toby Belch. Not only that. I spied with my little eye an egg-shaped depression in a snowdrift on the parterre surmounted by the lead soubrette who was grinding away for dear life in the woman-on-top position and it turned out the moaning recipient of her favours was who else but my now definitively ex-lover, his cap was gone, but his bells were all tinkling, and he made her a star in her own right in his next production.  (p. 103)

As in 'Overture and Incidental Music for *A Midsummer Night's Dream*', Carter presents a fantasy which appears to give us a realist interpretation of a fantasy. There is a confusion of roles here which leaves us wondering whether the people are themselves or the characters whose costumes they are wearing. The night of madness subverts the sense of decorum and sophistication which mediates the public's perception of theatre and the so-called serious arts. This view is suggested by the setting – a traditional English garden – where there is an emphasis on purity: there is a 'snowy rose-garden' and 'snow-caked sundial'. It is also conveyed through the contrast between the words which describe the features of the garden and the Anglo-Saxon description of the activities taking place. Coriolanus 'buggering' Banquo's ghost and Cleopatra having oral sex with Tony Belch seems somehow contrary to the kind of spiritual and moral uplift which Theatre is often thought to provide. However, this behaviour is exactly the kind of thing we might expect of Coriolanus. Cleopatra is actually behaving in character as is Toby Belch. The carnivalesque spirit of the episode is reinforced by the fact that much of the sex that is taking place – sodomy and oral sex – lies outside what is conventionally represented as the norm. In other words, from the perspective of established society these may be regarded as illegitimate activities:

> So there was an orgiastic aspect to this night of disaster and all around the blazing mansion, lit by the red and flickering flames milled the lamenting revellers in togas, kilts, tights, breeches, hooped skirts, winding sheets, mini-crinolines, like guests at a masquerade who've all gone suddenly to hell.  (p. 103)

Illegitimacy has always been an important trope in Carter's novels. Desiderio in *The Infernal Desire Machines of Doctor Hoffman* is the illegitimate son of a prostitute's relationship with an Indian, and Buzz in *Love* is the product of the sex his mother had, again while working as a prostitute, with an American serviceman. However, in *Nights at the Circus* and *Wise Children*, the convention whereby the theatre and illegitimacy were linked provided Carter with a means of developing illegitimacy in its various guises as a theme. As Alison Findlay (1994), points out, in the seventeenth century, the theatre and bastards were often seen as occupying an equivocal area, spatially and ideologically. Like the bastard, the theatre was perceived as socially disruptive and occupied a similar position to the bastard in the cultural landscape – 'a liminal area outside the law', making its subversive potential visible (p. 214).

The theatre in the seventeenth century was a much more carnivalesque institution than it is today. It was much more free as a place for meeting and drinking with people and performances were characterised by more interaction between the actors and the audiences and within the audience itself. As such, theatres were often spaces marked by internal difference, antagonism and cultural tensions. The ambience of the theatre is reflected in Shakespeare's plays themselves which combine solemn canonical words and riotously vernacular counterparts. However, as Carter herself was well aware, the more solemn aspects have often been stressed at the expense of the carnivalesque. The interest in the coexistence of two strands – the solemn and the carnivalesque – mirrors the coexistence of the illegitimate with the legitimate.

Both *Nights at the Circus* and *Wise Children* pursue the coexistence of these two strands at a number of levels. Carter herself said that *Nights at the Circus* 'is using the whole of Western European culture as though it were an oral tradition. . . . Folklore is the fiction of the poor, and therefore should be taken just as seriously as we take 'straight literature' (p. 92). In fact, the novel unites the serious and comic, the high and the low. In a single paragraph, it moves between Fevvers imaginings, the voice of an observer, and the way Fevvers slaps down those who come too close:

> Look at me! With a grand, proud, ironic grace, she exhibited herself before the eyes of the audience as if it were a marvellous present too good to be played with. Look, not touch.
>
> She was twice as large as life and as succinctly finite as any object that is intended to be seen, not handled. Look! Hands off! LOOK AT ME!
>
> She rose up on tiptoe and slowly twirled round, giving the spectators a comprehensive view of her back: seeing is believing. Then she spread out her superb, heavy arms in a backwards gesture of benediction and, as she did so, her wings spread, too, a polychromatic unfolding fully six feet across.   (p. 15)

In keeping with the spirit of the carnivalesque, there is no single, unified utterance. In its interweaving of different voices – Fevvers, Walser, Lizzie, the capitalist entrepreneur Colonel Kearney and so on – with allusions to Shakespeare, Milton, Poe, Ibsen Joyce, Foucault, the novel creates, as Palmer (1987) says ' a polyphonic interplay of European cultural attitudes and moments' (p. 197). Between them, Fevvers, Kearney, Walser, Lizzie all express different attitudes and ideologies so that, typical of the carnivalesque, the novel appears to proclaim the relativity of everything. Moreover, the way in which characters are envisaged in the novel accord, as Palmer points out, with the carnivalesque: Ma Nelson is 'The Mistress of The Revels', Buffo is 'The Lord of Misrule', God is 'the great ringmaster in the sky' and the saints are 'acts in a great circus' (p. 120).

In *Wise Children*, too, as in Shakespeare's plays, the language moves through a number of registers without violating the integrity of the work as a whole. Some of the prose is sharp and original as in the description of Melchior's eyes as 'warm and dark and sexy as the inside of a London cab in wartime' (p. 72); or the description of scrapbook cuttings 'turned by time to the colour of freckles on the back of an old lady's hand' (p. 78); or the description of how

'Nora threw her heart away as if it were a used bus ticket' (p. 80). However, at other times, Carter incorporates clichéd, colloquialisms such as the description of 'a face like a month of Sundays' (p. 82) or the description of Nora as 'a martyr to fertility' (p. 81). Nevertheless, the interweaving of the literary with the carnivalesque prose is successful. At the heart of the novel, is Dora's attempt to maintain a view of the world which, in describing a toy theatre, she sums up in terms of masked drama: ' the comic mask, the tragic mask, one mouth turned up at the ends, the other down, the presiding geniuses – just like life' (p. 58).

In both *Nights at the Circus* and *Wise Children*, the carnivalesque provides a social critique of patriarchy and, through the 'polyphonic interplay of European cultural attitudes and moments', a commentary on aspects of European socioeconomic history. Through, for example, Fevers' description of her experiences in a Victorian brothel, *Nights at the Circus* explores how the development of a sophisticated life of the emotions which is our cultural heritage has relegated certain aspects of sexuality to the social underground. In this respect, the location of the narrative at the end of the nineteenth century is especially significant for it was during this period, as Steven Marcus (1964) points out, 'that pornography and especially pornographic writing became an industry' (p. 2). However, it was also a time when fantasy – perceived as the illegitimate in cultural terms – came up against science, perceived as part of legitimate culture. The efflorescence of pornography during this period indicates not only a general disturbance of sexuality, but, as Marcus says, dysfunction (p. 262). Pornography in general amounted to a reversal of Victorian moral ideals and some of it, such as the pornography of sadism, a reversal of Victorian ideal moral standards for men (p. 263). Prostitution itself is seen in the novel as challenging traditional demarcations of reality and illusion. Afterall, the women assume a role and the men pay not for sex but for simulacra of sex. Hence, *Nights at the Circus* takes us through many positions of debasement, evidenced in worlds assembled and contained for the pleasure of men, and often betraying the influence of the Marquis de Sade.

*Nights at the Circus* also reflects the way in which the prostitute during the Victorian period was beginning to be seen in more humane ways. Reformers such as William Acton sought to educate or persuade the public 'to regard her not as some alien and monstrous creature but as a fellow human being' (Marcus, 1964, p. 5). Secondly, they sought to explode the popular myth of 'the harlot's progress'. The majority of prostitutes did not succumb to death or venereal disease as was popularly thought, but returned to a regular course of life – through finding work of some other kind, opening small shops or lodging houses, emigration or marriage (p. 6). In other words, the revised conception of prostitutes as 'fellow human beings' and of prostitution as a transitory state recommended acceptance of the interrelationship of the legitimate and the illegitimate whereas previously the latter had been denied or banished to the underground of 'civilisation'. The consequences of the latter is evident in the way in which Madame Schrek's subterranean museum is the darker side of Ma Nelson's. However, more importantly, the emergence of a more liberal and sympathetic view of prostitutes challenges the conventional opposition of subject and object in which prostitutes are an example of the way women are objectified by men. This is clearly alluded to, for example, in the episode in which a wealthy gentleman purchases Fevvers from the museum of women monsters and tries to kill her with his sword, a symbol of his phallic power, in a ritual which does not hide the thinness of the boundary between sacrifice and intercourse. Fevvers challenges him with her own blade, defying, as Michael (1994) says, 'accepted notions of women as naturally and inevitably passive objects' (p. 502). Moreover, *Nights at the Circus* pursues the implications of the revised ways in which prostitutes were being seen in late Victorian England in two further respects. Prostitution in the novel is seen as the product of economic need, disabusing the myth that the women involved take any pleasure in sex, and employed so as to confound the distinction between 'good' and 'bad' women – as Walser suggests when he admits that he has known many whores fine enough to have been his wife. Here, of course, Carter is blurring the distinction between what was often the only two alternatives open to women in the nineteenth century: prostitution or marriage. Indeed, the economic as well ideological oppression of women is kept to the fore throughout the novel by Lizzie, a strong Marxist and former prostitute herself. As Carter argues in *The Sadeian Woman*: 'The marriage bed is a particularly delusive refuge from the world because all wives of necessity fuck by contract. Prostitutes are at least decently paid on the nail ' (p. 9). In other words, wife and prostitute are both entrapped within an economic system that exploits women, but the prostitute is more aware of her position than is the wife.

In *Wise Children*, the interrelationship of a legitimate and illegitimate family lineage parallels the sometimes unexpected interrelationships between an official culture and its underside as evidenced, for example, in music hall, pantomime, popular song and television game shows. However, the novel also highlights and explores a fundamental difference between the interrelationship of the legitimate and the illegitimate elements in Renaissance drama compared with the twentieth-century mass media. Here the power of what might be regarded as the 'bastard culture' to transform serious culture is evident from the vulgarity of the Hollywood version of *A Midsummer Night's Dream*.

The extent to which Carter's last two novels are located in the theatre or circus, as sites of illegitimate power, is evident from the voices of Fevvers and Dora themselves. Dora's voice, as I suggested at the beginning of this chapter, is redolent of that of a music hall performer. However, it also possesses many of the characteristics of bastard speech in seventeenth-century theatre. She and her sister are, of course, the illegitimate, identical twin daughters of Melchior Hazard, the patriarch, who presides over the Hazard theatre dynasty. Like the bastard in the theatre, she occupies what might be described as a 'down stage' position. As she says herself, she and Nora seemed 'destined, from birth, to be the lovely ephemera of the theatre' (p. 58). During their professional life, they have danced the boards in music halls, have taken roles as extras in ill-fated Hollywood musicals and, stripped to G-strings, have taken part in strip shows. Like the bastard in the theatre, from this down stage position, Dora undercuts the authority of the multi-levelled reality represented, literally and metaphorically, on the stage. She, too, is positioned on the periphery, not fully integrated into the dramatic illusion of the stage world – Melchior denies his paternity.

Like the Renaissance stage bastard, Dora can move from one level of reality to another more easily than those who occupy a fixed position. Indeed, *Wise Children*, intertwining the different zig-zagging family, professional and social lines between the two families, the legitimate and the illegitimate, is a mirror of the Renaissance stage which, as Findlay (1994) says, 'was composed of very disparate modes which co-existed and intertwined' (p. 220). In particular, since Melchior and Peregrine, Dora's and Nora's father and uncle, are twins (which is the father and which is the uncle?) the novel reflects the way in which the Renaissance theatre disrupted the fixed nature of classic theatre. Of course, from a Puritan perspective, playhouses were seen as places of erotic exchange which destabilised clear distinctions between the classes and genders. Indeed, Dora's autobiographical narrative begins by bemoaning the loss of clear distinctions in London's social geography generally.

## IV

Of particular relevance to *Nights at the Circus* are Brecht's realisations that 'the oppressors do not always appear in the same mask' and that 'masks cannot always be stripped off in the same way' (p. 192). For at the heart of the novel is the central paradox which, according to Brecht, masked drama sought to uncover: 'The actors can do without (or with the minimum of) make-up, appearing 'natural', and the whole thing can be a fake; they can wear grotesque masks and can represent the truth' (Willett, 1964, p. 110). At the outset of *Nights at the Circus*, the reader is presented with a duality: the world of Fevvers and that of Walser who signs up to the circus in order to discover the truth behind her myth. It is a duality which brings Brecht's argument to mind especially since there is something grotesque about the way in which Fevvers is made up:

> In her pink fleshings, her breastbone stuck out like the prow of a ship; the Iron Maiden cantilevered her bosom whilst paring down her waist to almost nothing, so she looked as if she might snap in two at any careless movement. The leotard was adorned with a spangle of sequins on her crotch and nipples, nothing else. Her hair was hidden away under the dyed plumes that added a good eighteen inches to her already immense height. On her back she bore an airy burden of furled plumage as gaudy as that of a Brazilian cockatoo. On her red mouth there was an artificial smile.
>
> (p. 15)

So the question posed is Brecht's: whether she can wear such a grotesque mask and represent truth. In fact, Brecht's question is an intriguing one to apply to Fevvers because so much of her is an illusion. When we first encounter her, she is teasingly peeling off her false eyelashes. Moreover, we have to separate her from 'Fevvermania', the 'phenomenon' of Fevvers. Like Tristessa, she is a product of that complicity between the media and a 'persistence of vision' which Carter first began to write about in *The Infernal Desire Machines of Doctor Hoffman* but really began to explore in *The Passion of New Eve*. Fevvers, like Tristessa, brings to mind, once again, Mendoza's proposition from *The Infernal Desire Machines of Doctor Hoffman*, 'if a thing were sufficiently artificial, it became absolutely equivalent to the genuine' (p. 102). Her face is everywhere, shops are crammed with Fevvers products and she exists in all kinds of fictions about her. The novel develops the concern in *The Passion of New Eve* with femininity as a commodity. However, this occurs in a narrative constructed around a complex web of deceptions. At one point, for example, Fevvers poses as the winged victory; Mignon, enslaved by a medium, poses as Ape-man's woman; and pigs and monkeys pose as women.

From the perspective of the 'unmade-up' Walser, Fevvers is cast as the disturbing female presence which in American Hollywood films had to be eradicated. However, from Fevers' perspective, her advertising ploy – 'Is she fact or is she fiction?' – gives her control over her own subject position, subverting the place which narratives of sexual difference traditionally assign to women. As part bird, Fevvers is a means of exposing and subverting the misogynist cultural practices which designate women 'birds' in another sense. Indeed, through the idea of a winged lady, Carter manages to articulate the way in which women have been made the prisoners of cultural anxieties about female sexuality. Concerns pertaining to breasts, female genitalia and menstruation are displaced to another part of Fevvers' body:

> Now, Mr Walser, the day I first spread found me, as you might expect, much perplexed as to my own nature. Ma Nelson wrapped me up in a cashmere shawl off her own back, since I'd busted me shift, and Lizzie must needs ply her needle now, to alter my dress to fit my altered figure. As I sat on my bed in the attic . . . I fell to contemplating the mystery of those soft, feathery growths that were already pulling my shoulders backwards with the weight and urgency of an invisible lover.  (p. 27)

Fevvers appropriates the enigma of sexual difference, then turns her gaze on herself, producing herself as the object but also the subject of her own agency – as is evident in the combative assault on decorum in the first line; 'the day I first spread'. Like Leilah in *The Passion of New Eve,* she is a female masquerade. Her take-it-and-leave-it femininity appears to affirm but actually denies the masculinised imaginary of Woman. Here there is a parallel with seventy-five-year-old Dora's views in *Wise Children.* Dora and Nora dress up as they used to when they were younger, but they realise that even then they knew that it was all a masquerade. Now Dora observes wryly:

> Our fingernails match our toenails match our lipstick match our rouge. Revlon, Fire and Ice. The habit of applying warpaint outlasts the battle; haven't had a man for yonks but still we slap it on. (p. 6)

For Carter, Brecht's linking of alienation, mask and the grotesque begs questions pertaining to the masculine agency of the gaze. Throughout the novel, gender identity is the product of display and spectacle. A woman may masochistically identify with the spectacle. Or as in Fevers' case, construct femininity as a masquerade which ultimately deconstructs it in terms of the tyranny of the male Look. Mary Doane (1982) explains:

> The masquerade, in flaunting femininity, holds it at a distance . . . [its] resistance to patriarchal positioning would therefore lie in its denial of the production of femininity as closeness, as presence-to-itself, as, precisely imagistic. . . . The masquerade doubles representation; it is constituted by a hyperbolisation of the accoutrements of femininity. (pp. 81–2)

Indeed, Fevvers lives through entertainment, masquerade and spectacle by making a living from 'a hyperbolisation of the accoutrements of femininity':

> [Fevvers] cocked her head to relish the shine of the lamps, like footlights, like stage-lights; it was as good as a stiff brandy, to see those footlights, and beyond them, the eyes fixed upon her with astonishment, with awe, the eyes that told her who she was.

She would be the blonde of blondes, again, just as soon as she found peroxide; it was as easy as that, and, meanwhile, who cared! (p. 290).

The contrast with her in the novel is most obviously, Mignon, initially a Marilyn Monroe figure, who is the opposite of masquerade. She assumes the image but, unlike Fevvers, she does not realise that that is all it is. In fact, Fevvers is closer to Mae West than Marilyn Monroe. In *The Sadeian Woman*, the two – West and Monroe – are contrasted:

Mae West's joke upon her audience was, however, a superior kind of double bluff. She was in reality a sexually free woman, economically independent, who wrote her own starring vehicles in her early days in the theatre.   (pp. 60–1)

Carter herself says about Fevvers that she 'is basically Mae West with wings' (Haffenden, 1985, p. 88). Rendered silent as a female spectacle, Mignon is a version of 'the entranced maiden' who, as Judie Newman (1990) says, 'stand as emblematic of the patriarchal view of woman' (p. 116). The point is sharply made through the contrast between Mignon and the clowns; although both wear make-up, the clowns are still in charge of their personae. In fact, they actually achieve liberation through their masks. Women in the novel are seen in terms of binarisms – either goddesses and angels or as subhuman. Mignon becomes a battered wife who is beaten by the Ape Man and abandoned to a hungry tiger by her lover, the Strong Man. The subordinate position of the women performers in the circus is portrayed as comparable to that of the troupe of performing apes – although both troupes eventually rebel. A cruel parody of the 'patriarchal view of woman' as embodied in 'the entranced maiden' – 'totally under male control, veiled to deny her physicality, an idol obscurely in contact with spiritual mysteries, and yet exposed to prurient commercial exploitation' (ibid.) – are the women on display in the museum of death – the sleeping beauty who never wakes up or the miniature woman who never grows up. Eventually, through the intervention of Fevvers and Lizzie, Mignon rejects the role of victim and creates herself anew in a lesbian relationship with the Princess in the dancing tigers act.

Walser, blinkered through focusing on whether Fevvers is true or false, does not realise that masquerade engages with a phallic construction of femininity: 'She would be the blonde of blondes, again, just as soon as she found peroxide; it was as easy as that, and, meanwhile who cared!' (p. 290). Through her masquerade, Fevvers reverses the conventional masculine and female positions until, as I explained earlier, she turns her gaze on him: 'And she fixed Walser with a piercing, judging regard, as if to ascertain just how far she could go with him . . . It flickered through his mind: Is she really a man?' (p. 35)

As Desiderio's life changes when he falls in love with Albertina, Walser's life changes when he falls in love with Fevvers. In the course of the novel, he becomes insane but recovers to return to Fevvers' arms. For a while, Carter's narrative has the potential to develop along conventional lines: an ostensibly radical woman falls in love with a man and is transformed into Woman and marries him. Even though Carter reverses the gender roles, the potential ending is now the same as in the fairy tales where a prince rescues a maiden who falls in love with him. In fact, Fevvers begins to lose the control she has won over her own life – and begins to look like 'only a poor freak down on her luck' (p. 290). In a parody of ageing, her wings now become troublesome appendages – 'she could not spread two wings, she spread one – lopsided angel, partial and shabby splendour!' (p. 290). Failing against male images of female goddesses – 'No Venus, or Helen' – when she feels whole again it is in Walser's gaze. However, Lizzie warns Fevvers of the tyranny of the happy ending, observing with a candidness that borders on ruthless: 'You're fading away' (p. 280). It is also possible, though, to read the novel at this point with a focus on the transformation which Walser has undergone. As Carter herself explained he had 'to be broken down' before he could become 'not a fit mate for Fevvers at all, but a serious person' (Haffenden, 1985, p. 89). Running after the others as a 'human chicken', Walser soon forgets his quest 'in his enchantment at the sight of dappled starlight on the snow' (p. 224). Significantly, it echoes the flight from the House of Correction when 'the white world around them looked newly made' (p. 218). In order to become a reconstructed male, Walser has to become a 'blank sheet' upon which he can inscribe a new beginning. Turned upside down, literally and metaphorically, in a fireman's lift by the Shaman, Walser sees his past life in 'concrete but discrete fragments' (p. 238). Earlier, I suggested that the women's songs represent a reclamation of the 'joy' in language experienced by the babbling infant and by 'the mother tongue' which croons back those sounds to the child. In symbolic language which tends to privilege the male point of view, this 'joy' is often lost. Significantly, when turned upside down Walser begins to 'babble helplessly in a language unknown to the Shaman' (ibid.).

In the asylum which is structured as Bentham's panopticon so that each prisoner is held under permanent observation, the countess and the warders are also imprisoned and watched. The panopticon serves as an image of the way in which in society at large all are imprisoned. In many ways, *Nights at the Circus* takes up where *The Passion of New Eve* leaves off. It is located in a postmodern, postcultural space that is as much beyond America as it is beyond postwar Europe, 'the unfortunate bedraggled orphan' (Haffenden, 1985, p. 87). Indeed, the principal premises upon which twentieth-century America and the Americanised future for late capitalist society are founded are each collapsed in the course of the novel; Walser – post-Enlightenment, rational enquiry – is transformed through his experiences as a clown and through his love for Fevvers while Colonel Kearney's entrepreneurialism is left in ruins after the circus is seized by outlaws. Fevvers' laughter at the end of the book, as Michael Wood (1984) says, indicates that not only has she 'understood the joke of life' but 'the freedom that lives in jokes' (p. 16). At one level, the circus in the novel, as in Dickens's *Hard Times*, represents an alternative to what in *The Passion of New Eve* is 'the phenomena of the persistence of vision'. Fevers' boast at the end of the narrative – 'I fooled you then' – is partly a confidence trick as well as a description of her sense of being. When she says in the last line of the novel 'It just goes to show there's nothing like confidence' (p. 295), the word 'confidence' is double edged. As Carter commented: 'She's had the confidence to pull it all off, after all' (Haffenden, 1985, p. 90) It is a statement, which turns the book into a statement, about the nature of fiction and the nature of narrative. It invites the reader, as Carter intended, to take one further step into the fictionality of the narrative, instead of coming out of it and looking at it as though it were an artefact' (ibid., p. 91).

# 6

# Postscript

I have deliberately avoided writing a 'conclusion' to this critical study. A 'Postscript' seemed more appropriate because the book is not intended as a final word on Carter's work, as if there ever could be, and because I do not believe that Carter herself approved of conclusions.

Although, as I discussed at the beginning of this book, some critics, such as O'Day (1994), have suggested that the early novels invite readings from a realist point of view, her work is more appropriately approached as non-realistic, philosophical (some critics employ the term 'speculative') fiction. Steven Connor (1996), for example, has placed Carter outside the conventions of the 'English realist novel' (p. 33) and Alison Lee's (1990) study of the subversive techniques of postmodernist British fiction – of writers who deliberately use realist conventions in order to subvert them – does not even include Carter's Bristol trilogy.

As Pam Morris (1993) points out, the strength of the realist novel as it emerged in the nineteenth century is 'the detailed interaction of the moral and psychic development of the central characters with their determining social world'. But this means that the 'realist form' has 'to stay within the boundaries of the actual if it is to maintain its illusion to being true' (p. 77). Connor (1996), too, suggests that the characteristics of the English realist novel are also its limitations: 'levelness of tone', 'curbing fantasy' and paying attention 'to the particular and the plausible' (p. 33). Carter, however, favoured a mode of writing closer to Gothic, fantasy or the European Romance than the English realist novel and which drew increasingly on pre-novelistic forms such as the picaresque serial narrative, fairy stories, fable, folk tales, myth, legend, carnivalesque and theatre in its more 'illegitimate' forms. Her fiction involves magical trans-formations of identity, narrative leaps in space and time and a strong interest in the irrational and in violence. As Connor (1996) says, she chose 'a much more pushy kind of narrative [than the English realist novel], full of the disrespectful energies of exaggeration, travesty and masquerade' (ibid.).

The non-realist nature of Carter's writing does not mean, however, that she did not engage with the 'actuality' of people's lives, particularly women's lives. Like all feminist writers, she realised that this 'actuality' has been restricted in range. Like most feminist writers, she recognised that conventional modes of writing such as the realist novel were not always appropriate to envisaging alternative destinies and existences for women or to engaging with patriarchal culture from a feminist viewpoint. Haffenden (1985) maintains that Carter's 'gift of outrageous fantastification, resource-fully drawing on folklore and fairy tale, enables her to conjure fabulous countries which have close designs upon the ways and means of real men and women' (p. 76). As I have argued, her non-realist fiction presents the reader with new insights into how many societies are structured according to the interests of powerful groups. Indeed, Magali Michael (1994) points out that in *Nights at the Circus*, Carter posits a utopian liberating feminism, through postmodern forms of tall tales, inverted norms, carnivalisation and fantasy, against a sharp Marxist political edge in order to propose radical avenues of change (pp. 492–3).

Andrzej Gąsiorek (1995) and Isobel Armstrong (1994) both stress the analytical in Carter's fabulist work. Gąsiorek argues, that her fiction refuses to make a choice between fantasy and rationalism which he associates with the realist novel. Carter, he suggests, employs a fabulist mode, disrupting targets from within or ridi-culing them, but at the same time exposes the limitations of fantasy. Isobel Armstrong (1994), too, has placed Carter at one side of a binarism, this time in opposition to an 'expressive' mode of writing centred on a knowable core of self. The argument is developed out of a provocative comparison of Angela Carter's *Nights at the Circus* and Anita Brookner's *Hotel du Lac*, which were both short-listed for the 1984 Booker Prize. Provocatively because Carter and Brookner represent two antithetical traditions. Carter 'sports with displaced subjectivities performing themselves in the cultural debris of a multiplicity of histories and spaces' (p. 258), while Brookner holds 'to the core of self', attempting 'to stabilise the world of middle-class codes and practices with the particularities of documentary detail' (p. 257). Armstrong, finds an antecedent for Carter's work in Virginia Woolf's *Orlando* – the 'biography' of a man who lives from the Elizabethan period to the present (1928), becoming a woman before the nineteenth century begins. However, although she stresses that Carter writes from an 'objectifying, external manner, as if all experience, whether observed or suffered, is self-consciously conceived as *display*', she underscores that it is a 'rigorous, analytical, public self-projection' (p. 269). Having distinguished the traditions in which Carter and Brookner write, Armstrong argues, like Gąsiorek, that the combination of what she calls 'display' and of analysis in Carter's fiction creates a narrative space in which new possibilities for change can be explored.

Carter acknowledges that many of the traditional principles which have been associated with realism and which have governed our perception, and organisation of, 'reality' have been brought into question. There is a strong recognition throughout her work that identity, history, gender and sexuality are not as essentialist, as fixed and as stable as post-Enlightenment thinking has led us to believe. Boundaries and limits are perceived as signifying spaces in which identities, sexualities, histories, socioeconomic power and cultural status are contested, negotiated or reaffirmed.

At the end of *The Passion of New Eve*, as I noted in the previous chapter, Eve says: 'We start from our conclusions' (p. 191). In fact, this probably summarises Carter's approach to writing as a whole. In *The Passion of New Eve*, I take her to be referring, at one level, to the need for all us to subject our own, and our society's, conclusions – beliefs, assumptions and preconceptions – to scrutiny. But in her work, as I have tried to show, she does this in a bold, often mischievous and sometimes a theatrical way, that is not typical of English fiction. Inside her novels there seems to be the spirit of Marianne, the child 'who broke things to see what they were like inside' (*Heroes and Villains*, p. 4).

One of the most important 'conclusion' challenged throughout Carter's work is the system of differences upon which identities are predicated – particularly, the way in which 'man' has been seen as the norm, 'woman' has been seen as subordinate and all men perceived as having the same relationship to this norm. However, as I indicated in the first chapter, the extent to which Carter submits 'conclusion' to scrutiny has been a matter of debate among critics. Paulina Palmer (1989), for example, argues that the strategies which Carter employs to explore the distinction between biological sex and culturally constructed gender in *The Passion of New Eve* are contradictory. By focusing attention on the construction of the sign 'woman' and ignoring that of the sign 'man', Palmer suggests that Carter may be accused of representing masculinity as the behavioural norm. Thus she might be seen as promoting the essentialist attitudes she seeks to challenge. Palmer also argues that Carter erases femininity from the text by revealing the female characters to be either biologically male (as in the case of Tristessa) or to possess instrumental 'masculine' attributes (as in the case of Leilah) (p. 19). As an anomalous hybrid, Evelyn/Eve has also been challenged as a creation of a patriarchal culture with the aim of usurping women's place and power. Critics have had similar reservations over Carter's apparently conservative adaptation of fairy stories which left her working, supposedly, within the misogynist ideologies she sought to challenge.

Defenders of Carter's work, such as Merja Makinen (1992), have pointed out that the conceptual differences on which identity has been posited are subjected to scrutiny in her fiction. *The Passion of New Eve*, for example, challenges conventional binarisms which are seen as the cornerstone of a whole conceptual order. Assumptions as to what constitutes 'masculine' and 'feminine' behaviour are also challenged as are those about the norm and the range of sexual behaviour, especially female sexuality. Identity and sexuality in the novel are depicted as changing, unstable and contradictory. Armstrong (1994) hits the nail on the head when she writes of Carter sporting 'with displaced subjectivities performing themselves in the cultural debris of a multiplicity of histories and spaces, high-kicking with the conventions of class, gender and genre' (p. 258). Carter's post-1970 novels are set in locations which are geographically and temporally farther and farther from the England of the Bristol trilogy or the patriarchal Britain of *The Magic Toyshop* and are increasingly postcultural while the narratives themselves become more and more picaresque. Yet despite the apparent 'sporting' with 'displaced subjectivities' and the location of the post 1970 fiction in 'a multiplicity of histories and spaces', Carter sustains an unrelenting critique of identity and the conditions of existence in late twentieth-century capitalist economies.

Carter's novels are engagements with a whole range of issues such as the social construction of female subjectivity, biological essentialism, twentieth-century psychoanalytic theory and violence. She has a particular preoccupation with what we have tended to regard as 'natural' rather than socially constructed – sexuality, desire, motherhood, pain. It is typical of Carter's philosophical enquiry that she places sadism in the context of an extended exploration of the sources of evil. And that in doing so, she strikes a series of variations on different religious and political explanations. However, the evasiveness and ludism of Carter's feminism is also typical of her work. While some elements of feminism are treated satirically, her novels argue against the conventional assignment of gender roles and an essentialist concept of sexuality. For Palmer (1989), Carter's work in the 1970s, like that of Margaret Atwood, is problematic because it is so 'dismissive, contradictory and confused' (p. 130) in its attitude towards women's community and female relationships. These ambiguities, Palmer concludes express authorial unease and reflect the cultural climate of the time. This has to be taken in context, however, with Carter's reluctance to valorise any society, to mythologise any community or to homogenise any particular group of people. In *The Passion of New Eve*, sexual polarisation perpetuates a double illusion – in the inner world of the individual and in relationships with others.

The Gothic and fabulist modes of writing enable Carter to affirm the pluralist and shifting nature of 'reality', but also to explore the permutable boundary between consciousness and unconsciousness. For Palmer (1989) this is a weakness in Carter's fiction from the point of view of feminist criticism. Writers who adopt a psychoanalytic approach, Palmer notes, 'pay little if any attention to the collective, political aspects of relations between women' (p. 131). Carter's approach leads to an overemphasis on the motif of the fractured self, on the shifting meaning of the sign 'Woman' and problematises the concept of 'women'. More seriously still, Palmer alleges, it leads to a bifurcation of fictional representations of relationships between women into the psychoanalytic and the political. How far Carter separates the personal from the political and the private from the public is an issue which individual readers shall have to resolve for themselves. In the course of this book, I have tried to demonstrate that such bifurcations would be an anathema to Carter.

The novel as an art form, Michael (1994) reminds us, undermines the traditional demarcation between 'reality' and fiction' (p. 495). In Carter's novels phantasy is frequently a part of reality; or, as Carter herself said, 'there is certainly a confusion about the nature of dreams, which are in fact perfectly real' (Haffenden, 1985, p. 82). Generally speaking, we are able to cope with phantasy, magic and the preternatural when they are compartmentalised as fairy stories and folk tales. However, when they are incorporated into a novel as indistinguishable from the 'real' world they become disturbing – destabilising our perceptions of what is real, unreal, illusion or phantasy. Identity for Carter is constructed on the boundary between the social and the psychic. All of us live in a world which includes shadows of many kinds – fears, memories, phantasies, desires, images, illusions – some of which are repressed and some of which we are not even able to recognise let alone quantify. One of the possible functions of ghost stories as a genre at the end of the twentieth century, for example, is to remind us that what is repressed – such as a childhood memory or a deep-rooted fear – can destabilise our sense of identity and threaten our sense of coherence and stability. Carter recognised that our identities are more fragile than we often think and that reality is more shadowy than we care to admit. She is one of the few English novelists brave enough to write serious fiction from this proposition. Rather than a writer who eschews realism in favour of the fabulist, Carter is more accurately seen as one who engages with the core of realism, questioning the limitations of what is normally taken as constituting reality.

At the beginning of this book, I suggested that Carter's understanding of the Gothic came from her reading in Euro-American literature which was undoubtedly mediated by Leslie Fiedler's (1960) study. In fact, Fiedler's way of looking at the Gothic highlights the fabulist – the improbable and the marvellous – and the kind of analysis which we find in Carter. That is the kind of analysis that is not concerned with contemporary manners and modes as is much realist writing, but with the ideological and philosophical issues and assumptions that shape a milieu. As Fiedler says, in a sentence which might summarise *The Magic Toyshop*, the purpose of the Gothic novel was to 'shock the bourgeoisie into an awareness of what a chamber of horrors its own smugly regarded world really was' (p. 128).

David Punter (1996), one of the few critics to notice Carter's epigraph to Fiedler's book in *Heroes and Villains*, but without the space to pursue the implications of it for a reading of the novel, also suggests that Carter employs the Gothic mode in an engagement with realism. He points out that Carter does not parody the 'real' world, but exposes 'some of the ways in which the real world habitually parodies itself' (p. 141). This is a subtle distinction which is important, as I have tried to show, for *The Passion of New Eve*, *Nights at the Circus* and *Wise Children*, where Carter distinguishes between femininity and the masquerade of femininity. Both *Nights at the Circus* and *Wise Children* are concerned with 'showgirls' – women who are very much aware of femininity as a masquerade and of how their identities as women are constructed around flesh. Indeed, an example of Punter's observation of the world habitually parodying itself is the way in which Fevvers, a 'decolonised' woman, to employ Makinen's (1992) term, creates herself anew in a grotesque parody of unliberated women. For Punter, the Gothic mode is 'related to perceptions of the failure of accounts of the world and the mind predicated on the supremacy of subjectivity' (p. 143). In the course of this study, I have tried to take this argument further: examining how Carter's emphasis upon the body can be understood through Jameson's thesis that often this is all that is left in cultures where the larger narratives have lost their meanings and through Fiedler's observation that in American Gothic writing, when the communal myths collapse, individuals are left unsure of their relationship to the ego-ideals of the past.

Power, as theorists such as the French historian Michel Foucault has argued, is maintained through 'discourse' – accepted ways of describing and evaluating experience such as religious or medical discourses. At the heart of Carter's fiction is an interest in the way in which ideas, perspectives and insights are framed and con-ceptualised. Aware of how different frameworks create different perspectives and approaches to subjects, Carter's novels resist privileging any one paradigm. For Carter there isn't anything that is single or united. Although recognising that Britain after the war was plunged into a state of loss, she wrote edge-on to a culture which she increasingly saw as 'foreign' – a perception that was exaggerated after her return from Japan. This sense of the foreign-

ness of British culture fuelled a preoccupation with the artificiality
and plurality of culture generally.


## II

In some respects, it is irrelevant to judge Carter by criteria derived
from the English realist novel. From the outset, she seemed
indifferent to what constitutes the English tradition of fiction. Most
of the novels are self-denyingly short, perfunctory in dialogue
elements and limited in characterisation. I have argued that Carter's
early novels were influenced by Euro-American Gothic and that it
was probably Fiedler's (1960) study that brought its key elements
to her attention. Fiedler argued that the Gothic tradition achieved a
level of importance in the American novel which it only acquired
in poetry and drama in Europe. He attributed this to the failure of
love in American fiction and the special guilt which awaited projection in Gothic form (p. 134). The failure of love in the American
novel would certainly have appealed to Carter, an author interested
in the consequences of the polarisation of gender identities and the
essentialising of sexuality, as would the notion of projected guilt –
for her fiction, as I have tried to show, lends itself to being read
through a Kleinian theoretical framework concerned with projection
and introjection.

While in Carter's early fiction we find, as in Gothic writing, terror
as a central theme, there is also an increasing preoccupation with
two other elements that Fiedler associated with Gothic: firstly,
'sadist fantasy' – evident, for example, in Honeybuzzard in *Shadow
Dance*, Annabel in *Love* and Evelyn and Mother in *The Passion of New
Eve*; and secondly, a tendency to 'transcend the limits of taste and
endurance'. The latter is evident, for example, in Honeybuzzard's
mutilation of Ghislaine's face in *Shadow Dance* and in his suggestions
of taking turns with Morris to 'lay' her on a plastic crucifix and
afterwards to sell photographs to the colour supplements. Or in how
Zero denigrates and exploits the women in his harem in *The Passion
of New Eve* and in how they in turn humiliate and torture Tristessa.

Carter also seems to develop and challenge the association of
mythical evil with the male in Gothic writing. There are three ways
in which she rewrites the Gothic tradition in this respect. In arguing

for a view of feminine sexuality which allows for the full gamut of desires and 'perversions', Carter also revised traditional representations of the female psyche. In particular, she complicated the familiar villain/victim and active male/passive female binarisms while not eschewing the way in which pain and suffering are employed to dominate women. The man is the beast formula is also rendered more complex in novels which see men as trapped within conventional attitudes and ideologies. Carter may again have been influenced by Fiedler's book, this time his summary of how the American male emerged in American Gothic writing: 'Simply to be a man is to be impure, to betray; and there is nothing to do but to fall at the feet of the offended female and cry for forgiveness' (p. 276). She also appears to have recognised in, and developed from, American Gothic a further contradiction to which Fiedler draws attention: the emergence of a heroic feminist myth in contradistinction to the belief in the weakness of women in the hands of men. This is especially pertinent to *The Magic Toyshop, Heroes and Villains* and the last two novels.

An important characteristic of the Gothic which Fiedler highlighted was the replacement of the concept of 'nothing-in-excess' with the doctrine 'nothing succeeds like excess' (p. 126). However, this is an element of Carter's work which she developed in moving from Gothic as her source of inspiration to pre-novelistic forms such as myth, legend, the fairy story, the folk tale, the picaresque serial formula and pornography. And as I have tried to show, her later work is especially indebted to the theatre and the circus, particularly as sites of illegitimate power, and to her engagement with notions of the carnivalesque.

Given Carter's interest in the way in which gender and sexual identities have been constructed, assigned and essentialised, her interest in Renaissance drama is not surprising. As Mary Rose (1988) points out, the vitality of drama in this period was deeply enmeshed in struggles that characterised every aspect of English cultural life (p. 1). In the sixteenth and seventeenth centuries, an increasing emphasis on the conjugal couple and the isolated nuclear family was accompanied by changes in the official idealisation of sexual behaviour and the Protestant glorification of 'holy matrimony' as the eminently desirable sexual status (p. 2). In many respects, Carter's fiction can be seen as writing back not only to this idealisation of the private life and sexuality but the way in which the different dramatic forms represented discourses of sexuality. In particular, Carter sets the carnivalesque or more unstable hybrid forms of comedy against romantic comedy which performed, as Rose points out, 'a predominantly conservative function in Elizabethan culture by evoking potentially disruptive sexual tensions only to represent them as harmoniously assimilated with the existing social structure (p. 7).

It is difficult to think of many English novelists whose works are as consistently crammed with allusions as those of Carter. In this study, I have tried to draw attention to some of the more important of them, but there are many I have not had the space to trace and others which I have not been able to mention that readers will discover for themselves. All Carter's works are hybrids, as I have suggested throughout, and in each of her novels she seems to be aware of the different implications of pursuing one allusion rather than another for an interpretation of a particular text. However, it is important to recognise that Carter did not simply rewrite earlier texts whether fairy stories or Shakespeare's *A Midsummer Night's Dream* or John Ford's *'Tis Pity She's a Whore*. Her own explanation of the way in which she employed fairy stories, to which I referred in an earlier chapter, suggests how she used other texts generally – seeking 'to extract the latent content from the traditional stories and to use it as the beginnings of new stories' (Haffenden, 1985, p. 84).

Grafting into her novels elements from the prehistory of the novel, from popular culture, music, art, opera and technological forms of the twentieth-century is one of the means by which Carter seeks, as Connor (1996) says, to enlarge the novel's 'range and repertoire of effects' (p. 33). Thinking about her novels in this way was a product of her training as a medievalist as a result of which she thought of books as 'having many layers' (Haffenden, 1985, p. 87). In her last two novels, Connor sees Carter running the novel into unexpected collisions and collusions with circus, music-hall, pantomime, television game shows, pop songs and Hollywood musicals. Carter, following Brecht's cue, thought of the popular and the carnivalesque as creative sources which Shakespeare tapped but which have been marginalised by subsequent attempts to define Literature in terms of high moral and cultural values. As she herself remarked: 'we don't have an illiterate and superstition peasantry with a very rich heritage of abstruse fictional material. But I realise that I tend to use other people's books, European literature, as though it were that kind of folklore' (Haffenden, 1985, p. 82). However, in *Wise Children* popular and low cultural forms are associated with America, are regarded more ambivalently than Carter suggests in her interview with Haffenden and are part of the Americanised future on the threshold of which the West stands somewhat ambivalently.

Throughout her fiction, Carter, however, plunders the electronic media as well as pre-novelistic forms. Connor (1996) focuses on what he perceives as Carter's ambivalent attitude towards the electronic media, 'poised between fascinated identification with the self-replicating fantasies of modern life and mass culture and revulsion at their vacuity' (p. 35). Her interest as a novelist, though, is also in the way in which the electronic media contributes to the reversal of 'fiction' and 'reality'. As more and more information is received, and mediated, Carter suggests that we live in a fiction-alised and sensationalised world – like a novel. The boundaries between the world and fiction are increasingly blurred. Moreover, in her last novel the electronic media creates a postcultural space, associated with America, in which high and low culture, the legitimate and the illegitimate, are not only intertwined but lose definition and meaning as separate entities. It is the future which is already the present for much of the world.

Carter's interest in film – clearly evident in *The Passion of New Eve* – began in her childhood in south London when she was able to visit the National Film Theatre on a regular basis. There she became hypnotised by Hollywood's female icons. Indeed, it was at the NFT that she first began to acquire the critical edge on culture which her period in Japan confirmed and developed. She became aware of femininity as a social construction and of the artificiality of Woman. Fascinated by how these stars became what men perceived as goddesses she began to ask not how but why. Was it for fantasy, money or oppression? In *The Passion of New Eve*, the waxworks museum which Tristessa has set up, The Hall of the Immortals, contains the dead martyrs of Hollywood including Jean Harlow and Judy Garland. The Hall is intended to make a comment on the nature of illusion and personality as it is invented and reinvented in Hollywood. It presents us with the endless dis-posability of the commercial symbols which in effect 'fictionalise' our subjectivity.

In Carter's novels, all kinds of boundaries are blurred; her works are concerned with multilayered histories and spaces. Boundarylessness, however, can be disturbing. On the whole, critics prefer to deal with the kind of fiction that leaves us with no unresolved puzzles or inexplicable mysteries. As some of the notices which Carter's novels received demonstrate, authors who weave masquerades are not always understood and even more rarely appreciated. The characteristics of Carter's novels do not make neat packages: sportive recalcitrance and scutiny of any predictable orthodoxy; love of fantasy and theatricality; enthusiasm for spectacle, vaudeville and pageant; a preference for enquiry over conclusions; and the privileging of analysis over argument. Carter, however, tried to develop a novel form that, like Beckett's, would accommodate contradiction and confusion whilst remaining apodictically art. As Carter herself said in *Notes from the Front Line*: 'I am all for putting new wine in old bottles, especially if the pressure of the new wine makes the old bottles explode' (Wandor, 1983, p. 69).

# Select Bibliography

## MAJOR WORKS BY ANGELA CARTER

*Novels*

*Shadow Dance* (London: Heinemann, 1966; repr. as *Honeybuzzard*, New York: Simon & Schuster, 1966; London: Pan, 1968; London, Virago: 1995).
*The Magic Toyshop* (London: Heinemann, 1967; New York: Simon & Schuster, 1968; London: Virago, 1981).
*Several Perceptions* (London: Heinemann, 1968; New York: Simon & Schuster, 1968; London: Pan, 1970; London: Virago Press, 1995).
*Heroes and Villains* (London: Heinemann, 1969; New York: Simon & Schuster, 1969; Harmondsworth, Middx.: Penguin, 1981).
*Love* (London: Rupert Hart-Davis: 1971; rev. London: Chatto and Windus, 1987; New York: Viking Penguin, 1988; London: Picador, 1988).
*The Infernal Desire Machines of Doctor Hoffman* (London: Rupert Hart-Davis, 1972; repr. as *The War of Dreams*, New York: Bard/Avon Books, 1977; Harmondsworth, Middx.: Penguin, 1982).
*The Passion of New Eve* (London: Gollancz, 1977; New York: Harcourt Brace Jovanovich, 1977; London: Virago, 1982).
*Nights at the Circus* (London: Chatto and Windus, 1984; New York: Viking, 1985; London: Pan, 1985).
*Wise Children* (London: Chatto and Windus, 1991; New York: Farrar, Straus, and Giroux, 1992; London: Vintage, 1992).

*Short fiction*

*Fireworks: Nine Profane Pieces* (London: Quartet Books, 1974; New York: Harper and Row, 1981; rev. London: Chatto and Windus, 1987; London: Virago, 1988).
*The Bloody Chamber and Other Stories* (London: Gollancz, 1979; New York: Harper and Row, 1980; Harmondsworth, Middx.: Penguin, 1981).
*Black Venus's Tale* (with woodcuts by Philip Sutton) (London: Next Editions in association with Faber, 1980).
*Black Venus* (London: Chatto and Windus, 1985; repr. as *Saints and Strangers*,

New York: Viking Penguin, 1987; London: Picador in association with Chatto and Windus, 1986).

*American Ghosts & Old World Wonders* (London: Chatto and Windus, 1993; London: Vintage, 1994).

*Burning Your Boats: The Collected Angela Carter: Stories*, intr. Salman Rushdie (London: Chatto and Windus, 1995).

*Children's fiction*

*Miss Z. The Dark Young Lady* (illustrated by Keith Eros) (London: Heinemann, 1970; New York: Simon & Schuster, 1970).

*The Donkey Prince* (illustrated by Keith Eros) (New York: Simon & Schuster, 1970).

*Martin Leman's Comic and Curious Cats* (illustrated by Martin Leman) (London: Gollancz, 1979; London: Gollancz paperback, 1988).

*Moonshadow* (paintings by Justin Todd) (London: Gollancz, 1982).


OTHER WORKS

*Verse*

*Unicorn* (Leeds: Location Press, 1966).

*Radio plays, film and television*

*Come Unto These Yellow Sands: Four Radio Plays* (Newcastle upon Tyne: Bloodaxe Books, 1985; Dufour Editions, 1985).

Jordan, Neil (dir.), *The Company of Wolves* (ITC Entertainment/Palace Production, 1984).

Wheatley, David (dir.), *The Magic Toyshop* (Granada Television, 1987).

'The Kitchen Child', *Short and Curlies* (Channel Four, 1990).

*The Holy Family Album* (Channel Four, 1991).

*Non-fiction*

*The Sadeian Woman: An Exercise in Cultural History* (London: Virago, 1979; repr. as *The Sadeian Woman and the Ideology of Pornography*, New York: Pantheon, 1979).

*The Fairy Tales of Charles Perrault* (London: Gollancz, 1977; New York: Bard Books, 1979) (edited; includes a foreword by Carter).

*Nothing Sacred: Selected Writings* (London: Virago, 1982; rev. 1992).

*Sleeping Beauty and Other Favourite Fairy Tales* (London: Gollancz, 1982; New York: Schoken, 1989; London: Gollancz, 1991) (edited and translated).

*Memoirs of a Midget* (introduction to Walter de la Mare) (Oxford: Oxford University Press, 1982).

*The Puzzleheaded Girl* (introduction to Christina Stead) (London: Virago, 1984).

*Wayward Girls and Wicked Women* (edited) (London: Virago, 1990).
*Duck Feet* (introduction to Gilbert Hernandez) (London: Titan Books, 1988).
*Images of Frida Kahlo* (London: Redstone Press, 1989).
*The Virago Book of Fairy Tales* (edited) (London: Virago, 1990; repr. 1991).
*Jane Eyre* (introduction to Charlotte Brontë) (London: Virago: 1990).
*Expletives Deleted: Selected Writings* (London: Chatto and Windus, 1992; repr. London: Vintage, 1993).
*The Second Virago Book of Fairy Tales* (edited) (London: Virago, 1992; repr. 1993).

## CRITICISM OF ANGELA CARTER'S WORK AND OTHER RELEVANT SECONDARY SOURCES

Ackroyd, Peter, 'Passion Fruit', *Spectator*, 238/7760 (26 March 1977) 23–4.
Albinski, Nan Bowman, *Women's Utopias in British and American Fiction* (London and New York: Routledge, 1988).
Alexander, Flora, *Contemporary Women Novelists* (London: Arnold, 1989).
Alvarez, Antonia, 'On Translating Metaphor', *Meta*, vol. 38, no. 2 (September, 1993) 479–90.
Armstrong, Isobel, 'Woolf by the Lake, Woolf at the Circus: Carter and Tradition', in Sage, Lorna (ed.), *Flesh and the Mirror: Essays on the Art of Angela Carter* (1994).
Bakhtin, Mikhail, *Rabelais and His World*, trans. Helene Iswolsky (Cambridge, Mass.: MIT Press, 1968).
Baudrillard, Jean, *Symbolic Exchange and Death* (1976) trans. Iain Hamilton Grant (London: Sage, 1993).
Barker, Paul, 'The Return of The Magic Story-Teller', *Independent on Sunday* (8 January 1995) 14–16.
Bayley, John, 'Fighting for the Crown', *New York Review of Books* (23 April 1992) 9–11.
Bell, Michael, 'Narrations as Action: Goethe's "Bekenntnisse Einer Schonen Seele" and Angela Carter's *Nights at the Circus* ', *German Life and Letters*, vol. 45, no. 1 (January 1992) 16–32.
Belsey, Catherine, *Critical Practice* (London and New York: Methuen, 1980).
Boston, Richard, 'Logic in a Schizophrenic World', *New York Times Book Review* (2 March 1969) 42.
Brockway, James, 'Gothic Pyrotechnics', *Books and Bookmen*, vol. 20, no. 5 (February 1975) 55–6.
Brown, Richard, 'Postmodern Americas in the Fiction of Angela Carter, Martin Amis and Ian McEwan', in Massa, Ann and Stead, Alistair (eds), *Forked Tongues?: Comparing Twentieth-century British and American Literature* (Harlow and New York: Longman, 1994).
Bryant, Sylvia, 'Re-constructing Oedipus through "Beauty and the Beast"', *Criticism*, vol. 31, no. 4 (Fall 1989) 439–53.
Carr, Helen, *From My Guy To Sci-Fi: Genre and Women's Writing in the Postmodern World* (London: Pandora Press, 1989).

Clark, Robert, 'Angela Carter's Desire Machine', *Women's Studies*, vol. 14, no. 2 (1987) 147–61.

Collick, John, 'Wolves through the Window: Writing Dreams/Dreaming Films/Filming Dreams', *Critical Survey*, vol. 3, no. 3 (1991) 281–9.

Connor, Steven, *The English Novel in History 1950–1995* (London and New York: Routledge, 1996).

Cronan Rose, Ellen, 'Through the Looking Glass: When Women Tell Fairy Tales', in Abel, E. *et al.* (eds), *The Voyage In: Fictions of Female Development* (London: University Press of New England, 1983).

Crow, Thomas, *The Rise of the Sixties: American and European Art in the Era of Dissent* (London: George Weidenfield & Nicolson, 1996).

Dentith, Simon, *Bakhtinian Thought: An Introductory Reader* (London and New York: Routledge, 1995).

Doane, Mary Ann, 'Film and the Masquerade: Theorising the Female Spectator', *Screen*, vol. 23 (September/October 1982) 74–87.

Docherty, Thomas, *On Modern Authority: The Theory and Condition of Writing 1500 to the Present Day* (Brighton: Harvester, 1987).

Duncker, Patricia, 'Re-imagining the Fairy Tales: Angela Carter's Bloody Chambers', *Literature and History*, vol. 10, no. 1 (Spring, 1984) 3–14.

Duncker, Patricia, 'Queer Gothic: Angela Carter and the Lost Narratives of Sexual Subversion', *Critical Survey*, vol. 8, no. 1 (1996) 58–68.

Dworkin, Anthea, *Pornography: Men Possessing Women* (London: The Women's Press, 1981).

Fiedler, Leslie A., *Love and Death in the American Novel* (1960; repr. London: Jonathan Cape, 1967; Granada–Paladin, 1970).

Findlay, Alison, *Illegitimate Power: Bastards in Renaissance Drama* (Manchester and New York: Manchester University Press, 1994).

Fowl, Melinda G., 'Angela Carter's *The Bloody Chamber* Revisited', *Critical Survey*, vol. 3, no. 1 (1991) 67–79.

Freud, Sigmund, *The Interpretation of Dreams* (New York: Avon,1965).

Gąsiorek, Andrzej, *Post-war British Fiction: Realism and After* (London and New York: Arnold, 1995).

Gerrard, Nicci, 'Angela Carter is Now More Popular than Virginia Woolf . . .', *Observer, Life*, 9 July 1995, 20–23.

Haffenden, John, *Novelists in Interview* (London and New York: Methuen, 1985).

Hanson, Clare, 'Each Other: Images of Otherness in the Short Fiction of Doris Lessing, Jean Rhys and Angela Carter', *Journal of the Short Story in English*, vol. 10 (Spring 1988) 67–82.

Harman, Claire, 'Demon-lovers and Sticking-plaster', *Independent on Sunday* (30 October 1994) 37.

Hutcheon, Linda, *The Politics of Postmodernism* (London and New York: Routledge, 1989).

Irigaray, Luce, *This Sex Which Is Not One* (Ithaca, NY: Cornell University Press, 1985).

Jackson, Rosemary, *Fantasy: The Literature of Subversion* (London and New York: Methuen, 1981).

Jameson, Fredric, 'On Magic Realism in Film', *Critical Inquiry*, vol. 12, no. 2 (1986) 301–25.

Jordan, Elaine, 'Enthralment: Angela Carter's Speculative Fictions', in Anderson, Linda (ed.), *Plotting Change: Contemporary Women's Fiction* (London: Edward Arnold, 1990).

Jordan, Elaine, 'The Dangers of Angela Carter', in Armstrong, Isobel (ed.), *New Feminist Discourses: Critical Essays and Theories and Texts* (London and New York: Routledge, 1992).

Jordan, Elaine, 'The Dangerous Edge', in Sage, Lorna (ed.), *Flesh and the Mirror: Essays on the Art of Angela Carter* (1994).

Jouve, Nicola Ward, 'Mother is a Figure of Speech', in Sage, Lorna (ed.) *Flesh and the Mirror: Essays on the Art of Angela Carter* (1994).

Kappeller, Suzanne, *The Pornography of Representation* (London: Polity Press, 1986).

Kaveney, Roz, 'New New World Dreams: Angela Carter and Science Fiction', in Sage, Lorna (ed.), *Flesh and the Mirror: Essays on the Art of Angela Carter* (1994).

Klein, Melanie, *The Selected Melanie Klein*, ed. Juliet Mitchell (Harmondsworth, Middx.: Penquin Books, 1991).

Kristeva, Julia, *Black Sun: Depression and Melancholia* (1987) trans. Leon S. Roudiez (New York: Columbia University Press, 1989).

Kristeva, Julia, *Revolution in Poetic Language* (New York: Columbia University Press, 1984).

Kristeva, Julia, *Semiotike, Recherches pour une Semanalyse* (Paris: Seuil, 1969).

Lee, Alison, *Realism and Power: Postmodern British Fiction* (London and New York: Routledge, 1990).

Lee, Hermione, '"A Room of One's Own, or a Bloody Chamber?": Angela Carter and Political Correctness', in Sage, Lorna (ed.), *Flesh and the Mirror: Essays on the Art of Angela Carter* (1994).

Lee, Hermione, 'Angela Carter's Profane Pleasures', *The Times Literary Supplement*, 4655 (19 June 1992) 5–6.

Lewis, Peter, 'The Making Magic', *Independent* (3 April 1993) 24–6.

MacAndrew, Elizabeth, *The Gothic Tradition in Fiction* (New York: Columbia University Press, 1979).

Makinen, Merja, 'Angela Carter's *The Bloody Chamber* and the Decolonization of Feminine Sexuality', *Feminist Review*, vol. 42 (Autumn 1992) 2–15.

McLaughlin, Becky, 'Perverse Pleasure and the Fetishized Text: The Deathly Erotics of Carter's *The Bloody Chamber*', *Style*, vol. 29, no. 3 (Fall 1995) 404–22.

Marcus, Steven, *The Other Victorians: A Study of Sexuality and Pornography in Mid-Nineteenth Century England* (1964; repr. London: Weidenfeld and Nicolson, 1966).

Matus, Jill, 'Blonde, Black and Hottentot Venus: Context and Critique in Angela Carter's *Black Venus*', *Studies in Short Fiction*, vol. 28 (Fall 1991) 467–76.

Meaney, Gerardine, *(Un)like Subjects: Women, Theory and Fiction* (London and New York: Routledge, 1993).

Michael, Magali Cornier, 'Angela Carter's *Nights at the Circus*: An Engaged Feminism via Subversive Postmodern Strategies', *Contemporary Literature*, vol. XXXV, no. 3 (1994) 492–521.

Morris, Pam, *Literature and Feminism: An Introduction* (Oxford: Blackwell, 1993).

Newman, Judie, 'The Revenge of the Trance Maiden: Intertextuality and Alison Lurie', in Anderson, Linda (ed.), *Plotting Change: Contemporary Women's Fiction* (London: Edward Arnold, 1990)

O'Day, Marc, 'Mutability is Having a Field Day', in Sage, Lorna (ed.), *Flesh and the Mirror: Essays on the Art of Angela Carter* (1994).

Palmer, Paulina, 'From "Coded Mannequin" to Bird Woman: Angela Carter's Magic Flight', in Roe, Sue (ed.), *Women Reading Women's Writing* (Brighton: Harvester, 1987).

Palmer, Paulina, *Contemporary Women's Fiction: Narrative Practice and Feminist Theory* (London and New York: Harvester Wheatsheaf, 1989).

Peach, Linden, *British Influence on the Birth of American Literature* (London: Macmillan and New York: St Martin's Press: 1982).

Peach, Linden and Burton, Angela, *English as a Creative Art: Literary Concepts Linked to Creative Writing* (London: David Fulton, 1995).

Punter, David, *The Literature of Terror: A History of Gothic Fictions from 1765 to the Present Day: The Modern Gothic* (London and New York: Longman, 1996).

Punter, David, 'Essential Imaginings: The Novels of Angela Carter and Russell Hoban', in Acheson, James (ed.), *The British and Irish Novel Since 1960* (London: Macmillan and New York: St Martin's Press, 1991).

Reed, Toni, *Demon-lovers and their Victims in British Fiction* (Lexington, Ky.: The University Press of Kentucky, 1988).

Robinson, Sally, *Engendering the Subject: Gender and Self-representation in Contemporary Women's Fiction* (Albany, NY: State University of New York Press, 1991).

Roe, Sue, 'The Disorder of *Love*: Angela Carter's Surrealist Collage', in Sage, Lorna (ed.), *Flesh and the Mirror: Essays on the Art of Angela Carter* (1994).

Rose, Jacqueline, *Why War? – Psychoanalysis, Politics and the Return to Melanie Klein* (Oxford and Cambridge, Mass.: Blackwell, 1993).

Rose, Mary Beth, *The Expense of Spirit: Love and Sexuality in English Renaissance Drama* (London and Ithaca, NY: Cornell University Press, 1988).

Rushdie, Salman, introduction to *Burning Your Boats: Angela Carter: Collected Stories* (London: Chatto and Windus, 1995).

Sage, Lorna (ed.), *Flesh and the Mirror: Essays on the Art of Angela Carter* (London: Virago, 1994).

Sage, Lorna, *Angela Carter* (Plymouth: Northcote House in association with the British Council, 1994b).

Sage, Lorna, *Women in the House of Fiction* (Basingstoke: Macmillan, 1992).

Sage, Lorna, 'Breaking the Spell of the Past', *The Times Literary Supplement*, 4307 (18 October 1985) 1169.

Schmidt, Ricarda, 'The Journey of the Subject in Angela Carter's Fiction', *Textual Practice*, vol. 3 (1989) 56–75.

Schor, Naomi, 'Fetishism and its Ironies', *Nineteenth-Century French Studies*, vol. 17, nos. 1/2 (Fall/Winter 1988/89) 89–97.

Selmon, Stephen, 'Magic Realism as Post-colonial Discourse', *Canadian Literature*, vol. 116 (1989) 9–24.

Siegel, Carol, 'Postmodern Women Novelists Review Victorian Male Masochism', *Genders*, vol. 11 (1991) 1–16.

Suleiman, Susan Rubin, 'The Fate of the Surrealist Imagination in the Society of the Spectacle', in Sage, Lorna (ed.), *Flesh and the Mirror: Essays on the Art of Angela Carter.*

Studler, Gaylyn, 'Masochism, Masquerade, and the Erotic Metamorphoses of Marleine Dietrich', in Gaines, Jane and Herzog, Charlotte (eds), *Fabrications: Costume and the Female Body* (London and New York: Routledge, 1990) 229–49.

Turner, Rory P. B., 'Subjects and Symbols: Transformations of Identity in *Nights at the Circus*', *Folklore Forum*, vol. 20 (1987) 39–60.

Wandor, Michelene (ed.), *On Gender and Writing* (London: Pandora Press, 1983).

Warner, Marina, 'Angela Carter: Bottle Blonde, Double Drag', in Sage, Lorna (ed.), *Flesh and the Mirror: Essays on the Art of Angela Carter* (1994).

Webb, Kate, 'Seriously Funny: *Wise Children*', in Sage, Lorna (ed.), *Flesh and the Mirror: Essays on the Art of Angela Carter* (1994).

Williams, Linda Ruth, *Critical Desire: Psychoanalysis and the Literary Subject* (London and New York: Arnold, 1995).

Willett, John (ed. and trans.), *Brecht on Theatre: The Development of an Aesthetic* (London: Methuen, 1964).

Wood, Michael, 'Stories of Black and White', *London Review of Books*, vol.6, no. 18 (4 October 1984) 16–17.

Zipes, Jack, *Fairy Tales and the Art of Subversion* (London and New York: Routledge, 1988).

# Index